RISKING WHO ONE IS

RISKING
WHO
ONE IS

ENCOUNTERS

WITH

CONTEMPORARY

ART AND

LITERATURE

SUSAN

RUBIN

SULEIMAN

Harvard University Press ▸ Cambridge, Massachusetts, and London, England ▸ 1994

Library of Congress Cataloging-in-Publication Data
Suleiman, Susan Rubin, 1939–
Risking who one is: encounters with contemporary art and
literature / Susan Rubin Suleiman.
p. cm.
Includes index.
ISBN 0-674-77301-2
1. Suleiman, Susan Rubin, 1939– . 2. Art critics—United States
—Biography. 3. Conscience, Examination of. 4. Feminist art
criticism—United States. 5. Feminism and the arts.
6. Postmodernism. 7. Artists—Psychology. I. Title.
NX640.5.S85A3 1994
700'.92—dc20
[B]
93-38741
CIP

To my sister Eve Judith Rubin Sprotzer

who has taught me a thing or two about being contemporary

ACKNOWLEDGMENTS

This book was completed while I was in residence as a Fellow at the Collegium Budapest Institute for Advanced Study (February–July 1993), and it would have been a considerably different work without that experience. I wish to thank Lajos Vékás, Rector of the Collegium, and the other Fellows and members of the staff for providing indispensable intellectual and material support during this period.

Many people contributed valuable comments and suggestions about these essays at various stages. I thank them individually in the appropriate chapters. Here, I offer my grateful thanks to them collectively: readers do make a difference. My special thanks to the friends and family members who helped me in the search for a title, their generosity and patience sometimes far exceeding the call of duty: Dorothy Austin, Sheila de Bretteville, Elinor Fuchs, Marianne Hirsch, Alice Jardine, Deborah Jenson, David Lodge, Nancy Miller, Olivia Nicholas, Doris Sommer, Sam and Judy Sprotzer, Daniel Suleiman, and Michael Suleiman.

I have been lucky to have the devoted and intelligent research assistance of Sharon Bhagwan, Carla Mazzio, and Clare Parsons. Susan Fuerst has, as always, provided indispensable secretarial help.

Information about the publication of earlier versions of some chapters is given in the notes; I thank the various journals and presses for permission to reprint. My heartfelt thanks to David Avalos, Maria Magdalena Campos-Pons, and Eugenia Vargas for their generous permission to reproduce their work in Chapter 8; and to László Fehér for his generous permission to reproduce his work—which strikes me as so perfect for this book that it could almost have been painted for it—on the cover.

Finally, I wish to thank the efficient staff at Harvard University Press, especially Maria Ascher for her wonderful editing, and Margaretta Fulton, who as usual has been patient, effective, and superbly helpful.

CONTENTS

Introduction: The Risk of Being Contemporary   1

PART ONE · CONFLICTS OF A MOTHER

1. Writing and Motherhood   13
2. Maternal Splitting: "Good" and "Bad" Mothers
   and Reality   38
3. Motherhood and Identity Politics: An Exchange   55

PART TWO · THE CREATIVE SELF

4. Simone de Beauvoir and the Writing Self   67
5. The Passion According to Hélène Cixous   78
6. Artists in Love (and Out): Leonora Carrington
   and Max Ernst   89

PART THREE · ON BEING POSTMODERN

7. The Fate of the Surrealist Imagination in the Society
   of the Spectacle   125
8. Alternatives to Beauty in Contemporary Art   140
9. Living Between: The Loneliness of the "Alonestanding
   Woman"   169

PART FOUR · HISTORY/MEMORY

10. Life-Story, History, Fiction: Simone de Beauvoir's
Wartime Writings   179

11. War Memories: On Autobiographical Reading   199

12. My War in Four Episodes   215

Epilogue: The Politics of Postmodernism after
the Wall; or, What Do We Do When the "Ethnic
Cleansing" Starts?   225

Notes   245

Index   267

ILLUSTRATIONS

Leonora Carrington and Max Ernst in St. Martin d'Ardèche   90
Photo copyright © Lee Miller Archives, 1985

Leonora Carrington, *The Inn of the Dawn Horse*   95
Copyright © 1994 Leonora Carrington / ARS, New York

Leonora Carrington, *Portrait of Max Ernst*   97
Copyright © 1994 Leonora Carrington / ARS, New York

Leonora Carrington, *Femme et Oiseau (Woman and Bird)*   98
Copyright © 1994 Leonora Carrington / ARS, New York

Leonora Carrington, *The Horses of Lord Candlestick*   101
Copyright © 1994 Leonora Carrington / ARS, New York

Max Ernst, *Leonora in the Morning Light*   104
Copyright © 1994 ARS, New York / SPADEM / ADAGP, Paris

Max Ernst, *The Bride of the Wind (1927)*   105
Copyright © 1994 ARS, New York / SPADEM / ADAGP, Paris

Max Ernst, *The Bride of the Wind (1940)*   106
Copyright © 1994 ARS, New York / SPADEM / ADAGP, Paris

Leonora Carrington and Max Ernst, *Rencontre*   109
Copyright © 1994 Leonora Carrington / ARS, New York / SPADEM /
ADAGP, Paris

Leonora Carrington, *The House Opposite*   113
Copyright © 1994 Leonora Carrington / ARS, New York

Max Ernst, *The Robing of the Bride*   114
Copyright © 1994 ARS, New York / SPADEM / ADAGP, Paris

Max Ernst, *Europe after the Rain* (detail)   116
   Copyright © 1994 ARS, New York / SPADEM / ADAGP, Paris

Max Ernst, *Temptation of Saint Anthony* (detail)   119
   Copyright © 1994 ARS, New York / SPADEM / ADAGP, Paris

Leonora Carrington, *Temptation of Saint Anthony*   120
   Copyright © 1994 Leonora Carrington / ARS, New York

Juan Correa, *Allegory of the Sacrament*   149
   Courtesy of the Denver Art Museum, loan number 418.1989

David Avalos, *Hubcap Milagro—Junipero Serra's Next
Miracle: Turning Blood into Thunderbird Wine*   150
   Photo courtesy of the artist

Man Ray, *Gift*   152
   Copyright © 1994 ARS, New York / ADAGP/ Man Ray Trust, Paris

Robert Rauschenberg, *Coca-Cola Plan*   153
   Copyright © Robert Rauschenberg / VAGA, New York, 1993

David Avalos, *Café Mestizo*   155
   Photo courtesy of the Institute of Contemporary Art, Boston

David Avalos, *Hubcap Milagro—Junipero Serra's Next
Miracle: Turning Blood into Thunderbird Wine*
(installation)   155
   Photo courtesy of the Institute of Contemporary Art, Boston

David Avalos, *Hubcap Milagro—Combination Platter 2:
The Manhattan Special*   156
   Photo courtesy of the artist

Meret Oppenheim, *Ma Gouvernante, My Nurse, Mein
Kindermädchen* (*My Governess, My Nurse, My Nanny*)   156
   Copyright © 1994 ARS, New York / Pro Litteris, Zurich

David Avalos, *Hubcap Milagro—Combination Platter 3:
The Straight-Razor Taco*   158
   Photo courtesy of the artist

Maria Magdalena Campos-Pons, *I Am a Fountain*
(installation)   159
   Photo courtesy of the Institute of Contemporary Art, Boston

Maria Magdalena Campos-Pons, *I Am a Fountain* (close-up) 161
   Photo courtesy of the Institute of Contemporary Art, Boston

Ana Mendieta, *Body Tracks*   162
   Photo courtesy Galerie Lelong and the Estate of Ana Mendieta

Ana Mendieta, *Body Tracks* (performance)   162
   Photo courtesy Galerie Lelong and the Estate of Ana Mendieta

Eugenia Vargas, *Untitled 1*   163
   Photo courtesy of the Institute of Contemporary Art, Boston

Eugenia Vargas, *Untitled 5*   164
   Photo courtesy of the Institute of Contemporary Art, Boston

Frida Kahlo, *The Miscarriage*   165
   Photo courtesy of Mary-Anne Martin / Fine Art, New York

Frida Kahlo, *Self-Portrait with Cropped Hair*   166
   Photo courtesy of the Museum of Modern Art, New York;
   gift of Edgar Kaufmann, Jr.

The academic work of interpretation has traditionally flourished on past texts and ignored contemporary creations . . . This began to change in the second half of this century, presumably in relation to the loss of belief in univocal truth, but criticism of contemporary texts is visibly less "safe."

—Christine Brooke-Rose, "Illicitations"

It is so very much more exciting and satisfactory for everybody if one can have contemporaries, if all one's contemporaries could be one's contemporaries.

—Gertrude Stein, "Composition as Explanation"

We revise our own moral identity by revising our own final vocabulary. Literary criticism does for ironists what the search for universal moral principles is supposed to do for metaphysicians.

—Richard Rorty, *Contingency, Irony, and Solidarity*

INTRODUCTION: THE RISK OF BEING CONTEMPORARY

When I was in graduate school at Harvard in the early sixties, it was understood that good academic writing—in my case, literary criticism—aimed for impersonality and objectivity. What did a poem or a novel or an essay mean? Or, if you were more sophisticated: How did a work mean, how was it "put together" to produce a certain effect? These were the questions we were taught to ask, and the first rule we learned was that in answering them, one must never say "I." Nor, of course, should one make humorous remarks, or play on words, or try for "literary" or "poetic" effects, or in any other way seek to put one's own self, noticeably, into one's critical writing.

Today, those rules no longer exist. Thanks to a number of developments over the past twenty years—chief among which have been the demise of structuralism and the growth of a politically self-conscious feminist criticism, intent on confirming that "the personal is the political"—it is now all right to say "I" in writing about literature. Indeed, the line between "literature" and "writing about literature" has itself begun to waver, and there are critics (academic critics who write with footnotes) who

I was watching History pass by! It was my story. All of this is happening to me.
—Simone de Beauvoir,
The Blood of Others

1

are read as poets and novelists are read: not only for what they have to say, but for their personal voice and style. Nancy K. Miller, who qualifies as one of those, has spoken of a veritable "outbreak of self-writing" among American academics in the 1980s, and has wittily wondered whether this was "one of the many symptoms of literary theory's mid-life crisis."[1]

For many of us who have thought of ourselves as theorists as well as critics, "theory's mid-life crisis" has taken the form of a revulsion against metalanguage—in plainer English, a desire to write in plainer English. This does not necessarily mean that we have renounced theorizing, though I think that some of us have; rather, it is part of an attempt—really, a longing—to express our theories in a language that will allow nonspecialists to read us. It is a desire to speak to a larger public.

One way to speak to a larger public is to implicate yourself, your self, in what you write. "Reach out and touch someone": a cloying advertising slogan, but insofar as it recognizes a basic need for communication, for connections between selves, it rings true. Pursuing Miller's life-cycle metaphor, I would say that the earlier ideal of academic criticism was founded on not remembering who you were when you wrote, and, correlatively, not remembering that you were writing for people (as opposed to "the profession," or even "the community of scholars"). The new ideal, if ideal it is, is founded on the premise that since all writing is done by some-body for some-body, it is not merely permitted, but downright valuable, to remember who you are as you write. The "mid-life crisis" question then becomes: When are you old enough to remember who you are?

Remember? Who you are? The theorist in me bristles: Since when is the self a given, to be recollected, if not in tranquillity then at least all of a piece? What happened to postmodern (and modern) theories of the fragmented self and the constructed nature of reality? If "putting your self in your writing" and "speaking to a larger public" mean abandoning long-held theoretical positions, then, metalanguage or no, the theorist in me bolts for the door. To calm her righteous indignation, I will rephrase the question: When are you old enough to re-member who you "are"? The hyphen makes explicit and emphasizes what is always true about the activity of remembering: it is not a passive reception of memories fixed forever like a series of faded images in a scrapbook, but an active (re)construction, a putting together and shaping (the way an artist puts together and shapes certain materials) of a life or part of a life. Similarly, the self is not a fixed entity but an evolving process, not something discovered (or passively "remembered") but something made; which does not mean that it does not exist, but that its existence is always subject to revision (re-vision). Whence the quotation marks around the verb "to be," which indicate the necessary tentativeness, the necessary self-doubt, what Richard Rorty would call the necessary irony, in every discourse about the self.

Mollified, my theorist nods her head: You may continue.

Not only do the essays in this book argue, variously, for the above positions about memory and subjectivity; they also exemplify them—or, if you prefer, perform them. Written, for the most part, in the last few years, they were not planned from the start to form a single whole; but in the process of putting them together, occasionally rewriting them, and shaping them into this book, I became aware that I was also constructing one version of the shape of my own life. Since these are all critical essays dealing with the work of others (there is a single exception, which I will get to), they are not what I call "straight autobiography." Rather, they are a form of mediated autobiography, where the exploration of the writer's self (which I take to be a defining characteristic of autobiography) takes place not directly but through the mediation of writing about another. As the book progresses, one sees an increasing self-consciousness about the doubling between the writer/critic's self and the subject's self (using "subject" here the way art historians speak about the subject of a painting), and about the meeting of those selves on the collective ground of contemporary history.

What does it mean to write about the work of one's contemporaries, and what is the best way to do it? Why do it? These questions, sometimes explicitly stated, at other times merely implied, underlie all the essays in this book. The answers suggested are various, and I will not repeat them here. I will, however, mention three interrelated ideas that, for me, are closely linked to writing about contemporaries and also function as compelling reasons for doing so: self-recognition, historical awareness, and collective action.

But first you might ask: What, or rather who, is a contemporary?

Who are contemporaries of each other? And what does it mean to "be" contemporary? The dictionary is of limited help: "of the time, with the time." Those who are "of my time" ("of my place" is understood) are my contemporaries. In Hungarian, the word is *kortárs*—literally, "age-partner": contemporaries are people of the same age, who have experienced the same historical events, breathed the same historical air. But are all and only those who are my "age-partners" my contemporaries? What about people my age who view the world completely differently from me—who may even, in some circumstances, want my death and the death of others like me? Are they my contemporaries in any but the most narrow, most literal, least interesting sense? And what about people who are considerably older or younger than I, but who have shared an indelible historical experience with me—marched on Washington, or witnessed the shooting of Robert Kennedy on television, or survived the war in Europe? Even though they are not my "age-partners," are they not more appropriately called my contemporaries than those my age from whom everything separates me except, precisely, our age? Jan Kott has claimed that Shakespeare is "our contemporary."[2] Why not, if Shakespeare speaks to us in ways that make us recognize our selves, our own time and place?

Clearly, there is no single or simple way to define the word, whether one is talking about people or works. Are all works written or painted or composed around the same time and place contemporaries of one another? The same questions apply as to people. In this book, I consider as my contemporaries people whose life has in some way intersected with mine, even if they are much older or younger. Thus, Simone de Beauvoir is my contemporary even though she was older than my mother, and Maria Magdalena Campos-Pons is my contemporary even though she is young enough to be my daughter. When I say our lives have intersected, I don't mean it literally, although that is a possibility. I never met Simone de Beauvoir, and now unfortunately never will; I have met and consider as friends several of the writers whose work I discuss here. On a first level, "intersection" means that for a number of years we breathed the same air and participated in at least some aspects of the same material culture (for example, knowing what a telephone is, or an airplane, or a radio, even if you have never used one); on a second level, it means some common bond of experience, interest, curiosity, or allegiance. Since all of the people discussed in this book write or make art, this bond exists not only (not even primarily) with them as persons but also with their works.

One could argue that all great works are in some way contemporary and must be responded to that way. Yes, of course: Rembrandt's portrait of an old woman cutting her nails speaks to me across the centuries, about old age, about weariness, and about work and the beauty of concentrated attention, whether on the part of the artist or on the part of the woman he painted. But in the sense in which I conceive of that notion in this book (levels one and two above, combined), Rembrandt is not my contemporary: he never heard of World War II, or even World War I; he didn't know about telephones. Similarly, the definition excludes Shakespeare as my contemporary, even though I am prepared to grant that it is possible to *read* Shakespeare as "our contemporary," perform his plays in modern dress with modern props, and so on. (The question arises: Should I apply the term "contemporary" to a tribesman from a primitive Amazonian tribe who is exactly my age but has never heard of World War II and doesn't know about telephones, if such a person exists? I would say yes—or at least potentially yes, which is good enough—because he and I *could* end up sharing the same physical space; I would also note that "primitives" are fast disappearing.)

Lest my definition sound intolerably trivial (what do literature and art, or writing about them, have to do with telephones?), let me make clear that the contemporary, for me, is not by itself an evaluative category, although it is a valued one. There are contemporary works I consider great, and others I find worthless. But besides the great and the worthless, there is the category of the *interesting*—and it is sufficient if a contemporary work is interesting (to me) to warrant my writing about it and calling others' attention to it. In fact, I would argue that a contemporary work must be, before all else, interesting to someone. Only the future will tell whether it is great, or, if you will, timeless—able transcend its own contemporariness. But it is only in its own time that it can be found "interesting" in the full sense of that word: not only as an object of curiosity or even of intellectual passion, but as an object with some immediate relation to everyday life. My viewing of Rembrandt's old woman, and even more so of Vermeer's lady reading a letter or playing the lute, will never be like the viewing of people who *recognize* the world depicted in those works as materially similar to—or at least imaginable as—their own. (Note that it is not the question of "realism" that is at stake here: a seventeenth-century reader of Cyrano de Bergerac's *Trip to the Moon* could recognize it as contemporary, even though it was totally unreal; just as I recognize a novel by Angela Carter as contemporary, even though it may feature a giant heroine with feathered wings, or else a society of centaurs.)

It is because contemporary works can be interesting in the sense of appealing to one's "self-interest"—the opposite of disinterestedness as well as of indifference—that they are so exhilarating to write about. It is also why they are, to use Christine Brooke-Rose's expression, less "safe" to write about than works of the past. They bring the critic's self into play, and into risk. They stir up muddy waters. They can lead you into temptation and error—or into beatitude and bliss. In a word, they matter to you. The opposite of the contemporary is neither the timeless nor the out-of-date, but the uninteresting. Naturally, "to me" is understood—"the contemporary," as I use it here, is always in the end a subjective term. The challenge is to try to make *my* contemporaries interesting to *you* as well. I, after all, am your contemporary if you are reading me in 1994, or even later.

But let us return to self-recognition, historical awareness, and collective action. When I wrote the first of these essays (the only one written a long time ago), "Writing and Motherhood," which deals with the inner conflicts experienced by writing mothers who feel caught between the demands of work and child, I myself was the mother of two young boys, and had experienced that conflict (was still experiencing it) in an acute way. In the essay, I do not explicitly talk about my own feelings or experiences, though I do mention, in the beginning, that I am a mother of two sons. Despite my autobiographical discretion, anyone who reads the essay carefully will note a degree of personal investment, and an inflection of voice, that mark this work as mediated autobiography.[3] In writing about the essays and novels of other mothers who alternated between feelings of guilt and ecstasy, with many fine shades in between, I was in part working out my own ambivalence about the conflicting obligations of creativity and motherhood. In the works of the contemporary women writers I was discussing (works I read with bated breath, the way I used to read as a young girl and as I had done only once before in my life as a critic) I saw mirrored some of my own dilemmas and fantasies. This process of self-recognition (the theorist in me would probably want to say "self-construction") is a variant of the identification that all stories invite in their readers or listeners—we all want the hero or heroine to achieve some form of happiness. But it is stronger than mere identification, which most often disappears or dissipates when the reading or viewing experience is over. My self-recognition in the novels and testimonies of others was part of an attempt to understand and analyze both a personal conflict and some of its social and ideological components—for example, the role of normative psychoanalytic theories in devaluing, or positively ignoring, the mother's subjectivity and voice; or the absence of adequate social and material support for mothers in contemporary American society.

In short, the self-recognition that was involved in reading and then writing about these contemporaries led almost inevitably to larger considerations about culture and society—to the dimensions of historical awareness and collective action. In that particular essay, I did not dwell much on the latter—but by the time I wrote its sequel, "Maternal Splitting," I felt it necessary to insist on the inseparability of these issues: "Where motherhood is concerned, personal fantasy, fictional representation, and social and cultural reality are so interconnected that it is impossible to talk about one without the others." That essay ends with a call for a concerted social policy of universal child care—rather a long way off from "structural analysis of narrative," even though it was with the help of structural analysis that I developed the reading of Mary Gordon's novel *Men and Angels*, on which my cultural commentary was based.

Chapter 3, which consists of a dialogue with a reader of "Maternal Splitting," is even more explicitly oriented toward collective issues, since it deals chiefly with the question of motherhood as a category in relation to categories of race and class: Does the experience of motherhood constitute something like a potential "universal" among women, or do racial and class lines constitute an unbridgeable gap even in the experience of mothers? In some ways, the exchange of views with Raquel Portillo Bauman was a "collective action" (or at least a duet) of its own.

The notion of autobiographical reading, which I develop theoretically in Part IV, is closely linked to the idea of self-recognition and to writing about contemporaries. In Chapter 11 ("War Memories"), I define a mode of reading I call "strong autobiographical," which consists of reading another's story "as if it were one's own." *This could have been my story*, to paraphrase the insight of Simone de Beauvoir's heroine in her novel *The Blood of Others*. I contend that reading and writing about the work of contemporaries allows for the strongest kind of autobiographical reading, because the worlds and lives depicted in such work are (at least potentially) closer to the reader's own. To be sure, generalizations are extremely hard to make in this domain, and I explicitly reject a narrowly construed, strictly experience-based self-definition as the basis of autobiographical reading. Yet I am convinced both by my own reading experiences (in this instance, reading memoirs about World War II, especially by people who were children during the war) and by the responses of some readers to my own writing (including, most recently, "War Memories") that the self-recognition provided by contemporary work is very special indeed. It allows you to put your own life into historical perspective, establishing a link between individual and collective experience; this is especiallly important in the case of traumatic events such as war, forced emigration, or other experiences of radical loss.

Perhaps most precious of all, autobiographical reading can lead to more writing—your own. What I call "strong autobiographical reading" leads, in the best of cases, to autobiographical writing. That kind of writing is not the same as autobiographical criticism, or what some have called personal criticism—or what I am calling mediated autobiography. It is not necessarily practiced by professional writers, or critics; it does not have footnotes; it is not about "texts," though it may invoke them as part of a personal history; it may not even be written for publication. It is simply the logical consequence of a certain kind of reading. Strong autobiographical reading, correlatively, is not necessarily done by writers or critics; it is done by anyone who reads his or her contemporaries for the sake of self-recognition, an expanded historical awareness, and a sense of at least potential collective action.

Chapter 12, "My War in Four Episodes," is an example of what I consider autobiographical writing "without footnotes," or straight autobiography; it is the only independent example of such writing in the book. A few of the other chapters, notably the immediately preceding one, have some segments written in this mode, but they are not independent. They function as part of a larger ensemble that is different in kind.

Finally, I will say a few words about the overall shape of this book, especially insofar as it can be read as a mediated, fragmented, nontotalized, postmodern, and fortunately still unfinished autobiography. I find it significant (but of course it was I who arranged it this way) that the book begins with motherhood—that is, adult womanhood—and ends (leaving the epilogue aside for a moment) with childhood memories. This corresponds to a roughly chronological order of writing, but not exactly. It is as if, in discovering the autobiographical possibilities of critical writing, I first had to deal with the most pressing personal issues (for me at the time), which involved motherhood. After that, I could move on to more general, collective ones such as "becoming an artist" (Part II deals essentially with that question, especially as regards women) or "being postmodern" (a variant of the contemporary) or remembering World War II. But since World War II is also part of my own life, indeed contains my earliest childhood memories (1944–1945), one could see this evolution in the writing and arrangement of the essays as the gradual emergence of a buried past. This would correspond to a classic psychoanalytic paradigm, in which childhood provides a "key" to the present and is also the last to be recaptured, especially if it involved trauma. In this light, it is interesting that the later essays, which are also those that deal with the material relating to childhood and youth (Chapter 10 evokes my early days as a reader of Simone de Beauvoir), are those that are most free in their mingling of autobiography and criticism, or, to use my earlier terminology, of "straight" and "mediated" autobiography. An additional remark worth making is that it is the "History/Memory" section that moves the book away from being almost exclusively about women's work. Although women's work and its attendant gender issues dominate—which is hardly surprising, in a book that claims to be a mediated autobiography by a woman author—the issues raised by World War II bring to the fore other crucial preoccupations and categories, notably those of religion, political allegiance, and ethnic identification.

As originally conceived, the book was to end with Chapter 12, the piece of straight autobiography that went the farthest back in my own life (though not in historical time, since the essays that discuss people who are older go back further). But then, I had the unexpected opportunity to spend six months living and working in Budapest, and that experience ended up modifying the original scheme. Upon reflection, however, I find that it completes the scheme rather than modifying it. The epilogue, written chiefly in Budapest in May 1993, when the war in Bosnia was uppermost in many people's minds, including my own, is the closest I have come, so far, to theorizing the relations between a postmodern theory of subjectivity, personal experience, contemporary history, and collective or political action. As such, it belongs without a doubt in the concluding position in this book—but since it arrives more at painful questions than at firm prescriptions, I prefer to call it an epilogue rather than a conclusion. The epilogue also makes explicit the temporal pattern that underlies my "contemporary triad" of self-recognition, historical awareness, and collective action. Self-recognition can be said to exist most fruitfully in the present; historical awareness emphasizes the importance of the past, both for its own sake and for its role in understanding the present; collective action, like all action, impels us toward the future. This pattern suggests that "being contemporary" is necessarily an unstable condition, a process of movement toward an open future.

The fact that this book was completed in my native city, during a time of ethical and political anxiety but also of great personal freedom and intense self-exploration and exploration of "traces"— streets, houses, songs once heard and forgotten, foods savored long ago and rediscovered, flowers, shadows, scents—appears to me, here and now, as entirely fitting. The only thing that can follow, at least such is my hope, is more writing—both by me and by my readers, my contemporaries.

CONFLICTS
OF A
MOTHER

PART ONE

WRITING AND MOTHERHOOD

My epigraphs define the space I shall explore here. At one end, the confident assertion of a psychoanalyst who not only knows what mothers want and feel, but does not hesitate for more than an instant ("simply expressed"—a pause) in formulating the very words that mothers speak to themselves.[1] At the other end, a simple yet insidious question.[2] Does the question demolish the psychoanalyst's certitudes? That is not the point. My purpose is not to discredit psychoanalysis but, in the literal sense of the term, to put it in its place. It is a question not of distributing praise or blame but of seeing more clearly, of "knowing where it's at."

First, however, where am I at? Why did I choose to write about writing and motherhood? Is that a valid subject, is there really a connection there? Or am I indulging in a purely private pleasure, tracking a private mania, exorcizing private ghosts? I am the mother of two children, boys, aged nine and two (or so they were when these words were first written). I have written learned books and essays about fiction and the theory of literature. My first impulse, when faced with a problem or a text, is to analyze it, understand it.

With the approach of the climacterium, new motherhood is impossible, and the frustrated activity is directed toward other goals. Simply expressed, this attitude is: "If I cannot have any more children, I must look for something else."

—Helene Deutsch,
The Psychology of Women

What do we know about the (inner) discourse of a mother?

—Julia Kristeva,
"Un Nouveau Type d'intellectuel: Le dissident"

I am not the first to write about writing and motherhood, their conjunction or disjunction; I need not seek justifications for doing so. But necessarily, for better or for worse, I shall write about them in my own way.

Mothers/Writing: The Psychoanalytic Projection

The traditional psychoanalytic view of motherhood is indissociable from the more general theory of normal female development and female sexuality. According to Freud and his orthodox followers, the little girl's problem is to effect a satisfactory transition from the pre-oedipal phase of "masculine" (that is clitoral) eroticism to the properly feminine, vaginal eroticism that will prepare her for her role as a mother. In the process of this transition, the little girl must reject her own mother in favor of the father, whose child she longs to bear. She must reconcile herself to the "fact" of her castration, and must give up the active-sadistic impulses of the pre-oedipal phase in favor of the passive-masochistic gratifications appropriate to her female role. In the words of Karl Abraham, "The normal adult woman becomes reconciled to her own sexual role . . . She desires passive gratification and longs for a child."[3] According to Helene Deutsch, the sine qua non of normal motherhood is "the masochistic-feminine willingness to sacrifice" (pp. 411–412)—a sacrifice made easy by the impulse of maternal love, whose "chief characteristic is tenderness. All the aggression and sexual sensuality in the woman's personality are suppressed and diverted by this central emotional expression of motherliness" (p. 20). The mother's sacrifice is also made easy by the fact that through the child, especially if it is a male child, she compensates for the one great lack in her life, the lack of a penis.

Feminine masochism, feminine passivity, feminine castration, feminine penis envy—every one of these notions has been challenged, both by contemporary feminists and by such earlier revisionists as Karen Horney and Clara Thompson. Significantly, however, their arguments have borne not on the *fact* of feminine masochism, passivity, or penis envy in our society, but rather on their innateness versus their culturally conditioned character. More recently, such feminists as Juliet Mitchell and Elizabeth Janeway have salvaged Freud's insights by relativizing them: whereas for Freud the course of female development was a physiologically determined process and therefore inevitable (despite his well-known demurrals, his famous statements about not knowing what women are and what women want), for Mitchell and Janeway, as for Horney and Thompson before them, the fact of feminine masochism or penis envy reflects the devalued position of women in patriarchal society. It is the explanation of these facts that must be corrected and their inevitability that must be challenged. As Juliet Mitchell has written: "Freud's psychoanalytic theories are about sexism; that he himself propagated certain sexist views and that his work has been the bulwark of the ideological oppression of women are doubtless of great importance. But we can understand its significance only if we first realize that it was precisely the psychological formations produced within patriarchal societies that he was revealing and analysing."[4]

By and large I agree with this view, which also informs (by and large) Nancy Chodorow's important book *The Reproduction of Mothering*. As Chodorow shows, neither a biological-anthropological nor a behavioral role-socialization model is adequate to account for the permanence of women's mothering function: "Women's capacities for mothering and abilities to get gratification from it are strongly internalized and psychologically enforced, and are built developmentally into the feminine psychic structure. Women are prepared psychologically for mothering through the developmental situation in which they grow up, and in which women have mothered them."[5] This being the case, Chodorow argues that only a radical change in modes of parenting, so that fathers and men also "mother," can effect a change in the feminine psyche. If such a change should ever occur on a scale large enough to make a difference, the conjunction of writing and motherhood, like most other conjunctions involving motherhood, will become an altogether different subject. In the meantime, I shall argue that that particular conjunction is (1) a problem, (2) a woman's problem, and (3) a problem that must be considered as much in psychological as in sociological terms, if not more so.

Let me return, however, to the psychoanalytic view of motherhood as it exists in the traditional literature. The good and even the "good-enough" (Winnicott) mother is characterized, according to this literature, not only by tenderness and the "masochistic-feminine willingness to sacrifice" but above all by her exclusive and total involvement with her child. Chodorow quotes the psychoanalyst Alice Balint as representative in this respect. Balint states: "The ideal mother has no interests of her own . . . For all of us it remains self-evident that the interests of mother and child are identical, and it is the generally acknowledged measure of the goodness or badness of the mother how far she really feels this identity of interests." Chodorow comments: "This statement does not mean that mothers have no interests apart from their children—we all know that this kind of overinvestment is 'bad' for children. But social commentators, legislators, and most clinicians expect women's interests to enhance their mothering and expect women to want only interests that do so." Good mothering, in other words, "requires both a constant delicate assessment of infantile needs and wants and an extreme selflessness. Analysts do not consider their prescription difficult for most 'normal' mothers to fulfill."[6]

Melanie Klein speaks with great sympathy and understanding about the murderous impulses that every child feels toward its beloved mother; she does not speak about the murderous impulses that a mother may feel toward her beloved child.[7] According to Helene Deutsch, the one permanent tragedy of motherhood is that children grow up: "Every phase of the child's development ends with intensified tendencies to liberate himself. The mother—every mother—tries to keep him attached to herself and opposes the actions that tend to dissolve the tie" (p. 331). The notion that another tragedy of motherhood may lie in the conflict between the mother's desire for self-realization (a self-realization that has nothing to do with her being a mother) and the child's need for her selflessness seems never to have entered the psychoanalysts' minds.[8] Even Karen Horney, herself a mother and a writer, could devote a paper to the subject of "maternal conflicts" whose entire emphasis was on the harm a mother could do to her son if her own relations to her parents were not properly worked out.[9] It is as if, for psychoanalysis, the only self worth worrying about in the mother-child relationship were that of the child. How this exclusive focus affects the mother is something we are only now becoming aware of, as mothers begin to speak for themselves. "Most of the literature of infant care and psychology has assumed that the process toward individuation is essentially the *child's* drama, played out against and with a parent or parents who are, for better or worse, givens. Nothing could have prepared me for the realization that I was a mother, one of those givens, when I knew I was still in a state of uncreation myself."[10] That is Adrienne Rich's testimony; the feelings it describes are not unique to her.

Mothers don't write; they are written. Simply expressed (to quote Helene Deutsch), this is the underlying assumption of most psychoanalytic theories about writing and about artistic creation in general. According to Freud, the poet is a superior daydreamer, endowed with the gift of transforming his personal fantasies into aesthetically pleasing creations. The fantasies themselves, however, are always derived from the poet's childhood self: "a piece of creative writing, like a daydream, is a continuation of, and a substitute for, what was once the play of childhood."[11] D. W. Winnicott enlarged this view with his theory of transitional objects, which function essentially as substitutes for the mother. According to Winnicott, transitional objects exist in an intermediate area between the purely subjective world of the child and the external reality of the "not-me"—more exactly, in the "potential space between the baby and the mother."[12] Artistic creation, indeed all cultural experience, belongs to the realm of transitional phenomena. Successful creation, like all creative living, depends on the trust and self-confidence first developed in the child's earliest relationship to his mother.

In Melanie Klein's theory of artistic creation, the mother—or rather, the mother's body—functions as a "beautiful land" to be explored. The creative writer, like the explorer, the scientist, the artist in general, is impelled by the "desire to re-discover the mother of the early days, whom [he] has lost actually or in [his] feelings."[13] The work of art itself stands for the mother's body, destroyed repeatedly in fantasy but restored or "repaired" in the act of creation.

The fact that for Klein, as for Freud, the poet is always a "he" is worth remarking, but it is not the point I wish to stress here. For me it is more significant that psychoanalytic theory invariably places the artist, man or woman, in the position of the child. Just as motherhood is ultimately the child's drama, so is artistic creation.

In both cases the mother is the essential but silent Other, the mirror in whom the child searches for his own reflection, the body he seeks to appropriate, the thing he loses or destroys again and again, and seeks to recreate. A writer, says Roland Barthes, is "someone who plays with the body of his mother" (or her mother? The French is conveniently ambiguous on this point, but Barthes's own meaning seems clear enough).[14]

This is an extremely suggestive idea, one that is capable of renewing our understanding of a host of writers, such as Proust, Poe, Stendhal, Woolf (see *To the Lighthouse*), Robbe-Grillet (as I have tried to show elsewhere),[15] and many others. And yet . . . what about the writer who *is* "the body of the mother"? Is this a foolish question, since mothers, too, have mothers? Does the mother who writes write exclusively as her own mother's child?

Perhaps. Yet I contend that we know too little about what and how and why mothers write to answer the question one way or the other. We may even know too little to have asked the right questions. As Tillie Olsen has pointed out, mothers who have been "full-time" writers have been rare until our own century, and the great women writers have been, with very few exceptions, childless during all or most of their writing lives.[16] Kristeva is right: we know very little about the inner discourse of a mother; and so long as our own emphasis, encouraged by psychoanalytic theory and by the looming presence of (mostly male) mother-fixated writers, continues to be on the-mother-as-she-is-written rather than on the-mother-as-she-writes, we shall continue in our ignorance.

There are consistent reasons for the failure of psychoanalysis to see mothers writing (*as* mothers). First of all, psychoanalysis is nothing if not a theory of childhood. We should not be surprised if it locates artistic creativity, as it does every other aspect of adult personality, in the child the adult once was, and often continues to be. A second and more specific reason lies, as I suggested earlier, in the psychoanalytic theory of normal female development: mothers don't create works of art, because all of their creative, aggressive drives find an outlet in the production of children. As Helene Deutsch put it: "The urge to intellectual and artistic creation and the productivity of motherhood spring from common sources, and *it seems very natural that one should be capable of replacing the other*" (p. 478, emphasis added). So long as her motherly capacities are put to use, a mother does not need to write: "A motherly woman can give up her other interests in favor of the reproductive function, and she returns to the former when she feels the biologic restriction approaching" (p. 478). This might be called the menopausal theory of artistic creation—although when one reads Deutsch's description of the woman at menopause, one wonders what sort of creation she could possibly undertake: "With the lapse of the reproductive service, her beauty vanishes, and usually the warm, vital flow of feminine emotional life as well" (p. 481). The grave is not far off, it would seem. The menopausal theory is itself a subcategory of the more general "either/or" theory: writing or motherhood, work or child—never the two at the same time.

The either/or theory is, of course, older than psychoanalysis. As Elaine Showalter has documented, it was already invoked by the early Victorians. On the whole, Victorian critics were kinder to women writers who were mothers than to their childless sisters, but with the clear understanding that "mothers must not dream of activity beyond the domestic sphere until their families are grown."[17] This line of argument, adopted even by such writers as Mrs. Gaskell, who was the mother of four children (she published her first novel at age thirty-eight), was based on the moral obligations of the good wife and mother. "What most women rejected as unacceptable and unchristian," writes Showalter, "was the use of literary vocation to avoid the responsibilities of home life."[18] It took psychoanalysis to transform moral obligation into a psychological "law," equating the creative impulse with the procreative one and decreeing that she who has a child feels no need to write books.

By means of this "law," psychoanalytic theory not only offered an elegant explanation for and justification of the mother's silence (making any mother who did not wish to wait until menopause to write books feel "abnormal") but provided an equally elegant explanation for why some childless women (and men) did write books: books were obviously substitutes for children. Once the "law" was properly internalized by women (in a way it could not possibly be by men, since men cannot *choose* to bear children), its capacities for generating guilt and anguish were infinite: corresponding to the writing mother's sense of "abnormality" was the childless woman writer's sense of "unnaturalness." Not for nothing did Virginia Woolf, who knew her Freud, "fear that writing was an act that unsexed her, made her an unnatural woman."[19] Whereas the male writer, in comparing his books to tenderly loved children (a common metaphor, at least until the recent emphasis on writing as an autoerotic activity), could see his metaphorical maternity as something *added* to his male qualities, the childless woman whose books "replaced" real children too often thought (or was made to feel) that she had less, not more.

Here again, psychoanalysis cannot be held entirely responsible, since the derogation of childless and/or unmarried women writers was already common in the days of Austen and the Brontës. My point, however, is that psychoanalysis lent scientific prestige to a widespread cultural prejudice, reinforcing it and elevating it to the status of a natural law.

It is in this context that the protest against the "motherhood myth" perpetrated by psychoanalysis, and against the fact of motherhood itself—a protest that has characterized one branch of contemporary feminist writing and criticism—must be understood. We should also understand, however, that this protest is itself in a sense a victim of the either/or theory. The only difference is that the values attributed to book and child have been reversed. Thus, Nina Auerbach, in an article significantly titled "Artists and Mothers: A False Alliance," declares that "far from endowing Austen with second-hand motherhood, her identity as an artist represented an escape from confinement into a child-free world with space for mind and spirit, time for change, and privacy for growth." Auerbach celebrates Austen and Eliot *because* they "both turned away from motherhood and embraced a creativity they defined as more spacious, more adult, more inclusive."[20]

Is there no alternative to the either/or? Will we ever be forced to write the book and deny the child (not the child we were but the child we have, or might have) or love the child and postpone/renounce the book? Or is Kristeva right in insisting that "while a certain feminism takes its pouting and its isolation for protest and perhaps even for dissidence, genuine feminine innovation . . . will not be possible until we have elucidated motherhood, feminine creation, and the relationship between them"?[21]

It is time to let mothers have their say.

Writing and Motherhood: As Mothers See It

The picture is not all rosy.

> Try telling a child that Mamma is working, when the child can see with its own eyes that she is just sitting there writing . . . I dare not have music on when I am in the basement, writing, lest upstairs they think I am just sitting here loafing. I feel that to be respected I must produce pancakes and homebaked bread and have neat, tidy rooms. (Liv Ullman)[22]

> Since I had begun writing, I had sought time alone. That very self I had once sought to flee, . . . that dangerous, frightening self was precisely what I had learned to treasure, what I had begun to understand.
>
> In order to tame [the dangerous self], I had to write, regularly and consistently, and in order to write I had to be alone.
>
> Now suddenly I was always with Benjamin. (Jane Lazarre)[23]

> For me, poetry was where I lived as no-one's mother, where I existed as myself. (Adrienne Rich)[24]

> I just started pecking away at this story set during the American Revolution. It wasn't anything I could get completely absorbed in. I had three boys at home, and there were always dishes to put in the dishwasher. (Kathleen Woodiwiss)[25]

> Children need one *now.* The very fact that these are real needs, that one feels them as one's own (love, not duty); that there is no one else responsible for these needs, gives them primacy . . . Work interrupted, deferred, relinquished, makes blockage—at best, lesser accomplishment. (Tillie Olsen)[26]

> Every time I thought something would do, in the old days I'd race to the writing pad . . . and really be excited. Now I kept thinking: "Oh

no, I don't think that's very good." Then one morning I woke up and I thought: "It's gone . . . and I don't want it to come back." (Susan Hill)[27]

Guilt, desperation, splitting of the self, alienated role playing ("My writing is not serious; don't be offended by it—just look at my three children"), resignation to a lesser accomplishment, renunciation of the writing self—these are some of the realities, some of the possible choices that writing mothers live with.

Kathleen Woodiwiss is a rich woman, the author of historical romances for the "housewife market." Her latest book has sold more than two million copies. She calls herself "an ordinary housewife": "I enjoy cooking and cleaning, my family and home. Right now my husband is remodeling one of the bathrooms."[28] She represents what some would call the perfect accommodation between writing and motherwifehood. Perhaps she has no serious talent or ambitions; perhaps she has never allowed herself to ask whether she does.

Susan Hill was a highly respected "younger" British novelist—for the cultivated reader, not the buyer of best-sellers. In her late thirties she married, and she became pregnant soon after. She was working on a novel at the time, but never finished it. She no longer writes fiction.

Between these two extremes, each of which is in its own way a renunciation of the writing self, are manifold ways of coping. Some we know about because they have been written; others we can only guess at. We need more information—more interviews, more diaries, more memoirs, essays, reminiscences by writing mothers. I am sure I have missed many as it is, but exhaustiveness is not what I am aiming for. I wish merely to glimpse the possibilities, the principal recurrent themes in what some contemporary writing mothers have said discursively (poetry and fiction are a later question) about, or out of, their own experience of the relationship between writing and motherhood.

What are the major themes? I see them clustered into two large groups: opposition and integration, motherhood as obstacle or source of conflict and motherhood as link, as source of connection to work and world. The oppositional themes—guilt versus love, mother's creative self versus child's needs, isolation versus commitment—are the ones I emphasized in the above quotations. The daily conflict and self-doubt, the waste of creative energies these oppositions engender cannot be overestimated. What is involved here, furthermore, is not simply an institutional or social problem. Alternate nurturers will not necessarily relieve it (although they may eventually help) because the conflicts are *inside* the mother; they are part of her most fundamental experience. One can always argue, as Rich and others have done, that the internal conflicts are the result of institutional forces, the result of women's isolation, women's victimization by the motherhood myth in patriarchal society. But while this argument can help us understand *why* the conflicts are internal, it does not eliminate them. At the present time, any mother of young children (and I mean not only infants, but children of school age and beyond) who wants to do serious creative work— with all that such work implies of the will to self-assertion, self-absorption, solitary grappling—must be prepared for the worst kind of struggle, the struggle against herself. Here I am reminded of Karen Horney's description of a certain type of neurotic disturbance in work—the disturbance she sees as typical of the "self-effacing type":

> Without being aware of it, he is up against two kinds of chronic handicaps: his self-minimizing and his inefficiency in tackling the subject matter. His self-minimizing largely results . . . from his need to keep himself down in order not to trespass against the taboo on anything "presumptuous." *It is a subtle undermining, berating, doubting,* which saps the energies without his being aware of what he is doing to himself . . . As a result he works with the oppressive feeling of impotence and insignificance . . . His inefficiency in tackling the subject matter is caused mainly by taboos on all that implies assertion, aggression, mastery . . . His difficulty is not in being unproductive. Good original ideas may emerge, but he is inhibited in taking hold of them, tackling them, grappling with them, wrestling with them, checking them, shaping them, organizing them. We are not usually aware of these mental operations as being assertive, aggressive moves, although the language indicates it; and we may realize this fact only when they are inhibited by a pervasive check on aggression.[29]

Mothers, or women, are of course not the only ones to whom Horney's description applies.[30] She herself obviously had both men and women in mind. But I would suggest that in the case of the writing mother, the subtle undermining, the oppressive feeling of impotence and insignificance, the pervasive check on aggression that Horney talks about are intimately linked to a sense of guilt about her child. Jean-Paul Sartre once said in an interview, when asked about the value of literature and of his own novels in particular: "En face d'un enfant qui meurt, *La Nausée* ne fait pas le poids" (freely translated: "When weighed against a dying child, *La Nausée* doesn't count").[31] If this statement reflects the well-known guilt of the bourgeois writer with left-wing sympathies (Sartre being a specialist on *that* question), what are we to say about the guilt of a mother who might weigh her books not against a stranger's dying child but merely against her own child who is crying?

One way to appease the crying child (and my contention is that whether or not the child actually cries while the mother writes, he or she always cries in the mother's nightmares) is to tender her/him the book as a propitiatory offering. Phyllis Chesler's *With Child,* a diary of her first pregnancy and childbirth at the age of thirty-seven, is dedicated to her son: "To my son Ariel, this handmade gift to welcome you." (I am a good mother; I make my own presents.) Liv Ullman's autobiography, from which I quoted above, is dedicated to her daughter, Linn, with a frontispiece photograph of mother and child forehead to forehead. The back cover is a close-up photo of Liv, somber, alone. The last pages are a letter to Linn—a series of self-reproaches by the mother, culminating in the astonishing question: "Do you understand that I really have no valid reason not to run out to you and live your life?" This from one of the most serious actresses of our time, who is also a genuine writer.

Another way to propitiate the crying child is not to write the book, or to write it less well than one could. "Almost no mothers—as almost no part-time, part-self persons—have created enduring literature . . . so far." That was Tillie Olsen writing, in 1972.[32]

So much for the dark side. There is also a lighter one.

> Through you, Ariel, I'm enlarged, connected to something larger than myself. Like falling in love, like ideological conversion, the connection makes me *feel* my existence. (Phyllis Chesler)[33]

> And yet, somehow, something, call it Nature or that affirming fatalism of the human creature, makes me aware of the inevitable as already

part of me, not to be contended against so much as brought to bear as an additional weapon against drift, stagnation and spiritual death. (Adrienne Rich)[34]

A mother can be any sort of person, great or ordinary, given to moderation or intensity, inclined toward amazonian aggression or receptivity. But whatever type you are, being a mother forces you to accept your limitations. And when you accept your limitations as a mother, you begin to accept your limitations in other areas of life as well. The daily grinding friction of motherhood will give you the chance, at least, of relinquishing some of your egotism. You will finally cease to be a child. (Jane Lazarre)[35]

Through the coming of the child and the beginning of a love, perhaps the only genuine feminine love for another . . . one has the chance to accede to that relationship so difficult for a woman, the relationship to the Other: to the symbolic and the ethical. If pregnancy is a threshold between nature and culture, motherhood is a bridge between the singular and the ethical. (Julia Kristeva)[36]

What does it mean to love, for a woman? The same thing as to write . . . WORD/FLESH. From one to the other, eternally, fragmented visions, metaphors of the invisible. (Julia Kristeva)[37]

Integration, connection, reaching out; a defense against drift and spiritual death, a way of outgrowing the solipsism of childhood, a way to relate, a way to write—this, too, is motherhood as seen by mothers, often by the very same mothers who at other times feel torn apart by the conflicting pulls of work and child. Jane Lazarre, at the end of *The Mother Knot,* invents a debate between "the mother" and "the dark lady," the one urging Jane to have a second child, the other arguing against it. The dark lady says: "I am not speaking about mere details and practical responsibilities. It is the effect of those continuous demands on the spirit to which I commend your attention." The mother counters: "Don't you want the feeling of a baby moving inside you again?" But it turns out that the dark lady is the mother in disguise; the mother, the dark lady. And Jane is both of them: they are inside her head.

Have we simply arrived here at the point where Adrienne Rich began? "My children cause me the most exquisite suffering of which I have any experience. It is the suffering of ambivalence; the murderous alternation between bitter resentment and raw-edged nerves, and blissful gratification and tenderness."[38] Yes and no. For Rich, as she expresses it in this diary entry, ambivalence is an *alternation* between resentment and tenderness, negation of the child and reaching out for the child—as if these two impulses were unconnected to each other, locked in an insurmountable opposition, corresponding perhaps to the opposition between the mother's need to affirm herself as writer and the child's need (or her belief in the child's need) for her selflessness. There is something of this struggle in Lazarre's parable, but the parable also suggests a possibility of reconciliation rather than conflict between the warring elements. If the mother is the dark lady and the dark lady the mother, then the energies and aspirations of the one are also those of the other. The mother's tenderness and the dark lady's urge for self-expression may support, not hinder, each other.

This is precisely what is implied by Chesler, by Rich in another diary entry (the one I quoted above), and especially by Kristeva, who goes beyond implication to explicit statement: "Far from being in contradiction with creativity (as the existentialist myth still tries to make us believe), motherhood can—in itself and if the economic constraints are not too burdensome—favor a certain feminine creation. To the extent that it lifts the fixations, makes passion circulate between life and death, self and other, culture and nature."[39] Kristeva is prudent—she makes no absolute claims (motherhood *can* favor creation, but it doesn't necessarily do so); she is aware of the material obstacles (How will mother write if there is no one else to care for baby, or if she must work at other jobs to support baby?—Tillie Olsen's questions). Yet, in an important turn of French feminist theory, which we also see appearing in a less abstract version in current American feminist thinking, Kristeva rejects the either/or dilemma and suggests that motherhood and feminine creation go hand in hand.

Kristeva's argument, as stated in two essays in the winter 1977 issue of *Tel Quel*, is very complex and deserves a long analysis unto itself. This is not the appropriate place for that, but I wish to pause at least briefly in order to take a closer look.

Kristeva's argument can be summed up approximately as follows: the order of the symbolic, which is the order of language, of culture, of the law, of the Name-of-the-Father (in Lacan's terminology), is especially difficult for women to accede to, whether for historical or other reasons. Motherhood, which establishes a *natural* link (the child) between woman and the social world, provides a privileged means of entry into the order of culture and of language. This privilege belongs to the mother (if I read Kristeva correctly here) not only in contrast to women who are not mothers but also in contrast to men, whose relationship to the symbolic order is itself problematic, characterized by discontinuity, separation, absence. The symbolic, whether for men or for women, functions as the realm of the (unattainable) Other, the realm of arbitrary signs rather than of things; it is by definition the realm of frustated relations, of impossible loves. The love of God, that ultimate sign of the Other, is of the order of the impossible. But for the mother, according to Kristeva, the Other is not (only) an arbitrary sign, a necessary absence; it is the child, whose presence and whose bodily link to her are inescapable givens, material facts. If to love (her child) is, for a woman, the same thing as to write, we have in that conjunction a modern, secular equivalent of the word made flesh.

This straightforward summary is in a sense a betrayal, however, for the most interesting thing about Kristeva's argument is its quasi-byzantine indirection. The first of the two essays, placed as an introduction to the special issue of the journal devoted to "*recherches féminines,*" is not ostensibly about motherhood at all, or even about women, but about the possibilities of intellectuals and of intellectual dissidence in Western culture. The remarks about motherhood and its relation to feminine creation form part of a section on the possibly dissident role of women in relation to patriarchal law. Since the more elemental law of the reproduction of the species is essentially in women's hands, Kristeva wonders whether mothers are not, in fact, at the very opposite pole of dissidence—whether by maintaining the species they do not also maintain and guarantee the existing social order. She does not answer this question directly, but my sense is that, if pressed, her answer would be: "Yes and no." The mother's body, being a place of fragmentation, cleavage, elemental pulsations that exist *before* language and meaning, is necessarily a place of exile, a place of dis-order and extreme singularity in relation to the collective order of culture. At the same time, the mother's body is the link between nature and culture, and as such must play a conserving role.

What interests me, however, is another question that Kristeva poses: "After the Virgin [Mary], what do we know about the (inner) discourse of a mother?" The question is both provocative and bizarre, its bizarreness residing in the opening words. Do we know more about the Virgin's inner discourse than about any other mother's? At best we know the discourse that has been attributed to her, that has in fact *created* her—it is the discourse of Christianity, of the Fathers of the Church.

Kristeva is aware of this. Her second and much longer essay ("Héréthique de l'amour") is devoted to the question of how the myth of the Virgin Mother was gradually elaborated by Christian discourse, and how it has functioned in the imagination of the West. Above all, she seeks to answer this question: What is it about the Virgin that was satisfactory to women for hundreds of years, and why is that representation no longer satisfactory today? Her tentative conclusion is that in the image of the Virgin Mother, Christianity provided what for a long time was a satisfactory compromise solution to female paranoia: a denial of the male's role in procreation (virgin birth), a fulfillment of the female desire for power (Mary as Queen of Heaven), a sublimation of the woman's murderous or devouring desires through the valorization of her breast (the infant Jesus suckling) and of her own pain (the *Mater dolorosa*), a fulfilling of the fantasy of deathlessness or eternal life (the Assumption), and above all a denial of other women, including the woman's own mother (Mary was "alone of all her sex"). All of this was granted upon one condition: that the ultimate supremacy and divinity of the male be maintained in the person of the Son, before whom the Mother kneels and to whom she is subservient.

According to Kristeva, the compromise solution represented by the Virgin Mother provided a model that women could, however indirectly, identify with, and at the same time allowed those in charge of the social and symbolic order to maintain their control. (It may be worth noting that the Christian representation of the Virgin Mother has some affinities with, but is much more powerful than, the representation of ideal motherhood in psychoanalytic discourse. In both cases the mother is elevated precisely to the extent that she prostrates herself before her son. For Freud, the mother's greatest satisfaction is to see her favorite son attain glory, which then reflects back on her.) For today's women, however, Kristeva argues, the myth of Mary has lost its positive powers: it leaves too many things unsaid, censors too many aspects of female experience, chief among them the experience of childbirth and of the mother's body in general, the relationship of women to their mothers (and to their daughters), and the relationship of women to men (not to male children, but to adult men). So far as all of these relationships are concerned, motherhood provides a central point from which to ask the questions and to take a first step toward answering them.

As if to demonstrate this very thing, Kristeva intersperses her analytical, discursive text with lyrical, discontinuous fragments of an "other" text—this "other" text being the inner discourse of a mother, Kristeva herself. Since the lyrical fragments are surrounded, enveloped by the discursive text, it is tempting to see the two as "mother" and "child," with the lyrical fragments representing the child. (This idea was suggested to me by Carolyn Burke.) But paradoxically, in the "child-text" it is a *mother* who writes of her experiences: childbirth, playing with her infant, watching over the child who is sick for the first time, feeling separated from and at the same time united with the child, memories of her own mother (the "other woman"), her relationship to language, to the law. The lyrical fragments are thus in counterpoint, both stylistically and on the level of content, to the discursive text, as the mother's *inner* discourse is in counterpoint to the discourse given to her, constructed about her, by Christianity, the dominant order of Western culture.

These essays by Kristeva seem to me to be especially important for three reasons: she seeks to analyze and show the limitations of Western culture's traditional discourse about motherhood; she offers a theory, however incomplete and tentative, about the relation between motherhood and feminine creation; finally, she *writes* her own maternal text as an example of what such creation might be. This ambitious undertaking is part of the much broader context of contemporary French feminist theory, which over the past several years has been trying both to elaborate a theory of and to exemplify the specificity of *l'écriture féminine*. Luce Irigaray and Hélène Cixous (who is a mother) have insisted on the essentially subversive, disorderly nature of women's writing in patriarchal culture, without attempting to differentiate between the feminine and the maternal. This may be because—at least for Cixous—the very fact of being a woman means that one is "never far from the 'mother,'" that is, from a force of reparation and nourishment that is fundamentally "other" in relation to the desiccated rationalism of male discourse.[40]

Chantal Chawaf, on the other hand, much more radically than Kristeva, has tied the practice of feminine writing to the biological fact of motherhood. Chawaf is the mother of two children and the author of several books written in a lyrical autobiographical mode. The central experience around which all her writing turns is the physical and emotional experience of motherhood and of maternal love, which she endows with quasi-cosmic significance. One of her recent books, *Maternité,* is a series of sensuous prose poems celebrating the love between a mother who is on the verge of emotional breakdown and her two children, whom she perceives as her only link to communication and light, in opposition to solitude and eternal darkness. Chawaf has stated in interviews and in commentaries on her work that, for her, motherhood is the only access to literary creation. In *Maternité* she speaks of a "new syntax with fatty nouns, infinitive thighs," a language so physical that it would be a nourishment and "would make every sentence the close relative of the skin and of the mucous membranes."[41]

The work of the French radical feminists represents without a doubt the most ambitious attempt so far to theorize the relationship between writing and femininity, and more or less directly between writing and motherhood. Personally, my one reservation about their work—which is clearly work in progress and therefore impossible to make definitive pronouncements about—concerns its exclusionary aspects. To recognize that women, mothers, have been excluded from the order of patriarchal discourse, and to insist on the positive difference of maternal and feminine writing in relation to male writing, can only be beneficial at this time. But it would be a pity if the male gesture of exclusion and repression of the female Other were to be matched by a similar gesture in reverse. I do not mean only the obvious exclusion of men, for some French feminists (Hélène Cixous among them) are willing to admit that certain male poets have attained a "feminine" status in their writing. Rather, I mean the exclusion of a certain *kind* of writing and discourse arbitrarily defined as "male"—repressive, logical, the discourse of power, or what have you. Such a gesture necessarily places "feminine" writing in a minority position, willfully ex-centric in relation to power. I am not wholly convinced that that is the best position for women to be in.

I also have reservations about what might be called the fetishization of the female body in relation to writing. It may be true that femininity and its quintessential embodiment, motherhood, can provide a privileged mode of access to language and the mother tongue. What would worry me would be the codification, on the basis of this insight, of women's writing and writing style. In recent French feminist theory and practice, one sees tendencies toward just such codification, both on the level of themes and on the level of style: the centrality of the woman's body and blood, her closeness to nature, her attunement to the quality of *voice* rather than to "dry" meaning; elemental rhythms, writing as flow (of menstrual blood, of mother's milk, of uterine fluid), "liquid" syntax, lyricism at all costs, receptivity, union, nonaggression . . . We are reaching the point where a new genre is being created, and that may be all to the good. But to see in this genre the one and only genuine mode of feminine writing would, I think, be a mistake.[42]

Writing and Motherhood: The Mother's Fictions

After that ascent into theory, I would like to return to more concrete ground. Mothers write, and they write fiction as well as personal statements. Speaking of contemporary British and American novelists who are mothers, Tillie Olsen remarked that "not many have directly used the material open to them out of motherhood as central source of their work."[43] An interesting question is implied here. What fascinates me, however, is a more specific question: whether, and how, the conjunction of writing and motherhood is refracted in the fictions—as opposed to the more direct statements where the mother says "I"—of mothers who write. Here psychoanalysis may be of help, if only by analogy. Using as a starting point Freud's contention that the work of fiction is a distanced, formally disguised version of the writer's fantasy, we can ask: Is there such a thing as the writing mother's fantasy? And if so, what transformations does the fantasy undergo in the process of its fictionalization? To put it somewhat differently, what happens to the mother's discourse when it chooses not direct expression but the indirections of fiction?

Having asked the question, I am not quite sure just how to go about answering it. But no matter. I shall assume that mothers' fantasies exist, that they are formulatable, and that they can (can, not must) provide the impetus for fictional elaboration. I shall further assume that they are to be found, if anywhere, in the fictions of women writers who are mothers. To demonstrate the literary-critical, if not scientific, usefulness of these assumptions, I shall propose readings of two works by a single writer. The writer is the American poet and novelist Rosellen Brown. The works are a three-page short story titled "Good Housekeeping" and a novel titled *The Autobiography of My Mother*.[44]

"Good Housekeeping": the title is double-edged. A mother puts her baby down for a nap, first photographing his behind from close up. She is a photographer, working now after an interval long enough for all the chemicals in her darkroom to have dried up. But she is a professional, already imagining how she will hang the pictures in her next show ("utterly random, on flat matte. No implicit order, no heavy ironies"), and she works fast. After the baby's rear come the sludge-covered coffeepot, the inside of the toilet bowl, the mountain of laundry seen from the inside looking out, a bunch of peeled vegetables strewn among the peels, the rumpled bedsheets, her own vagina (seen only by the viewfinder of the camera), a handful of condoms found in a box and randomly arranged, the dirty window, fresh soil in which seedlings of vegetables are buried, a drawerful of household odds and ends, cigarette paper and the marijuana hidden in a spice jar, the inside of a pencil sharpener, a stretch of ugly wallpaper left uncovered, the welcome mat caked with mud. She rejects a row of lined-up cans and an omelet made for the occasion as inappropriate ("too much like *Good Housekeeping*"), as well as a pile of bird feathers left by the cat: their function is not clear without the cat, and besides, "are murdered birds a part of every household?"

Then the baby wakes, screaming. With the shades up it is so light "you could see the baby's uvula quivering like an icicle about to drop." When he sees the camera, the baby stops crying, fascinated. "Eyes like cameras. His mother looked back at herself in them, a black box in her lap with a queer star of light in its middle." The baby smiles, reaching for his mother (or for the camera?) through the slats of the crib. The mother's next action (and the story's final paragraph):

> She put her head in her hands. Then she reached in and, focusing as well as she could with one hand, the baby slapping at her through the bars, wheezing with laughter, she found one cool bare thigh, the rosy tightness of it, and pinched it with three fingers, kept pinching hard, till she got that angry uvula again, and a good bit of very wet tongue. Through the magnifier it was spiny as some plant, some sponge, maybe, under the sea.

I find this an extraordinarily powerful story, even after several readings. In trying to account for its power (its powerful effect on me), I invariably return to this last paragraph: the mother looking at her child not directly but through the camera, transforming him into an object; feeling his thighs not as flesh, her flesh, but professionally as a "rosy tightness"; then pinching until the cry comes, and with it the thing she wants to capture, the quivering uvula—the clinicalness of it, and at the same time its possibility for endless metaphorization: icicle, spiny plant, sponge under the sea. The rosy thigh, sentimental and cloying, would be at best appropriate for *Good Housekeeping;* the angry uvula, like the other exemplary objects ("part of every household") that preceded it, will hang in random order on flat matte. It is not propaganda ("Let us all be good housekeepers and have rosy babies") but art.

Art? And what about the crying child? The power of the story, for me, lies in the fantasy that I read in (or perhaps into) it: "With every word I write, with every metaphor, with every act of genuine creation, I hurt my child."

Surely I am overreacting? Perhaps not. To me this is not only a story about the inner world of motherhood *as it is felt,* instead of as it is mythologized in women's magazines (think of the mess and the jumble, the receptacles of every kind, the insides so carefully observed, the hidden things growing); it is also a story about the *representation* of motherhood by a mother, "seeing herself from a great distance, doing an assignment on herself doing an assignment." And finally, it is a story about the specular relation between mother-as-artist and her child: seeing herself reflected *as artist* (holding the camera) in his eyes, she reacts by pinning him down, turning him into an image, a metaphor, a text. Portrait of the artist as mother; or, the momentary triumph of aggression over tenderness.

I say momentary triumph, because the anguish and guilt that inevitably attend the real-life mother's fantasy of writing as aggression against her child are absent. The story ends at the precise moment when the artist affirms herself against both the child and her own maternal feelings, before guilt (or madness—for if she were to go on hurting the child, we would have to call her mad) has a chance to appear. The result, both in the fiction and in the effect its language produces, is a sense of freedom, of formal control, which blocks any possibility of sentimentalization or self-pity. This becomes clearer if one compares Brown's story to, say, Alta's long poem, *Momma*, which recounts a similar experience: the poet-mother chasing her child out of the room so that she can write about her, negating her physical presence in order to capture her as a name, a text. In *Momma* the tone is one of anguish, since the mother *feels* the child's pain and expresses, retrospectively, her own sense of guilt and self-reproach in the poem. By opting for a simultaneous rather than a retrospective point of view, Brown's story refuses, I think quite consciously, the relief—but also the sentimentalization—that comes from self-reproach. We do not know how the mother in the story felt about her action afterward; when she focuses her camera on the crying child (but significantly she does not *see* the child; she sees nothing but the "angry uvula"), we know only the cool concentration with which she snaps the picture. The language of the story "doubles" her own activity by means of the concluding metaphors.

Katherine Anne Porter once said about her own work that at the moment of writing "a calculated coldness is the best mood."[45] It is the dialectic between calculated coldness and intensity of feeling—a dialectic that characterizes the mother's problematic position between work and child—which is thematized in Brown's short story and which, present in the very language of the story, gives it its particular power.

Brown's novel *The Autobiography of My Mother* is a more extended and more complex treatment of the same theme. The novel consists of the alternating narratives of a mother and a daughter, herself the mother of a very young girl. The mother is a woman in her seventies, still actively involved in her work as a civil liberties lawyer, a public figure. The daughter is an ex-flower-child of the late sixties, an escapee of various communes and the California scene, who does nothing. She and her baby daughter return to New York, to her mother's Upper West Side apartment, after a ten-year absence.

Through the mother's narrative we learn about her own disturbed and loveless childhood, her conscious repression of passion and tenderness in favor of extreme self-control and rational action; we also learn of her solitude, her emotional sterility, her inability to make contact with people on any but the most abstract level. Through the daughter's narrative we learn about her feelings of abandonment, her pathological sense of failure and worthlessness, her inability to relate to others except on the most debased sexual level, and her deep hatred of as well as emotional dependence on her mother. During a televised mother-daughter talk show, she refuses to utter a single word. Her revenge on her mother, who is never at a loss for words, takes the form of total passivity and silence.

Between these two women, too much hurt and misunderstanding have accumulated to make any renewal possible. There is the granddaughter, however: stubborn and strong-willed like her grandmother, vulnerable like her mother, she appears to hold out the possibility of a reconciliation of sorts, or at least of a new start. She even manages to awaken her grandmother's seemingly nonexistent maternal feelings.

But it doesn't work out that way. The grandmother plans to take the child away from her mother by legal force. At a picnic where she intends to announce her intentions, she and the child walk down to a waterfall, while the child's mother watches from above. The old woman is not holding on to the child, the child is suddenly no longer there. She has been swept away, drowned. Earlier, the grandmother had stated: "In life there are no accidents."

What is one to make of this very disturbing book? Let's begin with the title: Of which mother, whose mother, is this the autobiography? And who is its author? The text clearly alludes to Gertrude Stein, who wrote *The Autobiography of Alice B. Toklas.* The grandmother's name in this novel is Gerda Stein, and at one point, in an extended allusion to Shakespeare, she refers to herself as Gertrude. She also mentions that her decision to be a lawyer came after her first desire, which was to be a writer. Is the fictional Gertrude a stand-in for the real one? Possibly. But it is Rosellen Brown who is the signed author of this "autobiography," just as Gertrude Stein was of the other one. Structurally, it is Rosellen Brown who is the stand-in for Gertrude Stein—authors both. Yet if one takes the title seriously ("the autobiography of *my* mother") then one must consider (the fictional) Gerda/Gertrude Stein to be Rosellen Brown's mother. Rosellen is thus both daughter to a Gertrude and a Gertrude herself, both author and author's daughter. The two narratives in the novel perhaps reflect this split, as does the fact that in the fiction, mother and daughter manage about equally to attract (and occasionally to repel) our sympathy.

But the question that plagues me is this: Why does the granddaughter, the beautiful and innocent child, have to die? And who is it who kills her?

I will propose a reckless interpretation. The child dies as a punishment to the "unnatural" mother—not her own mother, but her mother's mother, Gerda Stein. It is a self-inflicted punishment, for Gerda loves the child and "in life there are no accidents." It is also a punishment inflicted on Gerda by her daughter, whose own life has been a slow suicide and a permanent reproach to her mother. By not intervening in time, she allows her own daughter to perish as the ultimate reproach (thereby proving herself an "unnatural" mother too).[46] And she finally gets what she wants: for the first time ever, she sees her mother cry.

But of course it is neither Gerda nor her daughter who kills the child; it is the one who is both of them, Rosellen Brown. I read the ending of this novel as a gesture of self-punishment by the writing mother, and the novel itself as a dark companion piece to "Good Housekeeping." Here the aggressive impulse of the mother as artist is turned in on herself. Gerda is a writer *manquée,* and a failed mother as well. In her relationship to her daughter, she embodies the writing mother's most nightmarish fantasy: "I had not known we were to share but one life between us, so that the fuller mine is, the more empty hers" (p. 160).

Brown is the only contemporary novelist I know of who has explored, in fully rendered fictional forms, the violence and guilt as well as the violent energy that attend the artistic creations of mothers. Compared to Brown on this particular subject, I find Margaret Drabble, who has been called "the novelist of maternity,"[47] surprisingly simple. In Drabble's novels, the mothers who write or pursue a creative career (the older, famous novelist in *Jerusalem the Golden,* the thesis-writing heroine of *The Millstone,* the poet protagonist of *The Waterfall,* the archaeologist heroine of *The Realms of Gold*) all have an unproblematic, quasi-idealized relationship to their children. In *Jerusalem the Golden,* where the novelist's children are already grown, we see her mothering a stranger's baby. In *The Millstone,* the heroine writes better after her child is born. In *The Waterfall,* the narrator-heroine speaks of her feelings of ambivalence during pregnancy, but these feelings miraculously evaporate once the child arrives; her problems with writing are tied up not with her children but with her husband and her lover. As for the heroine of *The Realms of Gold,* she has no problems at all, once her love life is straightened out. If the complexity of exploration is any criterion to judge by, Drabble seems to me to be more the novelist of adult love than anything else. Her heroines are almost without exception mothers, but their motherhood is relevant above all to their relations—whether fulfilling or frustrating—with men. The question that I think underlies Drabble's novels is this: Can a creative woman with children have a satisfying, permanent relationship with a man? This question is fascinating in its own right, but it is another question.

So far as writing and motherhood goes, Drabble perhaps gives us the wish-fulfillment fantasies that correspond, in reverse, to the nightmare fantasies of Brown. In between, there remains a great deal of space to explore—in fiction and in life.

2

MATERNAL SPLITTING:
"GOOD" AND "BAD"
MOTHERS AND REALITY

When I first thought about writing this essay (from the beginning, it was linked in my mind to Mary Gordon's *Men and Angels*—a novel that aroused strong feelings in me even before I read it, on the basis of the reviews), I thought I would continue my exploration of the mother's subjectivity begun in "Writing and Motherhood." This time, however, I planned to focus not on the triangle of mother, work, and child, but on that of mother, mother-surrogate, and child. The first triangle involved a struggle between the mother's creative needs and the child's needs, the issue being work. The second triangle appeared as a logical and chronological sequel: no longer pitted against her child, the mother felt herself threatened by the intrusion of a third person, an "other mother" or maternal figure who might displace her in the child's affections while she was away pursuing her nonmaternal activities.

I knew from my own experience and from discussions with women friends engaged in self-absorptive creative careers that this anxiety does in fact exist, whatever its basis may be in reality. (Witness, most recently, the box-office success of *The Hand That Rocks the Cradle*—a

Hollywood nightmare version of the fantasy). Two popular books, Nancy Friday's *Jealousy* and Phyllis Chesler's *Mothers on Trial,* reinforced my conviction.[1] Friday shows, at great length, that jealousy, or the fear of the loss of love by the intrusion of a third party, is a well-nigh universal feeling. Chesler, in turn, documents with terrifying (and terrified) relentlessness a number of custody cases in which mothers have been legally deprived of their children by fathers who are often aided and abetted by what she calls "mother-competitors," women bent on replacing the child's biological mother both in the father's bed and in the child's affections. Even if such cases are statistically rarer than Chesler suggests, they still indicate that in contemporary America the mother's anxiety is not always a matter of fantasy but may be founded on a perception of real danger.

My beginning intention was to explore the question of the "other mother" not as a political issue but as a powerful maternal fantasy, especially as it is manifested in fiction by writing mothers. I soon realized, however, that where motherhood is concerned, personal fantasy, fictional representation, and social and cultural reality are so interconnected that it is impossible to talk about one without the others. My two triangles, too, turned out to be closely related. The notion of maternal splitting links maternal fantasies about the "other mother" with fantasies about the child and work, and in addition provides one perspective on the important question of the relations between maternal fantasy and the realities of mothering in our culture today.

Splitting the Mother: Some Psychoanalytic Views

As the fairy tales about wicked stepmothers and fairy godmothers tell us, the impulse to split the maternal figure into "good" and "bad" personae is very old indeed. Bruno Bettelheim has remarked that "far from being a device used only by fairy tales, such a splitting up of one person into two to keep the good image uncontaminated occurs to many children as a solution to a relationship too difficult to manage or comprehend . . . The fantasy of the wicked stepmother not only preserves the good mother intact, it also prevents having to feel guilty about one's angry thoughts or wishes about her."[2] Bettelheim is restating here what has long been recognized as a psychoanalytic truism: the child's feelings toward the mother are ambivalent, a conflicting mixture of tenderness, gratitude, and destructive rage. According to Melanie Klein, these feelings are already present in the very young infant, who experiences the mother's breast alternately as gratifying and pleasure giving, and (when it is delayed or withheld) as hateful and frustrating. "The baby reacts to unpleasant stimuli, and to the frustration of his pleasure, with feelings of hatred and aggression. These feelings of hatred are directed towards the same objects as are the pleasurable ones, namely, the breasts of the mother."[3] Later on, the child sees the mother as a whole person, but the coexistence of opposing feelings persists: "Feelings both of a destructive and of a loving nature are experienced towards one and the same person and this gives rise to deep and disturbing conflicts in the child's mind."[4]

In Klein's theory, these conflicts will, if all goes well, produce guilt in the child for her or his destructive fantasies, which in turn will lead to a desire for reparation. Or, as Bettelheim suggests, these conflicts may produce fantasies (such as that of the wicked stepmother) which deflect the child's destructive feelings away from the good mother. Or yet again, as Margaret Mahler has observed in the behavior of toddlers, ambivalence toward the mother may produce a splitting of the real object world around the child into "good" and "bad." One of the child's caretakers then becomes the "bad" mother, "protecting the good mother image from [the child's] destructive anger."[5] Splitting thus functions as a defense mechanism, enabling the child to preserve the image of a protective and nurturant mother—an image that must be preserved (so the theory goes), given the child's sense of total dependence on her. Ultimately, according to Mahler, if the child is to develop a stable and harmonious sense of self, splitting must give way to the "unifying of 'good' and 'bad' objects into one whole representation" (p. 110). This unifying might correspond to Klein's notion of repairing the mother's body or to Bettelheim's idea that, once a child grows older and more secure, no longer quite so dependent on her mother, she "can rework the double picture into one."[6]

If in these versions of splitting what is at stake is maternal nurturance, there exists another version, first analyzed by Freud, in which splitting refers specifically to the erotic realm: what is at stake is maternal asexuality. In his essay "The Most Prevalent Form of Degradation in Erotic Life," Freud diagnosed the "mother/whore" syndrome so common in men as the result of a dissociation of sensual and tender feelings, aiming to maintain the mother's asexual "purity" by deflecting all sensual feelings onto an other, degraded object. Recently, Jim Swan has analyzed Freud's own discovery of the Oedipus complex as resulting from a similar splitting: the splitting between Freud's Catholic "Nannie," who initiated him into sex (he called her his "first seductress and shamer"), and his mother, who remained the "pure object of desire."[7] It is perhaps explicable in historical terms, as a Victorian phenomenon, that the kind of splitting in which Freud himself was most interested and personally implicated was the splitting of the mother in the erotic realm. Object-relations theorists, on the other hand, seem less concerned with the child's view of the mother as asexual or sexual than with the child's view of the mother as benevolent or destructive.[8]

Whether of the strictly Freudian or the object-relations variety, all of the theories I have mentioned assume that the "unique love-object," as well as the single most powerful and important figure in the life of the infant and small child—and consequently, according to these theories, in the life of the adult the child will become—is her or his mother.[9] They also assume, by and large, that that is the natural and necessary way things should be. This is not the place to survey the various critiques and modifications that have been proposed with regard to this psychoanalytic model, whether one considers it as a model of child development (positing that the individual personality is fully formed in the first few years of life) or as a model of mothering (positing that the mother-child dyad is the determining one). Such critiques have come both from male psychoanalysts like Erik Erikson, who proposes a less infant-centered as well as a more socially oriented model of child development, and from feminist theorists like Nancy Chodorow and Dorothy Dinnerstein, who propose a less biologically based model of mothering, or Jessica Benjamin, who emphasizes mutual recognition rather than dependence and domination in the infant-mother relationship.[10] However, the dominant analytic and cultural discourse about mothers and their children—what Ann Kaplan has called the "Master Mother Discourse"—continues to emphasize the mother's crucial, determining role in the development and continuing welfare of the child.[11] This discourse fosters what Chodorow and Susan Contratto have called the "myth of maternal omnipotence"—the belief that whatever happens to the child on the way to becoming an adult is ultimately attributable to its "good" or "bad" mother.[12]

Chodorow and Contratto make an impassioned plea for an alternative to our "cultural ideology" of "blame and idealization of mothers," which has been internalized by so many women (p. 65). They mount an impressive critique of some of the more influential feminist writings by mothers about their experience of motherhood, showing that even feminists have not succeeded in freeing themselves from the myth of maternal omnipotence.[13] Although the feminist mothers "blame patriarchy" instead of "blaming Mom," they do not question the dominant assumption that Mom is all-important. Chodorow and Contratto claim that this assumption is itself based on fantasies about the omnipotent mother originating in infancy, but that such fantasies exist precisely because children in our culture are being "mothered exclusively by one woman." It seems that we are trapped in a vicious circle. The way out of the circle, Contratto and Chodorow suggest, is for feminists to be wary and self-critical about their own assumptions concerning motherhood and child development. They should seek models of development that "recognize collaboration and compromise as well as conflict" and that "look at times other than infancy in the developmental life span and relationships over time to people other than the mother to get a more accurate picture of what growing up is about" (p. 71).

Intellectually, I find myself very attracted to this conclusion, as well as to the analysis that precedes it. The idea that even feminists writing about motherhood are expressing infantile fantasies about the omnipotent mother, for example, could explain the phenomenon of maternal splitting *by* the mother, in which it is not the child who through fantasy splits the mother into "good" and "bad," but the mother herself who does so. Consider the guilt fantasy about work versus child which I formulated in "Writing and Motherhood:" "With every word I write, with every act of genuine creation, I hurt my child." This fear on the part of the mother that each moment of creative self-absorption is destructive to her child is widespread and powerful, and has found some powerful expressions in fiction. According to Chodorow and Contratto, this fantasy "repeats" both the infant's own fantasy and the cultural ideology of maternal omnipotence. If the mother did not somehow imagine herself omnipotent in relation to her child, she would not need to feel so guilty and murderous every time she turned away from the child to pursue other self-absorptive goals.

Carol Gilligan has noted that women with an absorbing career generally feel strong conflict "between achievement and care," even if they are not mothers. In her study of women pursuing advanced degrees, she found that "these highly successful and achieving women do not mention their academic and professional distinction in the context of describing themselves, and the conflict they encounter between achievement and care leaves them either divided in judgment or feeling betrayed."[14] If, as Gilligan suggests, the phenomenon of splitting is experienced by women in general, it is all the more strong when the care involved is that of a mother for her child. In both cases, however, cultural ideology plays at least as important a role as the feminine specificity one might wish to attribute to women or to mothers.

Sara Ruddick has suggested to me that the term "maternal omnipotence" does not accurately name what is involved both in the cultural ideology and in the maternal fantasy I have been describing. Ruddick proposes, instead, the term "maternal responsibility," which suggests not so much a feeling of power (mothers often feel powerless, even in relation to their infants) as the feeling that what happens to the child is ultimately attributable to the mother—hence the cultural "blame Mom" syndrome, but also the mother's own potential sense of guilt or self-blame. I find Ruddick's argument convincing, but I would propose the term "absolute responsibility" or "ultimate responsibility" to suggest the hyperbolic nature of what is involved. One could then say, refining Chodorow and Contratto's terminology, that what the young child perceives as maternal omnipotence, the mother perceives as absolute or ultimate maternal responsibility. The two perceptions are symmetrical and both are fantasies, for in reality the mother is neither all-powerful in relation to the child nor absolutely (exclusively) responsible for the child's fate.

Questions of terminology aside, I agree with Chodorow and Contratto's suggestion that a more reality-oriented attitude—an attitude reinforced or made possible by new theories of mothering and child development, a new cultural discourse—would be healthy for mothers. At the same time, when I think of my own experience as a woman with a commitment to intellectual creativity and to motherhood, as well as that of other women whom I have read or with whom I have spoken about this subject, I become painfully aware of the difficulties, both personal and social, that the realization of such a "program for mothers" entails. Can we choose or discard at will our most deep-seated fantasies and self-representations? Do we dare, in a time of increasing social conservatism and disintegrating family life, give up our sense of an absolutely privileged relationship with our children?

I am not going to try and answer these questions directly—at least not yet. Rather, I want to reinscribe them in my reading of *Men and Angels,* a novel that I think poses them in an extremely compelling and disturbing way.

Maternal Splitting: *Men and Angels*

About a month before the publication of *Men and Angels,* Mary Gordon published some excerpts from her diary in the *New York Times Book Review,* under the punning title "On Mothership and Authorhood." The diary entries covered the period from December 1983 to the fall of 1984. During this time, Mary Gordon gave birth to her second child, a boy, and also finished her novel and delivered it to the publisher. In the first entry, Gordon is in a New York apartment waiting for the birth of her son, who is late in coming; she has with her her unfinished manuscript and her other child, a three-year-old girl, who is sick. Sitting at her sick daughter's bedside, she thinks of the fact that she has not even looked at the manuscript: "I have not even looked at it, partly because any action is physically difficult for me; I could excuse myself this way. But the truth is, it is impossible for me to believe that anything I write could have a fraction of the importance of the child growing inside me, or of the child who lies now, her head on my belly, with the sweet yet offhand stoicism of a sick child."[15]

When I read that, my first reaction was, "Here we go again—not mothership and authorhood, but writing versus motherhood! The same old conflict, resolved here by a somewhat sentimental renunciation of the writing self. Will we writing mothers never get beyond this split, always having to choose the work or the child, always convinced that choosing one means sacrificing the other?" The rest of the diary entries show, however, that in reality Mary Gordon was able to choose both. After a few months of total immersion in/with her baby, she went back to writing and finished her novel. And when the novel was reviewed by Margaret Drabble (another famous writing mother) on the front page of the *New York Times Book Review,* a short boxed interview by Herbert Mitgang with Mary Gordon on an inside page showed a reassuringly unconflicted and practical author talking about her life. "I probably have it a lot easier than most writers with children. When the babysitter takes over after breakfast, I leave the house, get into my car and drive for 15 minutes to a little cabin on the Hudson River. There I light the fire and gain the physical separation that I need to work. Between 9:30 and 1:30, I turn into a writer." "In *Men and Angels,*" noted Mitgang, "Miss Gordon's heroine is happily married and has two children and a baby sitter. So does Miss Gordon, whose husband teaches English at the University of New York at New Paltz, where they live."[16]

In Margaret Drabble's review of *Men and Angels,* however, I read the following: "The bloody dénouement is both predictable and plausible. Presented with a stark choice . . ., Anne in effect saves her children and sacrifices Laura."[17] Anne is the writing mother, and Laura is the live-in babysitter; Anne writes, and Laura is sacrificed. It occurred to me then that "Miss Gordon's heroine" may lead a more complicated life, and be related to Miss Gordon in more complicated ways, than Mr. Mitgang realized.

A few weeks later, I went to hear Mary Gordon talk about the book and read excerpts from it at the Boston Public Library. "Who has written seriously about the inner world of mothers?" she asked, uncannily echoing a question by Julia Kristeva that I had used as an epigraph for "Writing and Motherhood": "Que savons-nous du discours que (se) fait une mère?" "What do we know about the (inner) discourse of a mother?"

In the first passage from *Men and Angels* that Mary Gordon read that afternoon, Anne Foster, the heroine, has just finished her day's work up in her study. She has recently accepted an important assignment: to curate and write the catalogue essay for the first major retrospective exhibition of an American expatriate painter, Caroline Watson, who lived and worked in Paris and died there in 1939. (Caroline Watson is an invented figure.) Anne has been poring over Caroline's letters and feels that she is beginning to know this woman "in the bone." Now, however, it is time for her to join her children in the familiar kitchen downstairs. Walking down the stairs, "hearing her heels on the wooden floor as if they were somebody else's," Anne feels the difference within herself: "In the room with Caroline she was weightless. Sometimes it frightened her, the speed of her blood, the giddy sense of being somewhere else, in some high territory, inaccessible. With the children, there was never any flying off, flying up. A mother was encumbered and held down. Anne felt that she was fortunate in that she loved the weighing down."[18] When she reaches the kitchen, the children are not there. They are out in the woods with Laura, the au pair girl Anne has hired to make her writing possible while her husband is away on a year's sabbatical in France. Anne feels disappointed, then happy when the children appear. But Laura is with them, diffident, watching her—an intrusive presence. Anne, intuitively understanding how starved Laura is for affection ("She was a girl who had not, it was clear, been held enough, been treasured"), tries to convince herself that her own discomfort is only momentary: "She was sure that when she got more used to living with a stranger, her unpleasant feelings would just disappear. She brought the cups to the sink, ashamed of herself for wishing Laura were not there" (p. 48).

The second passage Mary Gordon read occurs, in the novel's time, a few weeks later. Once again, Anne is reading Caroline's letters, and this time the text of one letter is quoted in full; it is from Caroline in Paris to her son Stephen and his wife Jane, who are in Cambridge, Massachusetts. It is a warm, witty, loving letter, but all the warmth is addressed to Jane, not to Stephen. Caroline did not love Stephen; she had barely ever lived with him, had left him in the care of others in the States while she chose to work in Paris, the only place where she could paint. Stephen died young, miserable. Jane is still alive, an old and vigorous woman, childless, flourishing, with a distinguished academic career behind her.

Whenever Anne thought of Caroline's treatment of Stephen she came upon a barrier between them that was as profound as one of language . . . She couldn't imagine Peter or Sarah [her children] marrying anyone she would prefer to them, as Caroline had preferred Jane to Stephen. You have done wrong, she always wanted to tell Caroline. Caroline, the ghost who had taken over her life, hovering, accepting worship . . . And even as she wanted to tell Caroline, "You have done wrong," an anger rose up in her as if the accusation had come from someone else. No one would have pored through a male artist's letters to his children as she had through Caroline's to Stephen. It was that Caroline was a woman and had a child and had created art; because the three could be connected in some grammar, it was as though the pressure to do so were one of logic. Then she wanted to defend Caroline from the accusation she herself had laid against her. What did it matter, she wanted to say to the shivering ghost whom she had left unsheltered. You were a great painter. You did what you had to do. Yet even as she shielded the ghost, she could not still the accusation: "You should not have let your child die young." For as a mother, she felt it was the most important thing in the world. You did not hurt your children. You kept your children safe. (pp. 68–69)

Hearing these two passages read by the author, I realized that *Men and Angels* was a book I had to read and write about. It is an extraordinarily powerful novel, and a veritable gold mine for anyone interested in the phenomenon of maternal splitting. That is a rather crude way of putting it, for I don't mean that Mary Gordon gives us a guided tour or a handy little catalog of maternal fantasies relating to children, creativity, and "other mothers." I mean, rather, that to those who share my current preoccupations, this novel reveals a rich and complex terrain, offering multiple paths for exploration. I want to explore here the direction of maternal splitting, to see how this notion makes possible both a detailed (albeit necessarily partial) reading of the novel[19] and a renewed consideration of the conflicts and dilemmas that real-life mothers face.

As the passages mentioned above suggest, the three principal characters in the novel variously mirror and read each other. More exactly, Anne is the central figure "doubled" on two sides by Caroline and Laura. Like Caroline, whose life and work she pores over, Anne is a creative woman and a mother. Unlike Caroline, however, Anne has a passionate commitment to motherhood. Whereas Caroline was a bad mother to her son, "allowing" him to die young (shades of the maternal omnipotence fantasy), Anne is a totally good mother to her children and has their safety uppermost in her mind. Caroline, on the other hand, was a good "other mother" to Jane, whose feelings toward her own biological mother were no warmer than (as she puts it) feelings toward "a rather distant cousin" (p. 167). Caroline is therefore split into a murderous and a nurturing mother, depending on whether one looks at Stephen or Jane as her child. But she can also be seen as the "bad" version or double of Anne, for she was a mother who chose to sacrifice her child to her work.

Structurally, Laura occupies the most interesting position, for she functions as a negative double both for Anne and for Anne's children: as the bad "other mother," she allows Peter and Sarah to walk on the thin ice of a pond while she herself sits engrossed in a book (as it happens, the Bible—which is the only book she reads); it is Anne herself who, rushing down to the pond, saves the children and then turns in a fury on Laura: "As strong as her love for her children, for her husband, stronger than the things that made the center of her life was her desire to inflict damage on the smiling face of this girl who might have let her children die" (p. 203). We can read Anne's destructive rage here as directed against the bad, murderous mother, who sits reading while the children are in danger; but the text emphasizes in various ways that this bad mother is a mirror image—what I call a negative double, and what in psychoanalytic terms might be called a split-off projection—of Anne herself. This is made most clear at the moment when, after Laura's suicide, Anne painfully drags the young woman's body to her own bed and proceeds to dress the body in her own bathrobe. It is also significant that the novel is divided into alternating sections with now Anne, now Laura as the center of consciousness. The narration thus mirrors in its language and point of view the psychological doubling between Anne and Laura.

If Laura is the negative double who must be destroyed in order to preserve the "good" Anne, the good mother, she is also the negative double of Anne's children. The novel emphasizes the adoring love that Laura feels for Anne. Having been rejected by her own mother, Laura is seeking a substitute; Anne knows this, but is unable to respond. Caroline, we recall, had one unloved child (her biological son) who died young, and another, chosen child (Jane) whom she loved. In Anne's case, the position of the unloved child is occupied by Laura, and it is this child who, like Caroline's son Stephen, is sacrificed by Anne to her work: "Each time now that [Anne] thought of her work on Caroline, she would have to wonder if Laura had been its sacrifice. Her death would touch even that. Had she not met me, she would not have died, Anne thought, listening to the priest. Had I not ignored her distress trying to finish my work" (p. 233). In destroying Laura, Anne destroys the bad mother, but paradoxically she also destroys a child, thus reintroducing the bad mother into herself. The young woman commits suicide like a child who has suddenly discovered, to her horror, that she possesses no "good" mother but only a murderously punitive one.

Although the complicated mirrorings among Anne, Caroline, and Laura dominate the novel, there are at least two more mothers who figure secondarily but significantly in the story. Anne's mother has two daughters; she has been a good, loving mother to Anne's sister, but a rejecting mother to Anne herself. In relation to Anne, the good-mother slot may be considered occupied by her father, and possibly also by the older woman, Jane (who enters her life quite late, however, through her work on Caroline). Laura's mother also has two daughters, of whom Laura is the unloved one. By their similar position in relation to their biological mothers, Anne and Laura again turn out to be structural twins—with the crucial difference that whereas Anne finds one, or perhaps two, good "other mothers," Laura does not. Laura's pathological attachment to Anne is an attempt to find in her a loving mother with whom she can identify. This attempt fails, however, because Anne cannot love Laura—Laura, like Stephen, is not lovable.

This may seem a highly problematic statement. Is there such a thing as an "essentially unlovable" child? Or are people like Laura and Stephen, who appear so unlovable, already the "products"—and victims—of a lack of maternal love? The very asking of this question entangles one in the fantasy of ultimate maternal responsibility, for if the child turns out unlovable because of the mother's care-less-ness, then the mother must be blamed for the child's fate. If this view appears unduly harsh, what shall we say about the alternative explanation that some people are "born unlovable"? Could the fantasy of ultimate maternal responsibility be one way to deflect the perhaps more horrifying notion (horrifying to a mother and to a child) that some human beings are unlovable by nature? At this point, the religious and theological dimensions of Gordon's novel, introduced by the character of Laura, take on a new resonance: Is grace given or withheld at birth, or is it acquired (or lost) through the course of one's life? And if the latter, who is the agent responsible for that process?

The web of connections among the characters in the novel suggests several observations. First, the structural similarity between Caroline and Anne is evident, but so is Anne's greater complexity (and more complicated splitting), which rightly confers on her the title of protagonist, if not necessarily of heroine. Caroline is divided internally into a good and a bad mother, with her work as a crucial element in both cases (it "kills" Stephen, but it creates an emotional and intellectual bond between her and Jane). Anne, too, is divided internally, but her work functions only in a negative way: it destroys Laura (as Anne herself thinks in a passage I quoted earlier), and it also, indirectly, harms Anne's own children. After Laura's death, nothing can ever be the same for them: "they would grow up knowing life was terrible and they were never safe" (p. 237).

In addition to this internal split, Anne is split in a quasi-pathological way: the bad mother in her is externalized in a separate figure, Laura, on whom she vents her murderous rage. One wonders whether this rage is only that of the good mother, whether it is not also, in some sense, the rage of a small child at her bad mother. Anne, Margaret Mahler might say, has never successfully integrated her own childish images of the good and bad mother. Or we could say that, if she experiences a kind of maternal schizophrenia, that is because she occupies, at one and the same time, the position both of the small child and of the mother. This would be a confirmation of Chodorow and Contratto's thesis that the maternal fantasy of omnipotence is a repetition of an infantile fantasy; only I would qualify that thesis by saying that the infantile fantasy of maternal omnipotence reinforces the maternal fantasy of ultimate responsibility, without being its only source. The other source is in the mother herself as mother—perhaps because she has internalized the cultural discourse about mothering, but also perhaps because the very fact of being a mother places her in a position symmetrical to the child. The psychoanalyst Alice Balint suggested in an essay published almost fifty years ago that "maternal love is the almost perfect counterpart to the love for the mother," both of them being archaic, instinctual, and absolute.[20] If there is even a slight bit of truth in this, then it may be too simple to declare that mothers should give up their "infantile" fantasies and become more "realistic." For the mother may always reply, "Yes, I know, but still." "Yes, I know I'm not the only one ultimately responsible for my child's life," says the mother; "I know it's only a fantasy, and a terrifying one at that—but I still need to pretend it's true." Some fantasies are felt to be too necessary to give up.

The second observation my reading suggests is a truism, but significant: in order to survive, a child needs at least one good mother, whether it is the biological mother or an "other" one. Stephen and Laura, who find no nurturing mother, die.

Finally, in this novel no child (except perhaps Anne) has more than one "good" mother. And that raises once again the question of maternal fantasy and its relation to social reality.

If Not Fantasy, What?
American Motherhood in the 1980s and Beyond

Reading *Men and Angels* as a multiple fantasy of maternal splitting, whose ultimate source or author is not so much the individual Mary Gordon as a collective contemporary American consciousness, one is led to ask: Why do mothers—even enlightened, creative, feminist mothers—in the United States today find it so difficult to acknowledge, in their deepest fantasies about their children, that they are not the only ones on whom the child's welfare, the child's whole life and self, depend? In reality, most mothers will readily admit that the father, grandparents, teachers, friends, aunts, uncles, and other adult figures can and often do play a significant mothering role. Many feminist mothers are ardent exponents of Dinnerstein's and Chodorow's thesis that fathers in particular must share that role. And yet, when we really dig down, when we really try to understand how we feel about our children, even the most enlightened among us will often discover in ourselves the stubborn belief that mother is the only one who really counts. Why?

Whatever psychological explanations one can offer (regression, identification with the child, internalization of the "Master Mother Discourse," and so on), I think that there is a specifically contemporary sociopolitical explanation as well. Erik Erikson has noted that in order to benefit both mother and child, "biological motherhood needs at least three links with social experience: the mother's past experience of being mothered; a conception of motherhood shared with trustworthy contemporary surroundings; and an all-enveloping world-image tying past, present and future into a convincing pattern of providence."[21] The third condition, which has religious overtones, is probably not specific to mothering: in order to do anything worthwhile, one has to have a certain sense of continuity and faith in the future. The first condition, we all more or less fulfill—which is not to belittle its importance, for we know that a mother's past history is crucial to her mothering. But it seems to me that as a social problem, the first condition merges with the second; and it is precisely Erikson's second condition that has become most problematic in American society today.

In order to relinquish her fantasy of ultimate responsibility, a mother needs a "conception of motherhood shared with trustworthy contemporary surroundings"; but we live in a society where divorce is rampant, where the old presumptions no longer hold (witness the conundrum of surrogate motherhood, as well as those posed by various reproductive technologies), where women who are mothers feel increasingly threatened financially, emotionally, and legally. Even if Phyllis Chesler's *Mothers on Trial* exaggerates in viewing all fathers as potential sadists and mother haters, and all mothers as potential victims, the fact that this view exists at all has both symbolic and social significance. (It is a similar perception of mothers as victims and its attendant fear that may account for the extraordinary popular success of Sue Miller's novel *The Good Mother*.) Lenore Weitzman has shown that in divorce negotiations fathers often blackmail their wives into accepting disadvantageous financial terms by threatening to sue for custody of the children, and that in any case mothers end up much more impoverished than fathers after divorce.[22] But if that is the case, if mothers cannot feel secure in their attempt to pursue full and integrated personal lives and remain mothers, if they feel or fear that society through its legal system is ready to punish them by depriving them of their children any time they stray from the traditional, constraining path of "true mother-and-wife," then it makes a certain practical and logical sense for them to hold on to one thing they can affirm with certainty: that they have a natural, biological bond and right, as mothers, to their children.

I read Chesler's book as a terrified reaction to what she perceives as a terrifying reality. To reaffirm, as she does, the biological bonding between mother and child and to claim that the mother is the child's "natural" guardian may be an ideologically and psychologically regressive move (one that overlooks, furthermore, the rights of adoptive mothers), but it is also a self-protective move, as regression often is.[23] Until and unless American women feel that society offers them a trustworthy surrounding in which they can safely pursue both their desire for self-creation and their desire to mother, they will be unwilling to share their child with "other mothers" and will cling to the fantasy of ultimate responsibility. It will appear to them as their best, perhaps their only, hope.

The popularity of Chesler's book underscores the connections between the fantasy of maternal splitting that I have analyzed in *Men and Angels* and women's real-life situations. Although it is theoretically hazardous to draw neat parallels between fiction and life, in practice we often do read fiction as an illumination of, and commentary on, real-life predicaments. That being the case, I would suggest that changes in the representation of maternal conflicts and fantasies in fiction by American women writers will have to be accompanied (perhaps even preceded) by efforts to create a trustworthy surrounding for women in American social life. As a first step, such efforts might be directed at the creation of a system of excellent, universally available day care that would allow biological mothers to rely on "other mothers" instead of feeling threatened by them, and would encourage all of us to think of motherhood and self-creation as complementary rather than as mutually exclusive categories in women's lives. In concert with other social policy reforms, this action would contribute to and reflect the broader thinking that is necessary about the family, the social roles of women and men (both those who are parents and those who are not), and how these will be linked to the needs, values, and ultimate goals of American society at the turn of a new century.

MOTHERHOOD AND IDENTITY POLITICS: AN EXCHANGE

3

Shortly after "Maternal Splitting" was published, in the fall of 1989, the editor of *Signs* received a letter from Raquel Portillo Bauman. Identifying herself as a Chicana woman married to a black man, Bauman reacted to my essay negatively because she felt that it did not take account of her experience or that of other minority women. To me, the questions she raised seemed especially important because feminists were just around then discovering the full import of the "race-class-gender" triad, both in its positive and negative effects. Positively, the realization that feminist theory, until then largely the work of white middle-class women, had not sufficiently recognized the specificities of race and class in its analyses was forcing white feminists to recognize their blind spots or their unconscious prejudices, and allowing black and other minority women to claim their own voices. Negatively, the splintering produced by identity politics threatened at times to disunite women, including feminist women, into hostile camps, thus enacting from within feminism the policy of divide and conquer that had effectively quashed many another progressive movement in the past.

The exchange of letters that resulted from Bauman's response, published in the spring 1990 issue of *Signs*, indicates the complexity of the issues involved. Besides the political issues, the most interesting question, for me, concerns the limits (or not) of psychoanalysis. Is a psychoanalytic understanding of human motivations and experiences limited to the privileged classes, applicable only to individuals acculturated in Western, Eurocentric societies? Implicated in this question is a large and ongoing philosophical debate about universalism, which has come to the fore in recent years with particular urgency as conflicts over human rights and tribal and ethnic clashes once again occupy center stage in Europe and elsewhere. Although the exchange of letters was more modest in scope, it resonated with these broad questions, for motherhood appears at least potentially as a "universal" pertaining to women. Are the experiences and the inner lives of mothers in Western and non-Western, mainstream and minority cultures so different that no common ground is possible? Or can one, without denying differences across cultures and subcultures, explore certain inner experiences of motherhood—notably in a psychoanalytic perspective—that are not limited to a single race or class?

In order to give full voice to both of the positions expressed in the exchange, I reproduce it here as it appeared in *Signs*. My thanks to Raquel Portillo Bauman for permission to reprint her letter.

Raquel Portillo Bauman

Susan Rubin Suleiman's article entitled "On Maternal Splitting: A Propos of Mary Gordon's *Men and Angels*" stirred a series of uncomfortable feelings. I was forced to think carefully of matters I often ponder but upon which I consider others better prepared to comment. I am a Chicana medical academic administrator (one of a very few), a painter, a teacher, a writer, a mother, and still the Suleiman article seemed not to be about me. It did not seem to be about my mother, not about my grandmothers (Mexican and Mexican American women from the region that is now, but has not always been, the American Southwest), nor did it seem to be about my mother-in-law, a black woman who has reared my husband and numerous nephews, nieces, a grandchild, and a great-grandchild while working, cared for an invalid mother, and long ago obtained her Vocational Nurse's License (perhaps the first black woman to do so in Muleshoe, Texas). When I reread the piece, I added the words "majority" or "advantaged" as adjectives each and every time the words maternal or motherhood appeared in the text, and the essay made more sense, but it still did not speak to my experience.

Yet there seemed more to my discomfort than the fact that an author once again excluded me and many other women from her deliberations, that an author once again assumed that my experiences were the same as hers. Many of the ideas presented in Suleiman's article troubled me: "self-absorptive, creative careers," "fear of loss of love by intrusion of a third party," "mother's asexual purity," the concepts of "maternal omnipotence" or of "ultimate responsibility." The assumptions about creativity, vulnerability, power, and safety that support such phrases have little to do with the history of people of color in the United States. For instance, in the same issue of *Signs*, Patricia J. Williams cited her own description of her great-great-great-grandmother Sophie. She said that Sophie was purchased by a white lawyer and that when she was about eleven she had a child. The child was taken from her to be raised as a house servant. How would the circumstances of power under which Sophie was a mother encourage the idea of maternal omnipotence? Tomás Rivera, in *Y no se lo trago la tierra*,[1] described a couple who wished to protect their children from the scorching sun while they labored in the fields. They thought their children would be safe in the migrant labor camp that they temporarily occupied, but their shack caught fire and the children were killed. It occurs to me that only a very few children are being mothered by women (or men) who are in a position to fantasize about omnipotence.

Buchi Emecheta, the Nigerian writer, was described by Thelma Ravella-Pinto in *Sage: A Scholarly Journal on Black Women* as a feminist who exposes the hypocrisy of patriarchal societies. Ms. Emecheta says during the interview that her novels are not feminist. She states that her work is part of the whole of African literature and that she is not affected by what critics say. She writes of war and colonialism, and the exploitation of Africa. She also has an interesting perspective on the concept of family. She says that in her country responsibility increases with education and wealth: "If I earn a lot of money, I also pay for the education of children who do not form part of my immediate family."[2] I propose that such a collective responsibility rather than an ultimate responsibility would be helpful to women, to mothers, to children, and to men.

Western models of thought describe and have perpetuated the notion of conflict between opposing forces, in this case the good mother and the bad mother, each concept exclusive of the other. Suleiman argues that in increasingly conservative times feminists should not relinquish the notion of "ultimate responsibility" or the concept of the "privileged relationship" mothers have with children. I argue that it is in these conservative times that we must look to other traditions and other histories. It is not possible to protect only our children and we cannot assist all children if we remain unwilling to learn from all women, if we try to measure ourselves and others against a single norm for "the good mother."

It was difficult to begin being a biological mother at thirty-nine. Before my son was born it was difficult to reconcile working at a demanding job I love and painting and writing short stories in my spare time. It remains difficult since his birth. Yet a part of my job is facilitating access to a professional education for women and people of color as well as influencing what and how future clinicians will be taught. Painting is about making my creative vision real, and writing is about giving voice to my history. For my son and my brothers and sisters and myself, no less can be done. Suleiman's ruminations about a divided self assume that the creative self is singular, individual, and that the conflicts exist within the woman. Yet my experience with mothering and with creating is different from hers. My own experience is that what I run out of is time and money, not creativity. While I am painting I do not love my son less. There is no guilt. When he is in another's care there is no fear that he will love me less and no concern that his love for my sister, sister-in-law, brothers, his father, his grandparents, or any other human will affect his love for me. Perhaps more important, however, is the sense that each of these people who love my son can give him a great deal. Perhaps most important, however, is the sense that my two younger brothers, both experienced parents, or my father, who is a hard-working laborer who loves horses, or my mother-in-law in Lubbock, Texas, all can enrich and empower my son.

I agree with Suleiman that women writers ought to be free to write and to mother; but the conditions that she thinks necessary to do this are too narrow. It is natural to be creative. All of us can learn from the "homeless poets in Nashville," some of whom work at a table inside the local hamburger stand (National Public Radio, August 8, 1989). I also agree with Suleiman that most mothers want to protect their children; indeed, most of us wish that reality were more merciful than it is. Yet it seems to me that the means mothers have available to be protective vary greatly. Latinas and Latinos, black women and men, and many others offer varied perspectives regarding how conflict, powerlessness, assimilation, culture, values, and exclusion affect parenting in American life. The conflict between mothering and creativity that Suleiman describes involves only one model of a protective mother. There are other models.

Susan Rubin Suleiman

Dear Raquel Portillo Bauman:

Contrary to convention, I am addressing these remarks to you—knowing full well, of course, that our exchange is indirectly addressed to the readers of *Signs*. By addressing my reply to you directly, I hope to emphasize our similarities without losing sight of our differences. I am interested not in drawing sharp, uncrossable lines—between women and men, between women of different races, classes or ethnic groups, between you and me—but in finding areas of common concern and, where possible, common action. Lest you think this means I'm going to be "nice" and not voice any disagreements with you, let me reassure you that that is not the case! But a good argument, I hope you will agree, is an exchange of views from which both parties emerge the wiser, with mutual respect, not a sparring contest in which opponents try to get the better of each other.

Besides describing your personal reactions to my essay and some of your own feelings about motherhood, your letter raises some important general questions. One of these is the relationship between collective responsibility and individual maternal responsibility for the well-being of children. Although you seem to believe that I adhere to the "exclusive maternal responsibility" view, I thought I had made more than clear in my essay that I consider collective responsibility both socially necessary and psychologically beneficial to mothers and children. Why did I argue, at the end of the essay, for universally available day care and emphasize Erik Erikson's notion of "trustworthy contemporary surroundings," if not precisely because I believe that mothers should not be made to bear child-rearing responsibilities alone? The "myth of maternal omnipotence" is, as I make clear (and as Nancy Chodorow and Susan Contratto, who coined that phrase in an article I cite, also emphasize) just that—a myth, not reality.

At the same time, I recognize and try to account for the power of this myth, or fantasy, as it manifests itself in works of literature ranging from traditional fairy tales to modern novels like Mary Gordon's *Men and Angels;*[3] and also as it manifests itself both in psychoanalytic theorizing about motherhood and in the life experience of mothers. Although I criticize, both here and in my earlier essay "Writing and Motherhood," the repressive ideological effects (for mothers) of classical psychoanalytic theories about motherhood, I do not reject psychoanalysis as an analytic framework. It is certainly not the only available framework for understanding the life experience of individuals, but I believe that it is a useful one; what in cultural terms is analyzed as myth can be analyzed in psychoanalytic terms as fantasy.

At this point, another general question rears its head: is a psychoanalytic perspective somehow inherently white and middle-class, inherently linked to privilege and "majority" status? This question occurs to me because of your response to a passage of my essay that you say troubled you but that you do not quote in full: "What the young child perceives as maternal omnipotence, the mother perceives as absolute or ultimate maternal responsibility. The two perceptions are symmetrical and both are fantasies, for in reality the mother is neither all-powerful in relation to the child nor absolutely (exclusively) responsible for the child's fate." What troubled you in this passage was the notion of "ultimate responsibility." As the last sentence indicates, I myself emphasize that this notion is "only a fantasy, not the real thing" (to quote a rock song I learned from my children). Still, it appears that the phrase "ultimate responsibility" troubled you because you did not feel that it corresponded to your own experience even as fantasy. In your experience, there is no guilt when you leave your baby in the care of someone else, especially another family member, in order to write or paint; you never have feelings of jealousy, because you know how beneficial contact with other adults is for your baby; in short, you do not experience inner conflicts or self-doubt relative to mothering.

Far be it from me to question the reality of your experience, or your sincerity in describing it. What I must question is the notion (which you assume from the beginning without ever arguing it explicitly) that your experience, or your description of it, represents the "real" experience of minority women, whether in the United States or in Africa or other parts of the Third World; and that it represents their experience more accurately than anything that I, writing from a chiefly psychoanalytic perspective, accomplish in my essay.

You accuse me of excluding you and many other women from my reflections. You suggest, both by your own example and by allusion to other minority or Third World women (like Buchi Emecheta), that "in these conservative times we must look to other traditions and other histories." As a general principle, I of course agree with your statement. I did not speak about work by women of color in my *Signs* essay, which, as its title indicates, deals with a novel by Mary Gordon; but if I *had* chosen as my subject the work of Buchi Emecheta, or Toni Morrison, I would surely have pointed to those aspects of their characters' experience that you yourself claim not to share with me—aspects that you claim are not relevant to the experience of minority women in general, but that merely typify my "advantaged" and "majority" point of view.

Take the fantasy of "ultimate responsibility," which makes you uncomfortable: What impels Sethe, in Morrison's *Beloved*, to kill her children rather than return them to slavery, if not a truly awesome sense that she is absolutely, ultimately, responsible for their fate? Why does the mother in *Sula* feel that she has the right to kill her hopelessly addicted, war-damaged son, if not because she feels ultimately responsible for his life, to the point of deciding when it should end? Or take the question of internal conflicts like jealousy, of which you are so suspicious: Why does Nnu Ego, the heroine of Emecheta's *The Joys of Motherhood*,[4] a traditional Ibo woman who labors all her life to support her children, experience feelings of jealous fear toward a younger woman ("She had worked herself up in her imagination to believe that Adaku would harm [her children] once her back was turned"—p. 133), guilt (when one of her babies dies at birth, she is horrified to think that she may have wished the baby's death), anger and frustration as a mother ("After all, I was born alone, and I shall die alone. What have I gained from all this?"—p. 186), if not because internal conflicts exist even among minority women and women in traditional African cultures?

You might want to argue, in response, that women like Sethe and Nnu Ego are the victims of social and economic oppression, which alone accounts for their troubles. I want to argue that it makes no sense to exclude either the social or the psychological dimension of experience in talking about motherhood (or about most other things), and above all that it makes no sense to claim that either of those dimensions is restricted to a particular race, class, or ethnic group. Obviously, significant differences exist among groups—the fact that white women in America never experienced slavery constitutes an enormous difference between any white woman and Morrison's Sethe; but it would be a mistake to claim, for that reason, that psychological categories are irrelevant in trying to understand Sethe's experience, or that only privileged white middle-class women can afford the luxury of having inner conflicts. Conversely, it would be a mistake to assume that, because of their "majority" status, white middle-class women contend with no social injustices or exploitation.

That brings me to the last of the important issues raised, for me, by your comment: the question of relative allegiances and alliances for women. Are racial or ethnic allegiances more significant, and ultimately more important, than allegiances among women? Does one have to choose between allegiances rather than try to combine them? Is your sense of being a Hispanic woman married to a black man so overriding that you cannot find any shared experience or understanding in an essay like mine?

Buchi Emecheta dedicated *The Joys of Motherhood* "To all mothers," not just to all Nigerian or all African or all black or all poor mothers. She evidently believes that motherhood is one experience sharable across racial, ethnic, and class differences; the fact that I, a white American middle-class academic woman and single mother of two sons, can share some of the joys and frustrations—and yes, fantasies—of an illiterate Ibo tribeswoman who is virtually the single mother of seven children (her husband fathers them, but does not "parent" them either emotionally or, for a number of years, financially) suggests to me that Emecheta is right.

Of the phrases in my essay that you quote as having troubled you, only two are actually mine, the others being either quotations or summaries of other people's views. About "ultimate responsibility," I have already said my piece; the other phrase is "self-absorptive, creative careers." I am fascinated and puzzled by the fact that it troubled you. No male writer or artist, I am certain of it, would be troubled by a characterization of his and other male artists' work as self-absorptive, creative, and a career. I wonder whether this may not be one area where you would find a feminist (or what Alice Walker has proposed as a more inclusive term, womanist) analysis, rather than an exclusively racial or ethnic one, helpful.

Thank you for having raised so many important questions by your letter. I would be pleased if our dialogue continued and continued to "make waves," both for ourselves and for the readers of *Signs*.

THE
CREATIVE
SELF

> > PART TWO

SIMONE DE BEAUVOIR AND THE WRITING SELF

4

How did Simone de Beauvoir conceive of herself—but I should really say, conceive her *self*—as a writer? "To conceive" has multiple meanings, all of them relevant: to form in the mind, to imagine; to understand; to express in particular words; to think; to become pregnant with. An autobiographer is one who imagines, understands, expresses, becomes pregnant with, and consequently gives birth to the self in writing. If the autobiographer is a writer in addition—which means, in this instance, not on the side but centrally—the self she or he conceives and gives birth to in the process of autobiography is the writing self: How did I become a writer? What does it mean, for me, to write? These questions are not always asked explicitly in a writer's autobiography, although they often are—in Sartre's *Les Mots,* for example, or in Beauvoir's *Mémoires d'une jeune fille rangée* (*Memoirs of a Dutiful Daughter*). But explicitly formulated or not, I believe they are always present when a writer sets out to write his or her life.

One important insight of contemporary critical theory has been that the very meaning of those questions, as well as the answers one might find for them, will differ not only according to individuals, but also, perhaps primarily, according to the *situation*—the race, class, gender, and historical moment—of the person who is asking them or about whom they are asked. This may sound too much like dubious pop psychosociology: "Who is the German-speaking Jew living in Prague in 1910, and how will his writing differ from that of the French homosexual thief living in a prison outside Paris in 1930?" What is at stake, however, is not a categorization or pigeon-holing, but rather the recognition that the subject of writing is not a disembodied, transcendental ego. Hélène Cixous has written about the coming to writing, "la venue à l'écriture"—a process in which the place where one feels oneself to be starting from is of crucial importance. "Everything about me joined together to forbid me to write: History, my story, my origin, my gender. Everything that constituted my social and cultural self—beginning with the essential, which I was lacking . . .: the language . . . I learned to speak French in a garden from which I was about to be expelled because I was Jewish. I was of the race of paradise-losers."[1]

Feminist critics, including Cixous, have laid particular emphasis on the role of gender in the coming to writing. One need not subscribe to a biologically deterministic view of femininity (or masculinity) to understand that a woman who writes will not have the same relation to language, and to that sacralized form of language we call literature, as a man, even a man of the same race and class. Here is Cixous again: "Writing was reserved for the elect. It had to take place in a space inaccessible to the lowly, to the humble, to woman . . . Writing spoke to its prophets from a burning bush. But it must have been decided that bushes would not converse with women" (p. 21). As Cixous' play with biblical allusions makes clear, one has but to look back with a certain ironic detachment at two thousand years of Western culture and at the discourses through which that culture has sought to define itself, to realize that sexual difference is not irrelevant to the writing self. But where is one to locate the difference? Does it reside in the body, male versus female, or in the places that have traditionally been assigned to the body by the culture and its discourses?

Most feminists, I think, would argue the latter. Beauvoir certainly did. And yet, the body (as physical entity, not merely as "sign") keeps intruding. We all have one; it is difficult to do without one. Our sense of who we are, and where we are in the world, necessarily passes through an awareness of ourselves as embodied beings. Even the language we use, no matter how abstract or metaphorical—one could even say *especially* when it is abstract and metaphorical—resonates with bodily overtones.

Take the word "conceive," for example, and put it next to the fact that in our culture the female body has been most consistently seen, and placed, as the body of the mother. What is the relation of a writer who could actually become a mother to the metaphorical conceiving and giving birth that occurs in autobiographical writing (and in much other writing as well, as I discussed in Chapter 1)? Beauvoir, as we know, refused motherhood—and she also refused, not by chance, the maternal metaphor for her writing. Would she have been happy with the way I formulated my starting question, "How did she conceive her self as a writer," knowing that the *first* meaning the dictionary gives for the verb is "to become pregnant with"? To imagine, to express in words, to think, are metaphorical derivatives of that first meaning; for Beauvoir, those were activities incompatible with the passive state (that is how she saw it) of being pregnant. To be a writer, to express in words and imagine and think, was precisely not to be pregnant, not to give birth.

Was it to be a woman? When she first started to write, she tells us in *La Force de l'âge* (*The Prime of Life*), "I did not deny my femininity, nor did I assume it: I didn't think about it." Since then, she adds, she has changed: "Today I know that in order to describe myself, I must begin by saying 'I am a woman'; but my femininity has not constituted for me either an embarrassment or an alibi" ("ni une gêne ni un alibi").[2]

Neither an embarrassment nor an alibi—simply a contingency, a fact of life. But as Beauvoir suggests in that most famous sentence of *The Second Sex*, "One is not born a woman, one becomes a woman," the contingent fact of being born female carries with it a whole cultural program. Can the contingency ever escape from the program? I suddenly think of the devastating pages at the end of the same book, which state over and over again that no woman has ever been a Kafka, a Rousseau, a Stendhal, a Dostoevsky, a Melville, a T. E. Lawrence. What does she mean?

She writes: "There are women who are mad and there are women of talent; none has the madness in talent that we call *genius*." She writes: "The men we call great are those who, in one way or another, took the weight of the world on their shoulders . . . That is what no woman has ever done, what no woman has ever been able to do." She writes: "The individuals who appear to us exemplary, whom we endow with the name of genius, are those who have sought to play out in their unique existence the fate of all humanity. No woman has believed herself authorized to do that."[3] A page later, she will add that the reason must be sought in woman's situation, not in "some mysterious essence. The future is wide open."

In the meantime, who is speaking?

Let's look at the pronouns: woman, she; women, they; the men whom *we* call great, the individuals whom *we* endow with the name of genius. I read those "we"'s as universal we's. Does she ever say "we" and mean women? Yes, at least once, when she is talking about autobiography: "There are feminine autobiographies that are sincere and appealing: but none can be compared to [Rousseau's] *Confessions,* to [Stendhal's] *Souvenirs d'égotisme.* We are still too preoccupied with seeing things clearly to try and pierce, beyond that clarity, other dark depths" (p. 474). Her own autobiography was still to come. Neither an embarrassment nor an alibi. But lacking in genius.

"Genius," Christine Brooke-Rose has noted, has the same Indo-European root as "gender," "genre," and "genesis": *gene,* to beget, to give birth, to be born.[4] Did Beauvoir know this etymology? If she did, she must also have known that, despite the common root, our culture has historically assigned quite different meanings to begetting and to giving birth: man is the begetter, woman the one who labors. Creation versus drudgery. Word versus flesh. Or, in the existentialist vocabulary that Beauvoir shared with Sartre, transcendence versus immanence.

Saint Theresa, she says, was the only woman who did it: "she lived, as a woman, an experience whose meaning goes beyond any sexual specification" (p. 422). Saint Theresa, in whom, twenty years later, Jacques Lacan was to see the very emblem of feminine *jouissance,* appeared to Beauvoir as the one woman, alone of all her sex, who accomplished the nearly impossible: who transcended the female body and the feminine condition and attained the universal, the human condition. Beyond sexual difference. In other words, male. For "until now it is in man, not in woman, that humanity has been incarnated" (p. 479).

Well, you will say, we know all this. Beauvoir was a male-identifed woman—everybody knows that. Just recall what she wrote in *Mémoires d'une jeune fille rangée*: "Barrès, Gide, Valéry, Claudel . . . It is normal that I should have recognized myself in them, for we were on the same side. Bourgeois like me, they felt, like me, uneasy in their body" ("mal à l'aise dans leur peau").[5] You think you're saying something new if you point out that the "like" elides precisely the difference between their body and hers? My dear, where have you been all these years? And besides, you claim to be talking about autobiography, but you've been quoting obsessively from *The Second Sex,* which is an essay. Can't you keep your genres straight?

I plead guilty on both counts. I wonder, however, whether juxtaposing my two intellectual transgressions—restating old knowledge as if it were new and rereading a familiar text in the improper place—might not produce something, an understanding or a question, that may be of value. Nancy Miller has argued that in order to "decipher the inscription of the female subject" in writing by women, we need to expand the corpus by breaking down the barriers of genre, by reading autobiography, essay, and novel together in their status as text.[6] Perhaps if we look at Beauvoir's male identification as it is inscribed in such an expanded text, we will find—what? Something.

Let us look, then, at *The Mandarins.* Again, this is not an autobiography, even though it has been read (and if so read, generally deprecated) as a *roman à clef* about Beauvoir's friends: Henri as Camus, Dubreuilh as Sartre, Lewis as Nelson Algren, the American lover. Anne, in that case, is Beauvoir, sort of. Sort of, because Anne does not write. *The Mandarins* is narrated in alternating chapters or sections, with two alternating characters as centers of consciousness or focalizers. Henri, who is a writer, does not narrate his own story; it is narrated through him, from his point of view, but not by him. He is not, technically speaking, the subject of enunciation of his story. (The subject of enunciation is the one who speaks or writes the narrative discourse; in Henri's story, it is an anonymous narrator.) Anne, by contrast, does narrate her own story, using the first person singular; but she is not a writer, and *does not write her story*—the text emphatically insists on that. She is thus the subject of enunciation, but the status of the discourse she produces is ambiguous: it starts out as an interior monologue, words spoken in her head while she is lying in bed unable to sleep. But very soon after that, it slips into classical first person retrospective narration, using the *passé simple* tense, and it is only at the very end of the novel, after several years of fictional time and more than a thousand pages of reading time have elapsed, that Anne once again (but in an altogether different situation, so that we can't "reattach" it to her initial situation of lying in bed) returns to a kind of interior monologue.

Emery Snyder has shown that Anne's retrospective narration is problematic because it is ostensibly neither written nor spoken to a dramatized narratee: it is addressed to no one—not to herself, or to anyone else. This kind of unanchored and unaddressed discourse is usual in interior monologue, but is aberrant in the formal retrospective first person narration that Anne practices.[7] Thus, literally, Anne's narrative discourse is impossible—ostensibly neither speech nor writing, even while having the form of a classical, generally written (as opposed to spoken) first person narrative. In a text like Chateaubriand's *René* or Prévost's *Manon Lescaut,* where the first person narrative is ostensibly spoken (René and Des Grieux both address their stories to a dramatized narratee), nothing distinguishes it formally from written discourse—it is writing masquerading as speech. Anne's discourse, however, is writing masquerading as non-writing. She produces a text, but she has neither a localized voice nor a pen.

Here, then, is a curious chiasmus: Anne, who is the subject of enunciation, neither speaks her narrative nor writes it. Henri, who in the fiction does practically nothing *but* speak and write (he speaks at public meetings, writes political journalism, is the author of a widely praised novel, and is shown conceiving, writing, and participating in the staging of an important play) is not the subject of enunciation of his story.

How can we account for this asymmetrical doubling, in which both centers of consciousness are at once endowed with and dispossessed of a crucial element? Let us leave that question in suspense for a moment and ask two simpler ones: Why are there two centers of consciousness in the first place, one male and one female? And why is the writer in the fiction male? These questions are the ones Beauvoir implicitly asks, and answers, in the pages she devotes to *Les Mandarins* in *La Force des choses* (*The Force of Circumstance*), written nine years after the novel.

I would like to look closely at two fragments from these pages, starting with the second, shorter one:

> Ce sont surtout les aspects négatifs de mon expérience que j'ai exprimés à travers elle [Anne]: la peur de mourir et le vertige du néant, la vanité du divertissement terrestre, la honte d'oublier, le scandale de vivre. La joie d'exister, la gaieté d'entreprendre, le plaisir d'écrire, j'en ai doté Henri. Il me ressemble autant qu'Anne au moins, et peut-être davantage.[8]

> It is above all the negative aspects of my experience that I expressed through her [Anne]: the fear of dying and the vertigo of nothingness, the vanity of earthly pastimes, the shame of forgetting, the scandal of living. The joy of existing, the gaiety of action, the pleasure of writing—these I gave to Henri. He resembles me at least as much as Anne, and maybe more.

This short sequence is structured by a single binary opposition, male versus female: the female character, Anne, is the subject through whom negativity, death, nothingness, vanity, shame, and scandal are expressed; the male character, Henri, is the subject of positive action, pleasure, and writing—pleasure *as* writing. But both characters, finally, are controlled and *used* by the writing self that is Simone de Beauvoir. ("*I* expressed through Anne"; "*I* gave to Henri.") It is a split self—not androgynous, for the androgyne suggests unity, whereas here all is opposition, stark and irreconcilable difference, positive and negative. At the same time, it is a triumphant self, mastering the opposition, making the split work for her. This is Beauvoir, the happy male-identified woman writer.

The first fragment, which occurs four pages earlier, suggests a less clear-cut story:

> Beaucoup de raisons m'incitèrent à placer auprès d'Anne un héros masculin. D'abord, pour indiquer l'épaisseur du monde il est commode

d'utiliser plusieurs regards; puis je souhaitais que les relations d'Henri et de Dubreuilh fussent vécues de l'intérieur par l'un d'eux; surtout, si j'avais chargé Anne de la totalité de mon expérience mon livre aurait été, contrairement à mon intention, l'étude d'un cas particulier. Peignant un écrivain, je désirais que le lecteur vît en lui un semblable et non une bête curieuse; mais beaucoup plus qu'un homme, une femme qui a pour vocation et pour métier d'écrire est une exception. (Ce mot n'est synonyme ni de monstre, ni de merveille; je le prends dans un sens statistique.) Je n'ai donc pas confié mon stylo à Anne, mais à Henri; elle je l'ai dotée d'une profession qu'elle exerce avec discrétion. (p. 284)

Many reasons incited me to place next to Anne a masculine hero. First, in order to indicate the density of the world it is convenient to use several gazes; then I wanted the relations between Henri and Dubreuilh to be lived from the inside by at least one of them; above all, if I had entrusted to Anne the totality of my experience, my book would have been, contrary to my intention, the study of a particular case. Depicting a writer, I wanted the reader to see in him a fellow human being, not a rare animal; but much more so than a man, a woman whose vocation and profession is writing is an exception. (This word is not a synonym either for monster or for miracle; I use it in a statistical sense.) I therefore entrusted my pen not to Anne, but to Henri; her I endowed with a profession she exercises discreetly.

The profession in question is that of psychoanalyst. But Anne exercizes it so "discreetly" that it seems to have no bearing at all on her story. Whereas the writer's profession is explored in great detail and from various points of view in *The Mandarins,* the psychoanalyst's profession appears simply as a label. One could speculate at some length on why Beauvoir chose it as Anne's profession only to ultimately ignore it (see my concluding note to this chapter). What concerns me at the moment, however, is not what Beauvoir gave to Anne (a profession), but what she did not give her. I read this sequence as Beauvoir's explanation of why she did not give Anne a pen, why she displaced her own profession onto a male protagonist—and what strikes me is a tone of increasing, albeit controlled, anxiety.

The sequence starts out calmly enough, enumerating reasons:

"d'abord," "puis" ("first," "then"). After that, the tone rises: "sur-tout" ("above all"), Anne would have been too particular a case if left to stand alone ("it is in man, not in woman, that humanity has been incarnated"). After that, the real nervousness begins. "I wanted the reader [*le lecteur*—but *la lectrice,* the female reader, is included] to recognize in the writer I depicted a fellow human being, not a rare animal." Semantically, the phrase "bête curieuse" does not refer here to a gendered being. The phrase is a cliché, meaning simply "curiosity," "rare creature"—an exception, a particular case. But as the genius of the French language would have it, a "rare animal" in this sense is always feminine: "bête curieuse" could not be replaced by, say, "animal curieux" (or even "curieux animal," another cliché meaning "odd fellow") and retain the same meaning.

Almost as if it were implicitly recognizing this semantic con-straint, the very next clause produces, for the first time in the passage, the word "woman": "But much more so than a man, a woman whose vocation and profession is writing is an exception." The abstract term "exception" has now replaced "bête curieuse," even while providing a gloss on it. But by now the text is visibly anxious, for it opens a parenthesis to explain its use of "exception," glossing the gloss. The parenthesis stands out all the more for wanting to remain discreet: THIS WORD IS NOT A SYNONYM EITHER FOR "MONSTER" OR FOR "MIRACLE"; I USE IT IN A STATISTICAL SENSE. Just as "exception" is a neutral, abstract sub-stitute for "bête curieuse," "statistical sense" is the neutral, abstract replacement for the alternative meanings of "exception" which recall "bête curieuse" semantically if not grammatically, and which have both been traditionally associated with woman: monster, miracle. It is as if Beauvoir were reenacting, in this series of glosses and qualifications, the gesture whereby, in *The Second Sex,* she ends her devastating put-down of women writers with the reassuring state-ment that "the future is wide open." Woman's situation (the "statis-tical sense"), not some mysterious essence ("monster" or "miracle") is to blame for her mediocrity. The situation may change. In the meantime, it is safer to bet on the man. "I therefore entrusted my pen not to Anne, but to Henri."

Therefore? Wherefore? To say that Beauvoir reinscribes here the "classic Western phallogocentric trope" of the penile pen[9]—and reinscribes as well the classic phallogocentric figure of woman as a castrated man—is merely to state the obvious. The question is: Why? Why was woman, in Beauvoir's eyes, too particular a case? Why, even endowed with a pen, would Anne never have been recognized by the reader—whether male or female—as anything but an exception, a "bête curieuse"?

Some feminists have argued that Beauvoir was too much under the influence of Sartre and Sartrean existentialism, which identified woman with immanence "for all eternity."[10] That may be true. Or maybe she was too much under the influence of the French proverb, "Qui peut le plus, peut le moins" (literally: "Whoever can do more can do less"). Henri, having "le plus," the extra part, can represent both those who have it and those who don't. In him, the reader—whether woman or man—will recognize a fellow human being, a "semblable"; Anne, who lacks the extra part, can represent only herself. Or maybe it is a matter not of ideology (a proverb is nothing if not ideological) but of rhetoric, a case of faulty troping. If the penis and the pen are the two terms of a metaphor, then Henri is privileged because his body can *display* one of the terms (is it the tenor or the vehicle?) and "call" the other to it by its resemblance. Anne, on the other hand, has "nothing to show," and therefore gets nothing. This hypothesis is interestingly confirmed, in a somewhat different context, by Jacques Lacan's analysis of the dissymmetry in men's and women's experience of the Oedipus complex: "Strictly speaking, we shall say that there is no symbolization of the woman's sex as such . . . And that is because the imaginary provides only an absence, whereas elsewhere [in the male sex] there is a very dominant symbol [*un symbole très prévalent*]."[11]

One can wonder whether Lacan is not lacking in imagination here, since artists like Georgia O'Keeffe and Judy Chicago have found powerful ways to symbolize the female sexual organs. It is true, however, that *at first glance* the male organ is more visible (or, as Lacan puts it, more "prévalent"—and a page later, more "provocant") than the female. Lacan's (and Freud's) emphasis on the visible and on visibility is, as Luce Irigaray has shown, part of the Western male philosophical tradition since Plato.[12] So long as the metaphor for writing is tied to the externally visible, there can be no feminine equivalent of the penile pen. That is why French feminists after

Beauvoir sought other empowering metaphors, not based on the externally visible: Cixous' "white ink" may be understood as an attempt to counteract, and counterweigh, the penile pen.

In choosing to entrust her pen to Henri, not Anne, Beauvoir reaffirmed the line of male subjects in whom she had recognized her self as a writer—from Barrès, Gide, Valéry, and Claudel to Sartre, who, as she writes in *Mémoires d'une jeune fille rangée*, "was the double in whom I found, carried to the point of incandescence, all my own obsessions" (p. 344). At the same time, though—and here we return to the question I left in suspense some time ago—she did not give Henri all, nor did she completely deprive Anne of subject-hood. Although she was never able to "entrust her pen to a woman" (even in her most active feminist phase of the 1970s, she refused to consider the possibility of a positively valued "woman's writing"), she came increasingly to recognize, and value, the specificity of women's struggle—"la lutte des femmes," if not an "écriture de femme." In the last decade of her life, she even spoke occasionally of what in *The Second Sex* she would have called impossible: a kind of feminine universal. "I think that a woman is at the same time universal and a woman, just as a man is universal and a male," she told Alice Jardine in an interview in 1977,[13] as if forgetting that everything she had written in *The Second Sex* suggested the contrary. And also forgetting, or simply not seeing, that the "just as" in her sentence was precisely what constituted the problem. For as she herself had so lucidly analyzed, it is not the case in our culture, or in any other, that a woman is universal-and-a-woman *just as* a man is universal-and-a-man. The "just as" can be read as the sign of a desire to transcend sexual difference by denying it; it may also be the sign of the aporia in Beauvoir's thinking, and in any thinking that tries to go beyond sexual difference without first working *through* it.[14]

5

THE PASSION
ACCORDING
TO
HÉLÈNE CIXOUS

One cannot not speak of the scandals of an epoch. One cannot not espouse a cause. One cannot not be summoned by an obligation of fidelity.

—Hélène Cixous, "From the Scene of the Unconscious to the Scene of History"

Ask any fashionable Parisian intellectual these days about feminism or feminist theory—let alone, heaven help you, "new French feminisms"—and you will be met by a pitying stare. "My dear, where have you been? Don't you know that no one does that anymore?" Nothing is more embarrassing, to a fashionable Parisian intellectual, than to be caught quoting last season's watchwords. Feminism, like Marxism, structuralism, poststructuralism (or like the narrow striped tie?) is definitely *passé.* No one—that is, no one fashionable, no one *dans le vent,* in the wind, knowing which way the wind blows—"does" it anymore.

Ah, well, so much for *la mode.* Some may have to resign themselves to being unfashionable (at least for a while, given fashion's fickleness), stubbornly clinging to what matters to them, repeatedly returning to the same subject, which turns out to be inexhaustible, upon inspection never exactly the same—like Hokusai drawing his two hundred and nineteenth lion or Rembrandt painting his hundredth self-portrait, or Monet painting his twenty-sixth cathedral or *n*th water lily. Or like Hélène Cixous, who cites these examples in her meditation on repetition and fidelity, "The Last Painting or the Portrait of God."

What does H.C. stubbornly cling to? What is the "same subject" to which she keeps returning? The essays in *"Coming to Writing" and Other Essays,* although representing only a tiny portion of her work over the past fifteen years, provide a surprisingly accurate, if necessarily shorthand, answer to that question. But first we must slightly modify the question, for what these essays present is not a single subject but a whole web of intertwined concerns and reflections: on the relations between writing, exile, foreignness, loss, and death; on the relations between writing, giving, nourishment, love, and life; and on the relations between all of the above and being a woman, or a man.

These concerns have been H.C.'s ever since she published her first works of fiction and criticism in the 1960s (the title of her first critical book was itself a whole program: *The Exile of Joyce, or the Art of Replacement*); but they have become, over time, by dint of repetition and fidelity, reworked, refined, at once complicated and decanted—I would be tempted to say "purified," were that word not so heavily overlaid with spiritualist and antimaterialist connotations, many of which I do not accept. H.C.'s latest book as of this writing, *Jours de l'an,* published in 1990, takes up again, in a complicated and decanted way, the "author's" problem (the author is not named; the word acts as both a proper and a common noun, though ungrammatically in the feminine, *auteure*): the problem of death and loss, in childhood and later. H.C. has often said that she "entered into writing" when her father died, she a young child and he still a young man. In *Jours de l'an,* the anniversary of his death is linked to other losses, other deaths, but also to the author's necessary choice to live, and write; and to her "passion for doors" that will allow her to get to the "other side." Or as the title of one chapter puts it, her passion for "breaking down the wall."

Walls

What exactly does it mean, in H.C.'s world and writing, to "break down the wall," or (in "Coming to Writing") to "get past the wall"? On an immediate, existential level, it means—as she explains in

"Coming to Writing," the most explicitly autobiographical of the essays in her book—daring to throw off the constraints, inner and outer, that join together to "forbid [one] to write." In H.C.'s case—but she is not the only one—the constraints were multiple: "History, my story, my origin, my sex." By what right did a "Jewoman" with a German mother(tongue), growing up in Algeria without a father, desire to enter the Sacred Garden of French Literature? No right at all, it seemed. But desire, like a breath struggling to get out after you have been held breathless, does not ask whether it has a "right" to exist. The passion to write can even get past triple walls of interdiction, triple walls of difference: foreignness, Jewishness, femininity. "As soon as you let yourself be led beyond codes, your body filled with fear and with joy, the words diverge, you are no longer enclosed in the maps of social constructions, you no longer walk between walls, meanings flow . . ." (pp. 49–50).

Interestingly, H.C. reinvents here, in describing the process of a free-flowing writing that she associates with femininity, some of the vocabulary of early Surrealism: "Let yourself go, let the writing flow, . . . become the river, let everything go, open up, unwind, open the floodgates, let yourself roll" (pp. 56–57). This could be a recipe for automatic writing, the poetic mainstay of the first Surrealist Manifesto. Like automatic writing, H.C.'s practice is "at once a vocation and a technique," "a practice of the greatest passivity" which is actually "an active way—of getting to know things by letting ourselves be known by them." Cagey H.C., to rewrite the avant-garde by feminizing it! "Continuity, abundance, drift [dérive, a favorite word of the Situationists, inherited as a concept from the Surrealists, and passed on to poststructuralism via the writings of Jacques Derrida], are these specifically feminine? I think so. And when a similar wave of writing surges from the body of a man, it's because in him femininity is not forbidden. Because he doesn't fantasize his sexuality around a faucet" (p. 57).

There is more than one way to get past a wall, and more than one kind of wall to get past. The wall of sexual difference, because it seems so impermeable, is one to which H.C. keeps returning. What fascinates her is the imagined possibility of getting past that wall: "Is there a man who can be my mother? Is a maternal man a woman?" (p. 50). "What interested me in Rossini's *Tancredi* . . . was the undeveloped mystery . . . of the existence of a character all the more man in that he is more woman, just as she is more man in that he is more woman" (pp. 147–148). Rossini wrote Tancredi's role for a female voice, woman singing as man; and he wrote Clorinda for a female voice, woman singing as a woman pretending to be a man. H.C. asks: "Where does man begin woman begin continue?" H.C. asks: "What do you call a person who looks rather more like a woman with dark blue eyes, with an icy look in appearance and who is burning inside . . ., who fights like a hero, would give up her life like a mother,. . . and who takes fortresses more easily than a kiss, and her voice is so deep and warm and moist, it sounds like the sea of human tears?" (pp. 96–97).

Is this poetry? Critical commentary? Autobiography? Ethical reflection? Feminist theory? Yes. One wall these texts most definitely get past is the wall of genres. Although H.C.'s formal "Bibliography," published in an excellent recent volume of essays about her work, divides "novels, stories, and fictions" from "essays, theory, criticism," this division strikes me as purely arbitrary—certainly insofar as the works published over the past fifteen years are concerned.[1] The texts published in *"Coming to Writing" and Other Essays* are all drawn from two books in the "essay" category; yet it is evident even on the most cursory reading that they are as much prose poems as critical or theoretical statements. And doesn't H.C. herself write, in "The Last Painting or the Portrait of God": "I am only a poet"? She means she is not a painter, only a "poor painter without canvas without brush without palette" (p. 106). But still, she calls herself a poet, rather than, say, a writer or theorist. And some pages later she explains: "I call poet any writing being who sets out on this path, in quest of what I call the second innocence, the one that comes after knowing, the one that no longer knows, the one that knows how not to know" (p. 114). Baudelaire called poetry "l'enfance retrouvée à volonté," "childhood rediscovered at will." H.C.'s "second innocence," the innocence of knowing how not to know, is something akin to this Baudelairean idea. "It is not a question of not having understood anything, but of not letting oneself get locked into comprehension" (p. 161).

H.C. loves to cite Kafka's mysteriously beautiful sentence, *"Limonade, alles war so grenzenlos."* Lemonade, everything was so infinite, so boundless (*grenze:* boundary). So wall-less. "Denationalization is what interests me," says H.C. in a recent interview with Françoise van Rossum-Guyon. I ask: Why did he say "lemonade"? What strange, impossible connection did Kafka see between "lemonade" and "everything"? H.C., same interview: "Our richness is that we are composite beings."[2] Breaking down walls does not necessarily—not desirably—lead to oneness. Rather, it leads to the recognition of composite selves, composite tongues ("Blessing: my writing stems from two languages, at least"—p. 21). Above all, it leads to the recognition of the stranger even in those one loves, or is.

Clarices

Sometimes, when one is lucky, H.C. has said, one finds the *unhoped-for other.* "Two people came to speak to me in 1977 of a writer named Clarice Lispector. I had never heard of her, *Editions des femmes* [headed by Antoinette Fouque] was preparing a book of hers. I glanced at some fragments of texts, I was dazzled . . . And then as I went on in the text I discovered an immense writer, the equivalent for me of Kafka, with something more: this was a woman, writing as a woman. I discovered Kafka and it was a woman."[3] If Kafka had been a "Jewoman" living and writing in a language that was not her mother tongue, in a country that was not the country of her birth, he would have been Clarice. (Clarice Lispector was Jewish, born in the Ukraine, emigrated to Brazil as a child, and wrote in Portuguese.) So, at least, thinks H.C. But who is H.C.? A "Jewoman" living and writing in a language that is not her mother('s) tongue, in a country that is not the country of her birth. Is finding the "unhoped-for other" but a way of finding one's other self?

Some painters, it seems, spend twenty years doing portraits of a single model. Thus the British painter Frank Auerbach: "To paint the same head over and over leads you to its unfamiliarity; eventually you get near the raw truth about it, *just as people only blurt out the raw truth in the middle of a family quarrel.*"[4] To see the most familiar face as unfamiliar is to see it in its truth. Such seeing requires time and concentrated attention: painting the same head over and over. Above all, it requires a kind of love—which can also be, in a family quarrel, a kind of hate; but which cannot be indifferent, for to reach the raw, the irreducible, the unfamiliar truth about an other, one has to be willing to take risks. As H.C. puts it, glossing Rembrandt's self-portraits: "One must have gone a long way in order to finally leave behind the need we have to veil, or lie, or gild" (p. 115). To see and love the other in her or his ungilded truth, which is his or her unfamiliarity, one has to be willing to see, without flinching, the stranger in oneself. As H.C. puts it, glossing Clarice's fictions: "Who are you who are so strangely me?" (p. 169).

For more than a decade, H.C. has been teaching and writing about Clarice, painting the same head over and over—nor is she finished yet.[5] We can get some sense of the ground covered in these years, these portraits, by comparing the first essay H.C. devoted to Clarice, "Clarice Lispector: the Approach" (1979) to the most recent one, "The Author in Truth" (1989). It's not that the first text is "less profound" or "less true" than the last, or that they present considerably different views of their subject. It's that in the last one there is more, and in more decanted form, of both H.C. and Clarice—two authors who are not one, but who are very close, very close; so close that in rereading Clarice's texts in order to understand the last work she wrote before she died (*The Hour of the Star*), H.C. is brought to reread, and rewrite, several of her own.

I am especially struck by the rewriting, in "The Author in Truth," of a story H.C. has often (re)written before, that of Eve and the apple. In one of her earliest versions, written before the encounter with Clarice, H.C. emphasizes irony and rebellion; her favorite character in that version is the "tall black serpent, all head and a tail covered with diamonds," whose beauty for her resides in his daring to break and defy the Law.[6] In the later version, written "after Clarice," H.C. emphasizes not rebellion but pleasure; the character in the story who counts for her now is Eve, struggling to choose between the absent, abstract Law and the present, concrete apple. "Myself, I would have eaten it," H.C. says about another apple, which Monet renounced (p. 130). Eve, too, ate it, discovering "the inside of the apple, and [that] this inside is good. The Fable tells us how the genesis of 'femininity' goes by way of the mouth, through a certain oral pleasure, and through a non-fear of the inside" (p. 151).

Of course, it would be far too simple to suggest (as I may appear to have done with my "before" and "after") that Clarice was the only, or even the most important, influence in what I see as one major development in H.C.'s mode of writing over the past fifteen years: the move away from a mode of ironic feminist polemic—as in what is undoubtedly her best-known text, that brilliantly explosive and angry essay/manifesto/poem titled "The Laugh of the Medusa"—toward what I want to call a mode of lyrical feminine celebration. (All these words should be between quotation marks, to indicate their tentativeness and my own aversion to labels or strict categorizations.) It is not the case that in 1975 H.C. was all anger and irony, whereas in 1990 she was all mansuetude and lyricism. "Coming to Writing," which dates from 1977, is a text in point, astonishingly varied in tone and mode. But I believe there has definitely been a gradual shift in emphasis over the years—one that H.C., too, is aware of. "Ever since I left the heterosexual scene, I feel less anger," she told me when we talked about this in June 1989. Some of the texts in this volume (especially "Tancredi Continues," published in the same year as *Le Livre de Promethea*) are beautiful love letters to femininity, as well as to a living woman. But as the very names Tancredi (a man's name) and Promethea (a man's name modified) indicate, H.C.'s notion of the "feminine" and its relation to the "masculine," or for that matter of women and their relation to men or to other women, is not a simple one. For example, it is not just ("just") a question of the male body versus the female body. That may be one reason why these love letters, written by a woman to a woman, can resonate so strongly even for a reader, man or woman, whose so-called sexual preference leans elsewhere. The "nostalgia for a happy love between two equal masculine and feminine forces," which H.C. sees embodied in Tancredi and Clorinda—and which, as she points out, is still feared as revolutionary—can take many different forms. And be embodied in more ways than one, or two.

That is where Clarice comes back in, after all. She comes back, that is, according to H.C. in "The Author in Truth": "The text [Lispector's *The Passion According to G.H.*] teaches us that the most difficult thing to do is to arrive at the most extreme proximity while guarding against the trap of projection, of identification. The other must remain absolutely strange within the greatest possible proximity." Absolutely strange, yet as close to me as my own self. Which means, at the right distance: "Love your fellow being as if he were your stranger . . . Yes, Clarice's ultimate project is to make the other human subject appear equal—and this is positive—to the roach. Each to her own species" (pp. 170–171).

We are rather far, here, from the question of "male/female," or even of "masculine/feminine." That question—which can never be ignored, or dismissed—has been subsumed (I stress: without being swallowed up) into the question of self and other. That is why Clarice, when painted by H.C.—over and over—can become plural, Kafka, Joyce, Rilke, Tsvetaeva, and all the others who are there without writing, each in her/his own species, at once familiar and absolutely strange.[7] That is why Clarice, as H.C. sees her, can even cease being a name and become a common noun: "Things of beauty come to us only by surprise. To please us. Twice as beautiful for surprising us, for being surprised. When no one is there to take them. It seems to us when they spring forth towards us that they are strokes of god; but when they come in we see by their smile that they are strokes of clarice."[8]

Her Story, Our Story, History

Luck: "I had the 'luck' to take my first steps in the blazing hotbed between two holocausts" (p. 17). Is it possible for a European born before 1939 to think of history, let alone individual life story, as anything but a form of luck? Is it possible for any Jewish European born in that time to think otherwise? Frank Auerbach, sent out of Berlin by his parents in 1939, never saw them again. He was lucky, they were not. H.C. had the luck—without quotation marks—to be born to a German Jewish mother in 1937 not in Germany but in Oran, Algeria. When Frank Auerbach sailed to England, she was two years old. At three, she discovered what it meant to be Jewish: "My father was a military officer during the war (temporarily, because he was a doctor), so suddenly we were admitted to the only garden in Oran (Oran is a very desert city), that of the Officers' Club. But the place was a hotbed of anti-Semitism. I was three years old, I hadn't the slightest idea that I was Jewish. The other children started attacking me, and I didn't even know what it was to be Jewish, Catholic, and so on."[9]

Before the awareness of being a woman, there was the sense of foreignness: "People said, 'the French,' and I never thought I was French . . . I felt that I was neither from France nor from Algeria. And in fact, I was from neither."[10] At home, her mother and grandmother spoke German—it was her language of nursery rhymes and songs, later of poetry. But in school, it was a language of rules, intolerable; for H.C., it had to remain private and sung—English became the school-learned tongue. Before that, there were Arabic and Hebrew, both interrupted when her father died. In Algiers, where the family had moved after the war, they lived in an Arab neighborhood where her father had his practice. But "since I didn't belong to the European community and wasn't admitted into the Arab community, I was between the two, which was extremely painful."[11] Many years later, in "Coming to Writing," she would sum it up: "No legitimate place, no land, no fatherland, no history of my own" (p. 15).

The miracle is that out of all this sense of lack, writing came. "At a certain moment for the person who has lost everything, whether that means a being or a country, language becomes the country. One enters the country of words."[12] Miraculous metamorphosis, when mourning becomes language, turns from emptiness to substance added to the world. "Exile makes one fall silent/earth [*taire/terre*]. But I don't want exile to make silence, I want it to make earth; I want exile, which is generally a producer of silence, extinction of voice, breathlessness, to produce its opposite."[13] *Taire/terre*, metamorphosis, wordplay. This is what another woman exile living and writing in Paris has called "transmuting into games what for some is a misfortune and for others an untouchable void."[14] H.C. says: "I lost Oran. Then I recovered it, white, gold, and dust for eternity in my memory and I never went back. In order to keep it. It became my writing."[15]

One aspect of H.C.'s recent work that is not represented, or even alluded to, in *"Coming to Writing" and Other Essays*, is her writing of historical epics for the theater. She wrote two short plays in the 1970s, *Portrait of Dora* and *Le nom d'Oedipe* (*The Name/No of Oedi-*

pus), which came directly out of her involvement, at once angry and passionate, with psychoanalysis. In the mid-1980s, she turned to a much vaster stage. For Ariane Mnouchkine and her renowned troupe, the Théâtre du Soleil, H.C. wrote two six-hour plays on national epic themes: *L'Histoire terrible mais inachevée de Norodom Sihanouk, roi du Cambodge (The Terrible but Unfinished History of Norodom Sihanouk, King of Cambodia)*, staged in 1985, and *L'Indiade, ou L'Inde de leurs rêves (The Indiad, or the India of Their Dreams)*, staged in 1987 and televised in three two-hour segments in 1989. Also in 1989, H.C. and Ariane Mnouchkine collaborated on a TV film commissioned by the French Ministry of Culture for the bicentenary of the French Revolution. H.C. coauthored the scenario and wrote the dialogues; A.M. coauthored the scenario and directed. The film that resulted, *La Nuit miraculeuse (The Night of Miracles)* is a modern-day fairy tale, at once poetic and full of comic touches, celebrating both the Revolution (past) and cultural and national diversity (present).

Although none of this work by H.C. is alluded to in the volume (most of the texts were written earlier), all of this work is in some sense implied by it. For breaking down walls and encountering Clarices will lead, if not inevitably, still with a coherence all its own, to a recognition of the other (of *others*) that is no longer limited to individual life-story. "It is when one has been able to reach the moment of opening oneself completely to the other that the scene of the other, which is more specifically the scene of History, will be able to take place in a very vast way."[16] For H.C., due to personal circumstances, writing the scene of History began literally with the "scene" of theater (*scène* also means "stage" in French). She has spoken with delight about the "depersonalization" of the author that writing for the stage both requires and makes possible, since the other in a stage production speaks necessarily with a voice different from the author's, and is physically someone else. But I believe that the scene of History, already evoked, if only fleetingly, in "Coming to Writing," was waiting to make an appearance in H.C.'s work, in whatever genre or mode. Indeed, it appeared full force in her non-theatrical writing in 1988, with *Manne, aux Mandelstams aux Mandelas*. In that book, exile, poetry, resistance, and fidelity—fidelity between a man and a woman (Nelson and Winnie, Osip and Na-dejda, "two equal masculine and feminine forces") and between individual human beings and transhuman ideals—come together textually as part of the "blazing hotbed" of twentieth-century history.

Who has spoken here? A "Jewoman" living and writing in a language that is not her mother tongue, in a country that is not the country of her birth: S.R.S.

ARTISTS IN LOVE (AND OUT): LEONORA CARRINGTON AND MAX ERNST

6

It would make a wonderful movie.

Max, forty-six, handsome, brilliant, a famous artist of the Parisian avant-garde and renowned ladies' man, arrives in London for an exhibition of his paintings and meets Leonora, twenty, a dark-eyed beauty with flowing black hair, rebellious daughter of a wealthy English industrialist and an aspiring artist herself. It's love at first sight, "mad love" as the Surrealists call it: tempestuous, irresistible, sweeping all obstacles before it, a melding of souls and minds as well as bodies. We are in June 1937, civil war is raging in Spain, and a sense of impending catastrophe hangs over the rest of Europe. All the more reason to cling to love: Max and Leonora run off for a vacation in Cornwall with friends, then "elope" to Paris. Max is married—horrible scenes of confrontation with his abandoned wife (his second). He and Leonora travel south. He leaves her in a small village, but soon calls her back to Paris—he can't live without her. She becomes part of the Surrealist circle; her paintings are included in their big exhibition in Paris. But the atmosphere is full of petty squabbles, and she and Max want tranquillity above all. They move back to their southern village, buy an old farmhouse together. Idyll: he paints and deco-

I'm sick of that. Those were three years of my life. Why doesn't anyone ask me about anything else?
—Leonora Carrington
Interview, 1990

It was a kind of paradise time of my life.
—Leonora Carrington
Interview, 1990

Leonora Carrington and Max Ernst in St. Martin d'Ardèche, 1939; photograph by Lee Miller.

rates the house with frescoes, sculptures, sculpted reliefs on the walls; she paints, and writes stories that he illustrates with his collages, published in limited editions in Paris. They receive visits from friends, fellow artists from Paris, London—scenes of feasts and merrymaking, outlandish costumes, games, dances. They work and they love. He does a painting he calls A Moment of Calm: *it is the summer of 1939.*

Then the screen darkens: on September 1, 1939, war is declared between France and Germany. Max, an exiled German who has lived in France for more than fifteen years and is a committed anti-Nazi, is nevertheless rounded up by French police as an "enemy alien." Leonora visits him at the detainment camp, where he continues to paint and draw; at Christmas he is released, thanks to the intervention of French friends alerted by Leonora. Return to their farmhouse in St. Martin; she paints his portrait, dressing him in striped socks and a merman's cloak and placing him in an icy landscape. The "phony war" drags on. In May, Max is denounced by a villager who claims he is in communication with the enemy. (In reality, if the Nazis found him they would not be nice: they have long considered him a "degenerate" artist, a menace to the Reich.) He is interned again, shuttled back and forth between camps; escapes and returns to St. Martin, but is taken away again. Leonora, anguished, starves herself and begins to hallucinate.

Meanwhile, the Germans occupy Paris: it's the real war this time. Leonora, in a state close to mental breakdown, is persuaded by friends to flee from St. Martin to Spain; in order to obtain the necessary travel permit, she signs over the deed of the house to a local official. When Max returns a few weeks later, he finds Leonora gone, the house no longer his. He stays for a while, painting her portrait over and over in mythical landscapes; he begins one of his greatest paintings, a cry of despair, Europe after the Rain. Then he leaves St. Martin, travels to Marseilles, where he meets Surrealist friends and is introduced to the rich American heiress Peggy G., who is on her way back to the United States and takes him under her wing: he must leave Europe. They go to Lisbon, to await the Clipper plane with a whole entourage: Peggy's children, her ex-husband, the ex-husband's estranged second wife.

Cut to Santander, Spain, where Leonora, having been diagnosed by Spanish doctors as incurably insane (she will later write about this experience, in a work called Down Below), is shut up in a mental hospital: delusions, mistreatment by the doctors and nurses, physical and mental torture. Finally, her parents send her old Nanny from England to take care of her. She is released, taken to Madrid, then shipped off to Lisbon; from there, they plan to send her to a sanitorium in South Africa. She succeeds, by a clever ruse, in escaping from her jailer and seeks protection at the Mexican embassy in Lisbon, where she knows a diplomat. Renato, the Mexican diplomat, is Max's age: he will protect her, but in order to get her to America they will have to marry. She agrees. (They divorce amicably a few years later.)

Then Max and Peggy and their entourage arrive in Lisbon, spring 1941. Leonora is reunited with Max and spends long, intense days of reading and drawing with him, but their love affair is over. Max is now Peggy's lover, although he does not love her and she knows it. Peggy, desperately in love with him and jealous, nevertheless realizes that he *and Leonora have a relationship nobody else can share: "Leonora was the only woman Max had ever loved." According to Peggy, who narrates this part of the story, Max begs Leonora not to marry Renato, to fly to New York with him and the rest of their group. She refuses, explaining that "her life with Max was over."*

It was not completely over, for Leonora and Max are both in New York during a whole year and they see a lot of each other, along with other exiled Surrealists. He lives with Peggy and she with Renato. But he continues to work on his paintings of her, and she continues to write about him and to paint pictures like the ones she did when they were together. An avant-garde journal in New York devotes a whole issue to Max, to which she contributes a story, "The Bird Superior, Max Ernst," accompanied by the portrait she painted of him in St. Martin; one of his large portraits of her, Leonora in the Morning Light, is also reproduced in that issue. His one-man show in New York that spring includes that painting and a number of others representing her, with less explicit titles. "Max was so insane about Leonora that he really could not hide it," says Peggy.

The end: in the summer of 1942, five years after their fateful meeting in London, Leonora leaves New York for Mexico. She and Max will both live to old age, but they will never see each other again.[1]

"It would make a wonderful movie," I told myself half ironically (but only half) as I drove to Leonora Carrington's apartment in Oak Park, Illinois, on a dark afternoon in late December 1990. I had visited her twice before there, aware each time of the incongruity: What was this extraordinary woman artist doing in that dreary Chicago suburb, whose only claim to art was that it had once been home to Frank Lloyd Wright? Leonora had moved there from New York a few years earlier, to be near her son Pablo Weisz-Carrington, a physician in charge of the pathology lab at the local Veterans' hospital. Her other son, Gabriel, was a professor of literature in Mexico City, where she had lived for many years and where she still returned for lengthy visits. (Her husband, the photographer Csiki Weisz, whom she married in 1946, still lived in their house; although no longer living together, they remained on friendly terms.)

On my two earlier visits, we had talked about Gnosticism and motherhood, cooking and the Cabbala, Jungian psychology, Tibetan Buddhism, humor (she values it highly), collage (she hates that word to describe her work—I had used it in connection with her novel *The Hearing Trumpet*, a "verbal collage"), writing and painting ("When I write, it's for others; when I paint, it's for myself"—but she has lots of unpublished writings, diaries, notes, and until recently even a number of stories written in St. Martin before the war), grandchildren (she has several, enjoys being a grandmother), chance ("There's no such thing as chance"), women's independence ("I earn my own way. No one keeps me"), feminism (she is a feminist, though not a dogmatist), Chicago, New York, Mexico. We talked about people she had known: André Breton, the great Surrealist poet and leader of the group ("A bit too formal with women—he kissed their hand in greeting"), Remedios Varo, her good friend and fellow painter in Mexico (I showed her a new biography of Varo by Janet Kaplan: "I don't want anyone to write my biography," she said firmly), and several other friends, old and new. The only person we did not talk about—studiedly avoided talking about—was Max Ernst.

Before I met her, I had heard from a few people that Leonora could be "difficult." I was all the more charmed by her warm reception on both my visits: she fed me, asked me questions about my family, my work, offered me her own opinions on a surprising variety of subjects ranging from politics to photography. I was especially impressed by her interest in current controversies, current work: she had read Rushdie's *Satanic Verses* before I did, as soon as the fuss began; and when I sent her two books by Angela Carter (whom she hadn't read—I was convinced she would find affinities between Carter's work and her own), she replied quickly to say she was enjoying them and thanked me for the introduction. I had long admired Leonora's writing, and had taught it and written about it before I met her. Many Surrealist artists (Ernst among them) wrote as well as painted, but few had as considerable a body of work in both domains as she did.

In short, I felt I had a good rapport with Leonora. That is what emboldened me, before my third visit to her, to call and ask whether I could bring along a tape recorder and do a formal interview. "I would like to talk to you about your early work," I told her on the telephone, "and also about your relations to the Surrealists." "All right," she said.

As soon as I stepped into her dark living room, I realized that it was not totally all right. Leonora was not as relaxed as she had been on my earlier visits. She was getting ready to leave for an extended stay in Mexico and the small apartment was cluttered with boxes. She told me she hadn't painted in a while, which bothered her. She felt isolated and lonely. "Who can blame you for feeling isolated in Oak Park, Illinois?" I remarked, not very diplomatically. "But what about the Chicago Surrealists? Don't they come around?" (Chicago is the last American outpost of Surrealism, with an "official" Surrealist group led by Franklin Rosemont, who met Breton as a young man.) Leonora shrugged her shoulders: "I'm interested in the present, not the past."

With a slightly sinking feeling, I turn on the tape recorder and pull out of my bag the small manila envelope in which I have brought two photographic reproductions: one is the portrait of Max Ernst painted by Leonora in 1939–1940, the other her famous self-portrait of 1937–1938, also known as *The Inn of the Dawn Horse.* It shows Leonora dressed in a riding outfit (tight white jodhpurs, green jacket, high-heeled black booties), sitting on the edge of a ladylike Victorian armchair in the middle of a large, otherwise unfurnished room; the feet of the chair are high-heeled women's shoes like her own; the armrest, too, echoes her own left arm and hand. Her unruly black hair, like a horse's mane, falls around her shoulders as she looks straight out at the viewer with a scowling air. Standing in front of her is a black-striped hyena with a highly expressive face and piercing blue eyes, its head also turned toward the viewer. Behind her, a white rocking horse is suspended in mid-air; outside the window framed by gold Victorian curtains like a stage set, a white horse, its legs extended like those of the rocking horse, runs free in a clearing surrounded by a copse of trees. "I wonder if you could comment on this painting?" I ask her, purposely vague. "No. Put it away, please. I know it quite well, I don't need to see it." "But . . ." "It's a good painting. Period." "Well, but what about your representing yourself in that particular pose?" "Well, that's what I did."

She will say no more: nothing about her love of horses, dating

Leonora Carrington, *The Inn of the Dawn Horse (Self-Portrait)*, ca. 1937; oil on canvas.

from early childhood; nothing about the white rocking horse bought at a second-hand shop in Paris shortly after she moved there with Ernst (there is a photograph of him sitting, long-legged, on that horse); nothing about the recurrent, highly overdetermined motif of horses in just about all of her paintings of that period, or about the horses that appear in some of her best-known stories written at that time. Nor is she willing to say anything about the figure of the hyena, another heraldic animal featured in what may be her best-known story, "The Debutante," in which a young society girl befriends a hyena at the zoo and gets the animal to take her place at a debutante ball. This story of adolescent rebellion and violence (the hyena eats the girl's maid and uses her face as a mask, like Hannibal the Cannibal in the recent Oscar-winning film *The Silence of the Lambs*) first appeared in 1939 in *La Dame ovale (The Oval Lady)*, a collection of stories illustrated by Ernst, and has often been anthologized since then, most notably by Breton in his *Anthologie de l'humour noir (Anthology of Black Humor)*, whose first edition contained only that single work by a woman writer.

About all this, Leonora refuses to speak. Daunted but not yet defeated, I try again. "And your portrait of Max?" "I have nothing to say about it." It, too, shows a white horse, but this time immobile, frozen; and if one looks carefully, one notices that what first appeared to be a lantern carried by the merman dressed in his gorgeous red cloak is actually a glass container in which a small gray-white horse is imprisoned in a greenish liquid. If the white horse is her emblem, could this be a negative commentary on her relationship with Ernst? I don't dare to ask the question, and she remains silent. I say: "What about those bird-like feet?" "They're striped socks," she replies. "Yes, but they look like bird feet." "That's true; there was something very bird-like about Max, although I didn't realize it at the time." This from a woman who in 1942 wrote a story titled "The Bird Superior, Max Ernst," about a man whose alter ego, appearing repeatedly throughout his paintings, collages, collage novels, and autobiographical writings, was Loplop, the Superior of the Birds, sometimes also called (as in the collage novel of 1930, *La Femme 100 têtes*, in English, *The Hundred-Headed/Headless Woman*), "Loplop l'hirondelle," Loplop the swallow. In her painting of around 1937 (the same period as *The Inn of the Dawn Horse*) titled *Femme et oiseau (Woman and Bird)*, Carrington depicts a horse-woman with black mane, looking down at a small black bird in whose plumage one sees the white figure of a headless woman.

In fact, no single figure is more closely associated with Ernst than that of the bird Loplop. In a well-known passage of his autobiographical notes, "Some Data on the Youth of M.E., as Told by Himself," he traces this association to an event in his adolescence, when the death of a beloved pet bird coincided with the birth of his sister: "The perturbation of the youth was so enormous that he fainted . . . A dangerous confusion between birds and humans became encrusted in his mind and asserted itself in his drawings and paintings. This obsession haunted him until . . . 1927, and even later Max identified himself voluntarily with *Loplop, the Superior of the Birds*. This phantom remained inseparable from another one called *Perturbation ma soeur, la femme cent têtes*."[2] Occasionally, the Ernst

Leonora Carrington, *Portrait of Max Ernst,* ca. 1939;
oil on canvas.

Leonora Carrington, *Femme et Oiseau (Woman and Bird)*, ca. 1937; oil on canvas.

bird appears as a flying man dangerous to young girls, as in the famous 1923 painting *Deux enfants menacés par un rossignol* (*Two Children Threatened by a Nightingale*), where the nightingale is a black-clad man on a rooftop, about to carry off a young girl in his arms, while below, a girl lies on the ground in a swoon and another one flees in fright. This painting was reproduced in Herbert Read's book *Surrealism,* which Leonora Carrington's mother gave her as a present in 1936, when she was an art student in London. She told the story to Paul de Angelis: "In the book I saw *Deux enfants menacés par un rossignol,* and it totally shocked me. This, I thought, I know what this is. I understand it."[3] Looking recently at a 1947 work by Leonora that I had not seen before, *Crookhey Hall* (exhibited at the Serpentine Gallery in London in 1991–1992), I was struck by the running figure of a young girl, whose stance and flying hair are similar to those of the girl in Ernst's painting.[4]

When Leonora told me, straightfaced, that she had never thought of Max as a bird, I acknowledged my defeat. There was nothing to do but put away the photographs and turn off the tape recorder. (Later, she agreed to have it turned on again, but only to talk about generalities.) It was around then, as I recall, that she uttered the words I have quoted in my epigraph. She exclaimed, in a tone of enormous frustration: "Those were three years of my life! *Why doesn't anyone ask me about anything else?*"

I have often thought about that failed interview—so much so that, curiously, I have come to consider it not a failure at all. For if it failed to yield the information I sought (one reason, I soon realized, was simply that Leonora had spoken at length about the subject with other interviewers: with Marina Warner in 1987, and, only a few months before I saw her, with Paul de Angelis), it gave me something more valuable: a way to think about the frustration itself—both hers and mine—as a vital piece of information. Leonora helped me in that regard, for she remarked later during my visit: "I don't know why I'm so hung up about not wanting to deal with those years. I just realized talking to you that I have not gotten reconciled—that is why I don't want to talk about my past." "Reconciled with what?" I asked. She didn't answer.

Frustration, lack of reconciliation: one feels a great urge to interpret psychoanalytically. Analysts would no doubt speak of ambivalence—unresolved, simultaneous feelings of love and hate directed toward the same object. But I will resist the psychoanalytic temptation in this instance, for I think it would yield only a truism: What, if not ambivalence, would characterize the feelings of a very young woman toward a much older man who appeared in her life at once as mentor, lover (both faithful and faithless), idealized father, and artistic brother-in-arms? Yet the notion of ambivalence, if used in a broad sense rather than in a narrowly psychoanalytic one, proves useful. Think of it as the simultaneous presence of equally strong positive and negative affects (and effects) in a single emotional and artistic relationship: suddenly, not only does the Ernst-Carrington relationship become illuminated, but the question becomes formulable in more general terms. What are the positive and negative consequences, for both parties, of any relationship between a young artist just starting out and an older, more established figure, possibly a "genius," who acts as both mentor and lover? Do gender and sexual politics play a role, making a significant difference whether the younger person is a woman or a man, of the same sex or of the "opposite sex"? What role does the specific historical and cultural context play: for example, the radical displacements and upheavals caused by the Second World War in Europe, or, on a different level, the assumptions about sex roles prevalent not only in a particular society or social class at a given time, but even within a particular subgroup like the French Surrealists between the wars? Perhaps most important, do these biographically slanted questions allow for a new or compelling understanding of the works produced during the relationship, by both the younger and the older artist?

In the case of Carrington and Ernst, it seems clear that the immediate positive consequences of their meeting were tremendous for both artists, if for somewhat different reasons. On the strictly practical, material level, the change was no doubt more radical for her: after years of struggling against her family's middle-class disparagement of art ("I was born into a hundred-percent philistine family," she told me) as well as against the "huge put-downs" she received as a beginning art student in London ("'Forget it, you're no good, and anyway there are no good women artists'"), meeting Ernst had inestimable importance. Here was a major artist whose work she understood and admired, who took her own work seriously and introduced her to others who did the same. Literally, he brought her into a new life—a new city, a new language (they spoke French together, as he knew no English at the time), a world where art was respected and women artists were not automatically dismissed.

Recent feminist criticism has rightly called attention to the subtle (and not so subtle) constraints placed on women even within the

Leonora Carrington, *The Horses of Lord Candlestick*, 1938; oil on canvas.

revolutionary, antibourgeois ideology of Surrealism; for example, by means of glorified but ultimately stifling roles like that of *femme-en-fant* ("child-woman") or "inspired madwoman" à la Breton's heroine in his best-known work, *Nadja* (1928). Carrington herself recently spoke of the role assigned to women as "slightly crazy muse."[5] Yet despite all this, there is no doubt that Surrealism also provided many women artists, including Leonora Carrington, with their first recognition, their first opportunity to exhibit their work. A few months after moving to Paris, she participated in the International Surrealist Exhibition of January–February 1938, and later that spring in the Surrealist exhibition in Amsterdam (where she showed *The Horses of Lord Candlestick*). That same year, the year she turned twenty-one, she published a short story in French, "La Maison de la peur" ("The House of Fear"), with a preface and collage illustrations by Ernst.

It is true that this early recognition and inclusion in the Surrealist circle also had negative consequences, and I will get to that. But considering the well-documented difficulty that many women artists—especially of Carrington's generation, but even today—have in taking themselves seriously *as* artists, I think it is important to acknowledge the positive consequences of recognition by an established, generally male "authority" before dwelling on its disadvantages.

Remaining on the practical level, we can see a "new life" offered to Max Ernst as well, by his encounter with Leonora. Although when he met her he was lacking neither in recognition by his peers nor in women's adulation (the autobiography of his son by his first marriage, Jimmy Ernst, offers instructive glimpses into Ernst's love life, as do the memoirs of Peggy Guggenheim, who supported him during his first years in New York and to whom he was married for a short time), Ernst was clearly reenergized and rejuvenated by his union with a young woman in whom he recognized a sister soul. By 1937, his marriage to Marie-Berthe Aurenche, a young Frenchwoman from a bourgeois Catholic family whom he had married ten years earlier, was foundering, possibly because she had become extremely devout. Ernst, himself the son of devout Catholics, took pleasure throughout his adult life in mocking the Church and everything connected with his own extensive Catholic education. He had been excommunicated by the bishop of Cologne for his blasphemous painting of 1926, *The Blessed Virgin Chastising the Infant Jesus before Three Witnesses,* which shows a sexy Madonna spanking a little boy whose halo has fallen on the ground (the fallen halo was what most outraged the prelate).[6] Ernst continued the provocation in his collage novel of 1930, *Rêve d'une petite fille qui voulut entrer au Carmel (Dream of a Little Girl Who Wanted to Become a Carmelite),* whose heroine, the curvaceous Marceline-Marie, is a most unlikely nun. Even his self-naming as "the Bird Superior" was a parody of convent terminology.

Like Ernst, Carrington came from a devout Catholic family whose religious and social convictions she found pleasure in lampooning; unlike Marie-Berthe Ernst, she never did return to the fold.

In 1934, Ernst published a short text in the Surrealist-dominated journal *Minotaure* which can be read both as a fable of disillusionment with his increasingly Catholic wife and as a premonitory evocation of a different woman. "Les Mystères de la forêt" ("The Mysteries of the Forest") contrasts two kinds of forests, fully exploiting the fact that the gender of that noun in French is feminine. First, there is the forest who, having been "a friend of dissipation" in her youth, suddenly "lets herself be touched by virtue" and becomes "geometric, conscientious, industrious, grammatical, . . . boring." This virtuous forest consults the nightingale (a stand-in for Ernst, as we have seen), who is not happy with her change of mood and advises her to go and see what forests are like in Oceania. She will not go, "being too proud." But the text continues: "Do forests exist over there? They are, it seems, wild and impenetrable, black and redhaired, extravagant, . . . negligent, ferocious, fervent and lovable . . . From one island to the other, above the volcanoes, they play cards with mixed-up decks. Naked, they dress themselves only in their majesty and mystery."[7]

As it happens, the forest—represented as a place of mystery and verdant nature, sometimes grotesque but always luxuriant—was a recurrent motif in Ernst's paintings, especially during the 1930s. Art historians have noted the link between these works and German Romantic painting, especially the subjective dreamscapes of Caspar David Friedrich, whose work Ernst knew well. His painting of 1936, *La Joie de vivre*, represents a forest landscape filled with fantastic animals and rampant foliage; surely not by chance, it is in a similar setting that he placed his 1940 portrait of Leonora, *Leonora in the Morning Light*. It seems clear that the young woman with the thick black hair whom he met in London in 1937 corresponded to a deeply embedded fantasy of "wild womanhood," already evoked in his "mystery of the forest" story of three years earlier.

With that observation, we have moved from the level of practical considerations to what might be thought of as the Surrealist equivalent of the mystical communion of souls. The Surrealists set great store by what they called "objective chance," a phenomenon that often took the form of a fateful encounter that had somehow been prepared by premonitory fantasies or visions. Breton, in his book *L'Amour fou* (*Mad Love*, 1938), described his first encounter with Jacqueline Lamba, who would become his second wife, as an event "foreseen" by a poem he had written eleven years earlier. In the same way, Ernst appears to have considered Carrington as the embodiment of some of his most powerful fantasies, reflected in work done years before he met her; reciprocally, she seems to have found in his earlier work (as in *Two Children Threatened by a Nightingale*) meanings that were immediately clear to her ("I know what this is,

Max Ernst, *Leonora in the Morning Light,* 1940; oil on canvas.

I understand it"), a visual language that corresponded to her own imagination and desires.

The single most powerful image joining them during those years was that of the wild horse.[8] In 1927, Ernst had painted a series of pictures all with the same title (he often explored a single theme or obsession in multiple versions): *La Mariée du vent (The Bride of the Wind).* Each picture represented two or more horses joined in ecstatic coupling, or in one case in a wild ride against a yellow sky. Uwe Schneede has pointed out that "la mariée du vent" is a literal translation of the German *Windsbraut,* a slightly archaic word meaning tempest or stormwind.[9] The great modernist painter Oskar Kokoschka had first exploited the metaphorical possibilities of the German word in his 1914 painting by that title, showing himself and his lover Alma Mahler lying side by side enveloped in a whirlwind. Ernst obviously knew that painting and seized on its erotic content. Quite probably, he was also familiar with the many Germanic leg-

Max Ernst, *The Bride of the Wind*, 1927; oil on canvas.

ends about a figure known as the "wild hunter," who drives before him the "wood-wives" and other inhabitants of the forest. One encyclopedia of Germanic mythology specifically mentions "the North German belief in the Wind's Bride, driven before the Hunter," citing Jacob Grimm's *Teutonic Mythology* as a source.[10] Ernst, like Grimm and the Romantics, was deeply interested in folklore; the legends of the "wild hunter" may provide one explanation for his association of unbridled (pun intended) sexuality with horses.

The horse as a symbol of sexuality functions equally well as male or female: the wild horse can symbolize male potency and sexual drive, but can just as well represent the female who is ridden by the male, carrying him on a whirlwind journey. In Ernst's 1927 "bride of the wind" paintings, the title does not seem to differentiate between stallion and mare, but refers rather to their coupling, their joint ride. However, whether for linguistic (*braut*/"bride" can only be feminine)

Max Ernst, *The Bride of the Wind*, 1940; pencil on paper.

or other reasons, the term eventually came to refer, for Ernst, specifically to a female: in the 1940 "bride of the wind" drawings he did at the detention camp of Les Milles, the figure is that of a hybrid creature standing on two curvy legs, seen from the back, with a horse's head and a long flowing mane that could also be the hair of a woman. This figure was later included as one of several female horse figures, some of them shown mating with the Loplop bird, in Ernst's visual poem "First Memorable Conversation with the Chimera," which appeared in the first issue of the journal *VVV* in New York in June 1942.

The next issue of the journal contained Leonora Carrington's story "The Seventh Horse," written in 1941. Before discussing that

New York story, however, I want to return to Europe. For we have not yet finished with Ernst's variations on the "bride of the wind," and we must also take the time to look again at some of Carrington's works done between 1937 and 1941.

In the early 1930s, Ernst did a series of self-reflective paintings and collages titled "Loplop presents . . .," in which the Bird Superior seems to offer the viewer a framed picture. One of these, *Loplop Presents a Young Girl* (it exists in three versions with small variations, 1931–1936), is a mixed-media work that was shown in his 1937 solo exhibition in London; featured prominently in it is a long black mane that could be the hair of either a horse or a woman. Once again, the Surrealists could see in this coincidence an example of premonitory vision; one of the "bride of the wind" pictures had also been exhibited in London the previous year, in the big International Surrealist Exhibition of 1936. As if in recognition of the "objective chance" that had brought together and materialized these two series of fantasy images in a single encounter, Ernst entitled his 1938 preface to Carrington's *The House of Fear* "Loplop Presents the Bride of the Wind." Here are the last three paragraphs of his preface:

> Who is the Bride of the Wind? Can she read? Can she write French without mistakes? What wood does she burn to keep warm?
>
> She warms herself with her intense life, her mystery, her poetry. She has read nothing, but drunk everything. She can't read. And yet the nightingale saw her, sitting on the stone of spring, reading. And though she was reading to herself, the animals and horses listened to her in admiration.
>
> For she was reading *The House of Fear,* this true story you are now going to read, this story written in a beautiful language, truthful and pure.

Well. On the one hand, there is enormous admiration and praise here for the work, as well as a deep personal infatuation with the mythologized figure of its author. On the other hand, there is a patronizing put-down, suggesting that the author is an inspired medium who "knows not what she does," rather than a self-conscious artist. True, the Surrealists set great store by "automatic writing" and other quasi-inspired states; nevertheless, it is doubtful that any male Surrealist would have been happy to see himself portrayed as a creature who has "read nothing," and indeed "can't read." A London journalist commenting on this text recently remarked, with a tartness that seems only slightly exaggerated: "he envisaged her . . . as a kind of holy idiot."[11]

On the one hand, on the other hand: we are back to the question of positive versus negative consequences. Looking at the work, both painting and writing, produced by Leonora Carrington between 1937 and 1941 with that question in mind, one sees an astonishingly even division between positive and negative, as if she were playing out in her imaginary representations the ambivalences of her relationship with Ernst. On the positive side, the figure of the wild horse and the identification between horse and young woman serves as a gesture of liberation, of power, or of rebellion against social and sexual constraints: thus, the white horse running free in the self-portrait, the group of horses resting in *The Horses of Lord Candlestick* (two of them, the brown and the white, seem to be exchanging sexual messages), and the strikingly phallic horse-woman of *Femme et oiseau* can all be seen as variations on the theme of sexual and creative power. A number of critics have pointed out that the power is linked to a certain androgyny, as in the pose and garb of the artist in the self-portrait. In *Femme et oiseau*, interestingly, it is the horse-woman who is phallic, and much bigger than the (presumably) male bird with whom she is joined. As for the published stories of this period, in "The House of Fear" the horse is a friend to the reclusive narrator-heroine; in "The Oval Lady," the rocking horse—who in the end starts to neigh as if "suffering extreme torture"—is an alter ego for the rebellious daughter, with the implication that no amount of punishment will succeed in taming her.

We might call these representations Carrington's own version of the "bride of the wind." In fact, she did not need Ernst to put her in touch with horses and their possible symbolic significance, for as she has stated in various interviews, she was "thoroughly obsessed with horses" long before she met him. She and her mother both had their own horses and rode frequently. At one time, as a little girl, she had even wanted to transform herself into a horse: "It would give me another kind of energy to become a horse."[12] Nevertheless, the meeting with Ernst and his particular obsession with wild horses could well have reinforced her own positive identification, and

Leonora Carrington and Max Ernst, *Rencontre*, ca. 1940; oil on canvas.

contributed to her preoccupation with that motif throughout the time they were together. There exists at least one painting from 1940 on which they actually collaborated, entitled *Rencontre (Encounter)*. Carrington did the left side, featuring a horse-woman similar to the figure in *Femme et oiseau*; she also painted the volcanic landscape in the background, which evokes (whether she was familiar with Ernst's text or not) the volcanoes he associated with the "wild and naked" forests of Oceania in "Les Mystères de la forêt."

But alongside these powerful positive images of the horse and the horse-woman in Carrington's work, there existed a far less happy version; it is significant, I think, that this negative version, although written around 1937–1938, remained unpublished until very recently. I refer to the long story, actually a novella, "Little Francis," which was first published in an abridged French translation (Carrington wrote it in English, unlike her other stories of that period) in 1986, then in its original version in 1988. The story is a transposition of the painful triangle formed by Ernst, Carrington, and Marie-Berthe Ernst during the first months after the breakup of the marriage. Carrington appears as a young English boy visiting his uncle in Paris; Ernst appears as "Uncle Ubriaco," the playful and unconventional, irresistibly attractive "drunken uncle," while Marie-Berthe figures as Amelia, Ubriaco's spoiled and possessive daughter. Carrington wrote this sad tale during the time when she found herself alone in St. Martin, abandoned by Ernst and uncertain of the future. In the story, after weeks of happiness spent with Francis in the south of France, Ubriaco returns to Paris with Amelia. Francis, in his grief, grows a horse's head and becomes a freak attraction in the local café; in one dreamlike sequence, he visits a fantastic castle and witnesses his own execution (himself before he grew the horse's head). Eventually, he is lured to Paris by Amelia just as Ubriaco has gone to rejoin him; Amelia attacks his horse's head with a hammer and keeps beating him until he dies, then has his body shipped back to England. Ubriaco, grief-stricken, follows, and in a last gesture of co-conspiracy and defiance, paints Francis' plain white coffin with black and yellow stripes.

In her perceptive analysis of this story, Marina Warner notes that Carrington's choice of a male alter ego is in this instance a sign not of androgynous power but rather of youthful vulnerability: "By changing herself into a youth, she uncovered a deeper truth about her relation to Max Ernst, revealing in the devotion and passivity of the boy Francis the tutelage in which Ernst and other masters held their *femmes-enfants,* their brides of the wind; similarly, by transforming Ernst's wife into his daughter, Leonora unveiled that relation of dependence and authority as well."[13] It is indeed true that in the story the emphasis is on Francis' vulnerability, his adoration of "Uncle Ubriaco," and his relation of pupil to teacher (Uncle Ubriaco "found Francis very ignorant indeed . . .," p. 117). Significantly, however, the critique of Ernst that Warner finds implicit in the story never rises to full consciousness; on the contrary, Ubriaco remains Francis' ally and fellow rebel, defying bourgeois convention even beyond death. The negative characters are Francis' English family and Amelia.

What I am suggesting is that although it is possible to read a critique of Ernst, and indeed of the whole relation of women to Surrealism, into this story, at the time of its writing that critique was not consciously available to Carrington. Her conscious energies were focused, rather, on her liberation from middle-class propriety and on attainment of an identity as an artist, a project in which Ernst and the Surrealists could only appear as allies. But—and this is the really interesting twist—it is also obvious that a certain unease with the *femme-enfant* role, and a certain ironic view of her male allies, including Ernst, was present, even if not always acknowledged, both in "Little Francis" and in several other stories that remained unpublished until very recently.

In "Little Francis," the mood is tragic rather than ironic (although there is a biting send-up of an "artistic" party at the castle Francis visits as a horse); the unease I refer to is evident in the significance accorded the horse's head. It transforms Francis into a hybrid figure, like one of Ernst's collages. But rather than becoming a strong sexual outlaw or a figure of potency like Ernst's hybrids or like the horse-woman of *Femme et oiseau,* the horseheaded boy is simply a freak, the object of other people's curiosity. Note that the Francis of before, the one with the human head, is guillotined while the horse-headed Francis watches; the horse's head thus functions as an alienation from self, a "loss of one's head" that is a kind of death rather than a positive metamorphosis.

Still, one could argue that Francis loses his head only after Ubriaco leaves him, not because of Ubriaco's presence. Another story written between 1937 and 1940, however, leaves no doubt as to the target of the author's ironic critique. This one, entitled "Pigeon, Fly," was written in French, and was first published in French in 1986 before appearing in *"The Seventh Horse" and Other Tales.* There are no horses in this tale, but there is a man who takes himself for a bird; and he is chillingly portrayed. The story is stunning, difficult to summarize briefly despite its own brevity. The narrator, a woman artist, is summoned by a certain Monsieur Airlines-Drues (he looks like a sheep and is surrounded by other men with high-pitched voices like those of sheep), who asks her to paint the portrait of his "adored" dead wife before she is buried. The artist accepts the commission, only to notice, to her astonishment, that the portrait she has painted is of her own face. Monsieur Airlines-Drues offers her a room in his house where she can finish the portrait; it is his wife's studio, where the narrator finds a profusion of costumes and the diary of the dead woman. In it, the young wife describes her husband, Célestin, who comes to her dressed in a feather robe and wears "blue stockings with red stripes." Later, he tells her: "You will always be a child, Agathe. Look at me. I am terribly young, aren't I?"[14] Living in his house, she has the feeling of becoming transparent: "Every day, . . . I lose myself a little more . . . I try to paint my portrait so as to have it near me still . . . But . . . I can't. I elude myself" (p. 27). The diary comes to an abrupt end after she describes a game of "Pigeon, Fly" in which Célestin terrifies her by actually flying up in the air. After reading this, the narrator turns to her portrait of Agathe, but the canvas is empty. "I didn't dare look for my face in the mirror. I knew what I would see" (p. 29).

Here, as clear as in a polished glass, is the nightmare image of what it was like to be a *femme-enfant* among the Surrealists: robbed of one's face, one among a series of replaceable women, each "adored" in turn, then buried by a band of bleating sheep who want never to grow old.

In Oak Park, Illinois, in 1990, Leonora said to me during our taped conversation: "There is always a dependency involved in a love relationship. I think if you are dependent, it can be extremely painful." And a bit later: "I think that a lot of women (people, but I say women because it is nearly always women on the dependent side of the bargain) were certainly cramped, dwarfed sometimes, by that dependency. I mean not only the physical dependency of being supported, but emotional dependency and opinion dependency." When, the question arises, did she come to this understanding? I have tried to suggest that she already possessed it, albeit in an unacknowledged form, even during the most euphoric period of her relationship with Ernst; but at that time, as so often happens in life, the emotional attachment and other undeniably positive effects of their life together kept this understanding in the background. Only after being separated from Ernst, against her will, by the brutal forces of history, and only after undergoing a harrowing experience of mental breakdown from which she emerged perhaps as a different person, did she realize what she must do.

Peggy Guggenheim, who is not necessarily the most reliable wit-

Leonora Carrington, *The House Opposite*, 1945; oil on panel.

ness so far as Ernst is concerned, seems to me entirely believable when she reports that, in Lisbon in 1941, Leonora refused to return to Max despite his pleading: "She felt that her life with Max was over because she could no longer be his slave, and that was the only way she could live with him."[15] Although this decision did not immediately manifest itself in her work (the writing and painting she did in New York do not represent a radical break with the earlier work), a few years later her painting looked quite different: a much lighter palette than before, more of a miniaturist attention to detail, and an entirely new set of images inspired by her interest in Celtic, Mayan, Egyptian, and Tibetan mythology. It is only after 1945 that she attained her mature style as a painter—as evidenced, for example, in one of the earliest paintings she did in Mexico, *The House Opposite* (1945). To attribute this maturation entirely to her separation from Ernst would be too simple, for there were many other changes in her life as well, including the sheer passage of time and the growth of experience. Still, it is not unlikely that coming into her full identity as an artist and abandoning the *femme-enfant* role were closely related. In 1946, she became a mother, yet another way of moving beyond the childlike role.

This does not mean, of course, that Carrington's separation from Ernst was easy, or free from pain for either of them. The stories she wrote in New York and published there ("Waiting," "White Rabbits," "The Bird Superior, Max Ernst," "The Seventh Horse") testify to the contrary, so far as she is concerned. As for Ernst, the testimony of

Max Ernst, *The Robing of the Bride*, 1940; oil on canvas.

his son is eloquent: "I don't recall ever again seeing such a strange mixture of desolation and euphoria in my father's face [as] when he returned from his first meeting with Leonora in New York . . . Each day that he saw her, and it was often, ended the same way. I hoped never to experience such pain myself."[16] The series of paintings Ernst did between June 1940 and the spring of 1942, most of them exhibited in his one-man show at the Valentin Gallery that year, include some of the greatest in his *oeuvre*—for example, *The Robing of the Bride, The Anti-Pope, Europe after the Rain*. I call them the "Leonora pictures," for each one contains, quite clearly, a fantasy portrait of Leonora Carrington. In the center of the ruined landscape of *Europe after the Rain,* the last picture to be completed in this series, we see a tall, slim, dark-haired woman turning her back on a bird-headed man. It was his version of their farewell, not only to each other but also to Europe. (Ernst eventually moved back to France, but not until the mid-1950s; Leonora has remained in the New World, save for a few visits to England and France many years ago.)

That could be an ending, but I promised earlier to return to "The Seventh Horse," published in the second issue of *VVV*; it can be read as Carrington's version of farewell. The story features three main characters: Hevalino, a "strange-looking creature" with a long mane, actually a young woman accompanied by the lord of the manor's six horses; Philip, "the friend of the horses" and lord of the manor; and Mildred, his very proper wife, who disapproves of Hevalino and whom Philip despises. After a dispute at the dinner table, during which Mildred claims to be pregnant and Philip insists she cannot be, since he hasn't slept with her in five years, he leaves and calls his horses: "He counted seven horses as they galloped by. He caught the seventh by the mane, and leapt onto her back. The mare galloped as if her heart would burst. And all the time Philip was in a great ecstasy of love; he felt he had grown onto the back of this beautiful black mare, and that they were one creature." The story ends cruelly: at dawn, Mildred is found dead, apparently "trampled to death" despite the gentleness of Philip's six horses. In the empty seventh stall, there is no black mare, only a "small misshapen foal" whose presence "nobody could explain" (p. 71).

"The Seventh Horse," with its suggestion of an extremely powerful but aborted love, is the last of Carrington's works in which the

Max Ernst, *Europe after the Rain* (detail), 1940–1942; oil on canvas.

figure of the horse-woman appears. By the time it was published, in 1943, she had left New York for Mexico and Ernst had met the American artist Dorothea Tanning, whom he married in 1946 (his fourth marriage) and with whom he spent the rest of his long life. He died, covered with honors, on April 1, 1976, the day before his eighty-fifth birthday.

Decidedly, I am having trouble saying good-bye to this couple (no doubt my own fantasies of an ideal partnership, sexual and intellectual, between a man and a woman, are strongly in play), for I would like to try yet another ending—this time, a less bleak and heartbroken one. It involves a story about Hollywood in the 1940s, in the days when the popular-movie industry and the "high art" avant-garde were not as separate as they later became. (Today, we may be seeing a renewed rapprochement in the carnivalesque arena of postmodernism, where one aspiring Hollywood production company calls itself Propaganda Films, pseudo-nostalgically evoking the days of the Soviet avant-garde.)

Around 1945–1946, the Hollywood director Albert Lewin decided to make a movie version of Guy de Maupassant's novel *Bel Ami,* which required for its plot a distinguished painting by a contemporary (that is, late nineteenth-century) painter, on a Christian subject. Lewin, who had already successfully commissioned an original painting for his previous film, *The Picture of Dorian Gray* (1945), decided to do it again. In Maupassant's novel, the painting is of "Christ walking on the waters," but since the Hollywood Code Authority did not allow representations of Christ on film (things have changed since then, although the fuss made over Scorsese's *The Last Temptation of Christ* shows that it is still a very touchy subject), Lewin decided to change the subject to one that had inspired many great artists of the past: the temptation of Saint Anthony. Furthermore, instead of commissioning a single artist, he came up with a more novel idea, over lunch one day with Harriet Janis, wife of the distinguished New York gallery owner Sidney Janis. His company, Loew-Lewin, would sponsor a limited competition, inviting a number of distinguished contemporary artists to submit work. Each artist would receive $500, as well as the right to retain ownership of his or her painting; the paintings would be on loan for two years to Loew-Lewin, who would arrange a traveling exhibition in the United States and England during that time. The winning painting would be used in the film, and the artist would receive an additional $2,500 as first prize.

This being the 1940s, the Hollywood moguls enlisted no lesser representatives of the New York artistic vanguard than Marcel Duchamp, Alfred H. Barr, Jr. (director of the Museum of the Modern

Art), and Sidney Janis to serve as jurors. And the dozen artists they invited included no lesser luminaries of Surrealist art (the subject, they decided, required artists working in the figurative mode, who were sympathetic to the Victorian sensibility of Maupassant's story) than Salvador Dali, Paul Delvaux, and Max Ernst, as well as Leonora Carrington, Dorothea Tanning, and Leonor Fini.[17] The judges, by their own account, had a hard time reaching a decision. Ernst won first prize.

From my point of view, the most comforting thing about this last cohabitation of the two artists' work is that they both produced first-rate paintings, which are unmistakably their own mature expression.[18] Ernst's gloss on his painting (all the artists were asked to write comments on their picture for the exhibition catalog) was very short: "Shrieking for help and light across the stagnant water of his dark sick soul, St. Anthony receives as an answer the echo of his fear: the laughter of the monsters created by his visions" (p. 9). Carrington's commentary on her work was longer. Besides giving a detailed, almost parodically conscientious explanation of the picture's iconography, her text displayed the Lewis Carrollesque humor that had already been suggested in some of the stories of *La Dame ovale* and that would find its fullest expression in *The Hearing Trumpet*, a novel she wrote a few years later in Mexico.[19] Since this lovely text on the *Saint Anthony* has never been reproduced and is hard to find, I shall quote it in its entirety:

> The picture seems pretty clear to me, being a more or less literal rendering of St. Anthony complete with pig, desert and temptation. Naturally one could ask why the venerable holy man has three heads— to which one could always reply, why not?
>
> You will notice the veteran's suit to be whitish and of an umbrallaoid form which would lead one to believe that the original colour had been washed or bleached out by the vagaries of the weather or that the monkish apparel had been cleverly constructed out of used mummy wrappings in umbrella or sunshade form as a protection from sand storms and sun, practical for someone leading an open air life and given to contemplation (as Egyptologists apparently didn't exist in those days, mummy wrappings were no doubt to be gathered like

Max Ernst, *Temptation of Saint Anthony* (detail), 1946;
oil on canvas.

Leonora Carrington, *Temptation of Saint Anthony*, 1946; oil on canvas.

blackberries and therefore to one of an economical and modest turn of mind they would provide a durable and apt clothing for the desert).

The Saint's traditional pet pig who lies across the nether half of the picture and views the observer out of its kindly blue eye is adequately accounted for in the myth of St. Anthony, and likewise the continually flowing water and the ravine.

The bald-headed girl in the red dress combines female charm and the delights of the table—you will notice that she is engaged in making an unctuous broth of (let us say) lobsters, mushrooms, fat turtle, spring chicken, ripe tomatoes, gorgonzola cheese, milk chocolate, onions and tinned peaches. The mixture of these ingredients has overflowed and taken on a greenish and sickly hue to the fevered vision of St. Anthony, whose daily meal consists of withered grass and tepid water with an occasional locust by way of an orgy.

On the right, the Queen of Sheba and her attendants emerge in ever-decreasing circles out of a subterranean landscape towards the hermit. Their intention is ambiguous, their progress spiral.

And last to the ram with the earthenware jar one could only quote the words of Friar Bacon's brazen head: Time was—Time is—Time is past. I was always pleased with simple idiocy of these words.

Carrington's *The Temptation of Saint Anthony*, after years of languishing at her mother's house in England and then her brother's, showed up resplendent in the retrospective exhibition at the Serpentine Gallery in December 1991. In May 1992, it was put up for auction at Christie's in New York and was bought by a Mexican collector for $440,000, the highest price ever paid for one of her works.

The ripeness is all.

ON BEING
POSTMODERN

PART THREE

THE FATE OF THE SURREALIST IMAGINATION IN THE SOCIETY OF THE SPECTACLE

7

What does Japan have to do with it? That requires a little story. In 1991, I decided to write an essay on an early novel by Angela Carter, *The Infernal Desire Machines of Dr. Hoffman* (1972), for a panel at the International Comparative Literature conference to be held in Tokyo that summer. The general theme of the conference was "Imagination"—perfect, I thought, for this novel, which I had long wanted to write about because it was so obviously inspired by Surrealism, a subject in which I have a deep interest. Carter, like a number of other contemporary women writers I think of as feminist postmodernists, had a particular affinity with Surrealism. This was my chance to explore that affinity in some detail.

Here the plot thickens. It turned out that Carter wrote *The Infernal Desire Machines of Dr. Hoffman,* a novel whose title points insistently to European art and literature (from the *Tales of E.T.A. Hoffmann* to the "bachelor machines" of Duchamp and the Surrealists), in Japan. It was in Tokyo, moreover, around 1970, that she first came upon two books about Surrealism and cinema that had a tremendous effect on her. Ado Kyrou, a "true believer" in Surrealist

Imagination alone offers me some intimation of what *can be.*
    —André Breton,
    First "Surrealist Manifesto"

In Japan, I learnt what it is to be a woman and became radicalized.
    —Angela Carter,
    "Tokyo Pastoral"

theories of liberation through desire and through the exercise of the faculty of the imagination, wrote his books *Surréalisme et cinéma* and *Amour-érotisme et cinéma* during the listless 1950s, the last years of the Fourth Republic, in France.[1] A decade or so later, the Situationists and other revolutionaries of May 1968 reformulated some of the Surrealist theories into slogans on the walls of the Sorbonne and elsewhere: "Power to the imagination!" "I take my desires for reality because I believe in the reality of my desires." By the time Carter discovered Kyrou's books in Tokyo, the "events of May" had come and gone in Paris, but (in her words) "extraordinary things were happening in Japan—they had their own version of 1968." That, at least, is how she experienced it. Japan, in her eyes, was both a link to Europe and a country of absolute otherness, not only because she saw it as Other in relation to what she knew, but because she herself was seen, in the "completely Japanese environment" in which she lived, as an unassimilable Other, a foreigner, "*Gaijin.*"[2]

The country that Roland Barthes, at just about the same time, was calling the "Empire of Signs" because of its expansion of the notion of writing to nonverbal modes of communication, became, for Carter too, a place where the decoding of signs passed through vision rather than through language: "Since I kept trying to learn Japanese, and kept on failing to do so, I started trying to understand things by simply looking at them very, very carefully, an involuntary apprenticeship in the interpretation of signs."[3]

The Infernal Desire Machines of Dr. Hoffman, I am going to suggest, is a novel *of* as well as *about* the Surrealist imagination, seen from the doubly distant perspective of an elsewhere and another time. "The early 1970's, when Japan was just starting to boom," is how Carter described the time and the place (she wrote the novel in three months, in a Japanese fishing village on an island where she seems to have been the only European). A few years earlier, Guy Debord had diagnosed the "boom" that Japan would soon adopt as the latest stage of world capitalism, the "society of the spectacle." Carter's novel stages, in a wonderfully inventive way, the question I ask more abstractly in the title of this chapter: Is there a future for the totally free imagination espoused by Surrealism ("Only the word 'liberty' still thrills me," wrote Breton in the first "Surrealist Manifesto" in 1924) in a society ruled by images?

One last remark, by way of introduction: When I first decided to write an essay about *The Infernal Desire Machines of Dr. Hoffman* and came up with a title, I had no inkling about the circumstances of the novel's composition. It was Angela Carter who informed me, after I told her on the telephone in London in May 1991 that I would be presenting a paper on *Dr. Hoffman* in Tokyo. "Interesting coincidence. I wrote that novel in Japan," she said, and proceeded to tell me about the two years she spent in Tokyo, her discovery of Kyrou's books, and the "completely Japanese environment" of the island where she wrote *Dr. Hoffman*.[4] The Surrealists would call this coincidence "objective chance." I will be content to think of it as an auspicious start.

Postmodern Reflections

Since I have called Carter a feminist postmodernist, I shall follow the classificatory impulse for a moment and consider in what ways *The Infernal Desire Machines of Dr. Hoffman* is a postmodernist work. Brian McHale has proposed that despite the great variety of postmodernist novels, one major preoccupation they all share is with ontology, the nature of being: "What is a world? What kinds of world are there . . .? What happens when different kinds of worlds are placed in confrontation, or when boundaries between worlds are violated?"[5] If McHale is right that such questions are implicit in all postmodernist fiction, then *Dr. Hoffman* is the very model of the genre, for it explicitly thematizes those questions and uses them as major plot elements. Desiderio, the narrator-protagonist, is thrown into several different, incompatible kinds of world; and the story he tells is essentially about a conflict between two Masters, a war of possible worlds. On one side, the Minister of Determination, whose totally rational world tolerates no slippages, no "shadow between the word and the thing described"; on the other side, the "diabolical Dr. Hoffman," who tries to do away with the very distinction between shadow and thing. In the Minister's world (which is what would generally be called the "real" world), every object or person has a clear identity, guaranteed by an unchanging name and a place in an elaborate logical and social hierarchy. Consistency rules and boundaries are strictly observed, especially the boundary between reality and dream, actuality and imagination. In Dr. Hoffman's world, it is just the opposite: his ruling principle is that "everything it is possible to imagine can also exist."[6] Thus, peacocks can suddenly invade the audience at a performance of *The Magic Flute* ("It was [his] first disruptive coup," recounts Desiderio, who was in the audience), rivers can run backward, clocks can "tell everybody whatever time they like," a man's hat can become his head, and "in the vaulted architraves of railway stations, women in states of pearly heroic nudity, their hair elaborately coiffed in the stately chignons of the *fin de siècle,* might be seen parading beneath their parasols as serenely as if they had been in the Bois de Boulogne" (p. 19). The allusions to Dali's soft watches, Magritte's bowler hats, and Paul Delvaux's dreamlike nudes are, of course, not accidental.

The battle between the Minister and the Doctor is, in Desiderio's words, a "battle between an encyclopedist and a poet" (p. 24). But it might be just as true to say "between a realist and a surrealist," for as Desiderio's examples make clear, the Doctor-poet is a Surrealist image-maker. (Besides Dali, Magritte, and Delvaux, elsewhere the novel evokes Ernst and Duchamp, among others.) In one sense, all of *Dr. Hoffman* can be read as a reflection on the opening pages of Breton's first "Surrealist Manifesto," with its celebration of dream and the imagination and its indictment of "real life" and the "realist attitude" toward life. Equally relevant is the essay Breton wrote shortly before the Manifesto, the "Introduction to the Discourse on the Paucity of Reality," which rhetorically asks: "What prevents me from jamming the order of words, from attacking by that means the merely illusory existence of things?"[7] The notion of an "alchemy of the word" goes back to Rimbaud, whom the Surrealists greatly admired. Dr. Hoffman's version of this notion is formulated as the "Third Theory of Phenomenal Dynamics: the difference between a symbol and an object is quantitative, not qualitative" (p. 96). If one imagines something—that is, desires something—with sufficient energy, it will exist.

If *Dr. Hoffman* is a postmodernist novel in its preoccupation with possible worlds or ontologies, it is postmodernist in another, somewhat different sense as well, which I can best elucidate by recalling what I wrote a few years ago about the "postmodern moment": "that moment of extreme (perhaps tragic, perhaps playful) self-consciousness when the present—our present—takes to reflecting on its relation to the past and to the future primarily as a problem of repetition. How to create a future that will acknowledge and incorporate the past . . . without repeating it? How to look at the past with understanding, yet critically—in the etymological sense of criticism, which has to do with discrimination and choice *for* and *in* the present?"[8] From this perspective, postmodernist fiction can be defined *formally* as a hyper-selfconscious mode of writing that insistently points to literary and cultural antecedents or (as we say in the trade) intertexts; and *thematically* as a kind of fiction that reflects, implicitly or explicitly, on the historical and social present in its relation to the past and, if possible, the future. A double orientation—toward other texts, and toward the world—can be said to characterize all works of literature; or perhaps it represents two possible modes of reading. Still, I am suggesting that postmodernist fiction is distinguished by its high degree of formal self-consciousness *and* by its thematic preoccupation with present and past history. Linda Hutcheon has proposed the term "historiographic metafiction" to define "novels which are both intensely self-reflexive and yet paradoxically also lay claim to historical events and personages."[9] I would simply emphasize that in order to be "historical," events and personages don't necessarily have to appear in history books.

So far as my formal criterion is concerned (self-consciousness and intertextuality, the recognition of literary or artistic antecedents), *Dr. Hoffman* is a veritable collage of preexisting genres and verbal or visual quotations. I have already mentioned a few evocations of Surrealist writing and painting, but there are literally dozens more—including, toward the end, the evocation by Dr. Hoffman himself of the Surrealist notion of "objective chance" (p. 210). In addition, the novel abounds in allusions to German Expressionist film, particularly *The Cabinet of Dr. Caligari*, on which one whole chapter (Chapter 2, "The Mansion of Midnight") and an important character (the "peep-show proprietor," alias the Professor) are modeled. Moving backward to the German Romantics, the *Tales* of E.T.A. Hoffmann are not only alluded to in the novel's title, but provide one structural model for the overall story. This model, which one finds realized in many of the best-known tales of Hoffmann, can be summed up as follows: a powerful father with magical powers keeps his beautiful but potentially deadly daughter (who is not necessarily human—she can be a doll, all the more alluring and deadly) tantalizingly out of the reach of a desiring young man, a situation that eventually leads to the death of the daughter (as in the tale titled "Councillor Krespel"), or of the young man (as in "The Sandman"). Carter's novel conforms to the first pattern, but adds a new twist: it is the young man himself who kills the daughter, as well as the father. (By a curious coincidence, Carter told me, Hoffman is also the name of the inventor of the hallucinogen LSD, which led quite a few early reviewers to speak of the novel as a "drug book." Being a "bookish person," she said, she was aware only of E.T.A. Hoffmann, not of the LSD Hoffman, when she invented her visionary character.)

Besides the clearly designated intertexts in *Dr. Hoffman*, one finds, pell-mell, echoes of Proust ("I remember everything" is the opening sentence, and the beloved "lost object" is named Albertina); Sade (quoted directly, as well as parodied in the character of the Count, who "rides the whirlwind of [his] desires" until he lands in a cannibal soup); *Gulliver's Travels* (one of the societies Desiderio discovers is a society of centaurs—who, being all too human, "were not Houyhnhnms," he tells us); and any number of unspecified Gothic romances, tales of piracy, travel narratives, sci-fi thrillers, porn novels, and picaresque adventures.

Such are the virtuoso, playful aspects of postmodernist collage. One could spend a long and pleasant time tracking down all the allusions and quotations, direct and indirect, and untangling the various generic threads. But it is equally pleasant simply to admire the web, even bask in it, without trying to untangle it. One extremely self-conscious textual moment I relish occurs in the beginning of Chapter 6. Desiderio, having temporarily thrown in his lot with that of the Count, has just spent a night with him in a brothel that evokes (with no small degree of parody) any number of pornographic novels, from Sade's *Justine* to *The Story of O*. As they are about to embark on a new adventure (Chapter 6 bears the title "The Coast of Africa"), Desiderio remarks: "I had not the least idea what time or place the Count might take me to though, since his modes of travel were horseback, gig and tall-masted schooner, I guessed, wherever it was, it would be somewhere in the early nineteenth century" (p. 143). The narrative, playing its mirror game (the technical term is *mise-en-abyme*), "duplicates" its own procedures, taking the reader in a single sentence from an unspecified future time (Desiderio's present) into the early nineteenth century and from a porn novel into a tale of adventure on the high seas; and, for good measure, it also "duplicates" the response of a reader who consents to being led along, without much analysis ("I had not the least idea what time or place the Count might take me to"), by the meanderings of the story and the author's luxuriant imagination.

Clearly, Carter takes extreme delight, as well as a kind of swaggering pride, in her ability to play with and on a long, varied literary and artistic tradition. But where, one might ask, does this novel reflect on the historical and social present and their relation to the past and future? That reflection, I suggest, is to be found in the thematization of Surrealist ideas about desire and the imagination, on the one hand; and, on the other, in the descriptions of "what it is to be a woman" in various societies. As we shall see, the two hands are not unrelated.

Laws of Desire

"My name is Desiderio," says the narrator by way of introduction. His name means "desire" in Italian, although he lives in what appears to be a Latin American country where the official language is Portuguese and where the indigenous Indian peoples speak their own Amerindian dialect. Desiderio-Desire is the child of a European prostitute and an unknown Indian father, a young man of mixed blood and mixed loyalties. He works for the Minister of Determination, but falls in love with the "magician's daughter," Albertina Hoffman. He admires the Minister, a man as "clear, hard, unified and harmonious as a string quartet," but defines himself as "a man like an unmade bed" (p. 13). He refuses to surrender to the "flux of mirages" proposed by Dr. Hoffman, yet embarks with nary a glance backward on a journey that will turn out to be nothing if not full of mirages and miraculous visions. Although lacking all of the traditional heroic qualities (certainty, determination, ambition, aggression), he ends up a hero by ridding the city of its archenemy—and in the process also kills, to his eternal regret, the object of his desire, the woman he loves, his emotional double.

In short, Desiderio is ambivalence itself, a perfect emblem of the Romantic, but also no doubt the postmodern, subject. What characterizes him, further, is a kind of paradoxically active passivity—for although he does nothing to initiate action, he is thrown into it; and once in it, he keeps going, as if his very passivity made it possible for adventure to seek him out. He has no fixed opinions, yet in the end is forced to make an impossible choice: "I might not want the Minister's world but I did not want the Doctor's world either . . . I, of all men, had been given the casting vote between a barren yet harmonious calm and a fertile yet cacophonous tempest" (p. 207). He chooses the calm by killing Dr. Hoffman; yet his choice is hopelessly compromised by his regret at killing the Doctor's daughter as well. In a sense he had to kill her, for "Oh, she was her father's daughter, no doubt about that!" (p. 13). But this does not prevent him from desiring her all the remaining days of his long life, or from dreaming about her every night. In the end, Dr. Hoffman, although defeated, has in some fashion won: he has imposed the power and reality of dreams, if not on the whole city, at least on the "hero" who killed him.

It is difficult to resist an allegorical reading of this novel. Auberon Waugh, one of its first reviewers, praised its success in combining "allegory and Surrealism," something very few works had achieved (Waugh mentioned *Gulliver's Travels* and *Alice's Adventures in Wonderland;* I would add Leonora Carrington's *The Hearing Trumpet,* among recent works in English). Waugh then proceeded to define the Minister as personifying "the forces of logic, reason, law and order, but also the excesses to which these properties are liable," while Dr. Hoffman "represents poetry, and the liberation of the spirit but also anarchy and the 'creative nihilism' of the rebel without a cause."[10] In a more specifically historical mode, David Punter suggests that "we can read the text [leading to Desiderio's rejection of Dr. Hoffman] as a series of figures for the defeat of the political aspirations of the 1960's, and in particular of the father-figures of liberation, Reich and Marcuse."[11] Punter does not say so outright, but he seems to find Desiderio's choice itself a kind of failure: "it is [Desiderio's] fate to will away pleasure for fear of the damage it might do to him and to others" (p. 214).

What Punter fails to mention is that the kind of pleasure offered to Desiderio by Dr. Hoffman is extremely drab: the Doctor, scientifically literalizing the Surrealist dictum that desire makes the world go round, succeeds in channeling sexual energy to fuel the huge machines that bombard the city with mirages. To this end, he employs lovers who voluntarily spend all of their time copulating in "love pens," the energy they release being immediately collected and transformed into fuel. (As I have said, *Dr. Hoffman* is a novel "of" as well as "about" the Surrealist imagination!) Desiderio, desire itself, would be the prize energy producer if he consented to enter the love pen that awaits him and Albertina. Instead, appalled at the contradiction between a "liberation philosophy" that depends on slavery (even if the slaves are willing love slaves), he turns and runs, killing both father and daughter.

Ricarda Smith, reading this ending, criticizes Punter for what she considers his celebratory view of Marcuse (for she, too, sees Dr. Hoffman as an allegory of the 1960s philosopher). According to Smith, Carter is quite critical of Marcuse, indeed "contradicts Marcuse's optimistic view that . . . highly advanced productivity makes a 'non-repressive civilization' possible."[12] As for me, I find both Punter's and Smith's readings plausible. I am surprised, however, that neither one mentions Surrealism, even though the character of Dr. Hoffman is, both textually and representationally, much more of a Surrealist than a Marcuse. Marcuse himself, in a crucial passage of *Eros and Civilization*, where he argues for the social and liberating value of fantasy, can think of no better support for his argument than to quote a passage from the first "Surrealist Manifesto," in French, ending with the sentence I have chosen as an epigraph: "La seule imagination me rend compte de ce qui *peut être*."[13]

To say that Carter "contradicts Marcuse's optimism"—more exactly, the optimism Marcuse shared with the Surrealists about the liberating potential of fantasy and desire—is, I think, to miss an important point. For if it is indeed true that Dr. Hoffman is no hero and that his method of liberation mocks its own proclaimed aims, it is not at all certain that he is an allegory of either Marcuse's philosophy or the Surrealists'. I would suggest that if he is an allegory of anything, it is of the technological appropriation (but I prefer the gallicism "recuperation") of Surrealism *and* liberation philosophy—precisely that recuperation which Marcuse himself, not at all optimistically, analyzed as early as the 1961 preface to the re-edition of *Eros and Civilization* (first published in 1955). Marcuse called this mode of recuperation "repressive desublimation" and saw in it, with something close to despair, the latest ruse of capitalism. He himself had hoped for something quite different: "non-repressive sublimation," or the diffusion of the erotic impulse to all aspects of life, with an attendant decrease in aggression and release of the creative faculties. In his terms (but also in Surrealist terms), this would be the triumph of the Pleasure Principle over the Reality Principle: work itself would become a form of play. Instead, repressive desublimation turned this project on its head, and made even play—or love—into a form of work.

The "methodical introduction of sexiness into business, politics, propaganda, etc." is one example Marcuse cites of the way instrumental rationality encroaches on the realm of the erotic. Another example is the organization of "fun and leisure," which he identifies as simply the other face of repression, the social control of docile bodies. Marcuse's conclusion, in the 1961 preface to his book, is stark: "The events of the last years refute all optimism. The immense capabilities of the advanced industrial society are increasingly mobilized against the utilization of its own resources for the pacification of human existence." As he saw it, the very technologies that were to have made nonrepressive sublimation possible by releasing human beings from alienated labor were being used to enslave them further: "The modes of domination have changed: they have become increasingly technological, productive, and even beneficial; consequently, in the most advanced areas of industrial society, the people have been co-ordinated and reconciled with the system of domination to an unprecedented degree" (p. vii).

Reading Marcuse's preface today, one is struck by the way his analysis of the double-edged possibilities of technology dovetail with the even more pessimistic analyses of Guy Debord's *La Société du spectacle*, published six years later. For Debord, there is no question that the society of the spectacle is the product of a technology gone bad. One thing such technology makes possible is the reign of images, which Debord defines in a broad sense as the increasingly abstract relation of people to each other and to their environment. The opening lines of *La Société du spectacle* could have been written by Marcuse: "All the life of societies in which modern conditions of production dominate presents itself as an immense accumulation of *spectacles*. Everything that was directly lived has distanced itself in a representation."[14] Like Marcuse, Debord and the Situationists were caustic in their critique of organized "fun and leisure," especially as it was archetypally embodied in the Club Med, founded in the mid-1960s.

If we now think of Dr. Hoffman's machines for projecting representations on the world, fueled by the "acrobats of desire" in their "perpetual motion" of disciplined copulation, we may see in Carter's mad scientist the nightmarish synthesis of repressive desublimation and the society of the spectacle. The fact that this character was conceived in the country that would become the world's leading manufacturer of advanced electronic equipment takes on a particularly prescient, ironic cast.

Given the current interest in technology in both feminist and postmodernist circles, it is worth nothing that Carter's position is not "antitechnology." Indeed, despite their pessimism, Debord's and Marcuse's critiques are not directed against technology either; rather, they are aimed at the uses to which it has been put. Contemporary celebrations of technology by postmodernist theorists, such as Donna Haraway's famous paean to the cyborg or, earlier, Jean-François Lyotard's hopeful pages about computer information networks, have generally not been much concerned with the ways technology, even a potentially revolutionary one, can *fail* to change the status quo.[15] Carter's novel, perhaps because it was written not long after the dissipation of 1968's revolutionary euphoria, is closer in mood to the pessimism of Marcuse and Debord. But Carter's pessimism, or what one can take to be such, is not the result of a disenchantment with technology; rather, it results from her sense (which I share, on the whole) that questions about technology cannot be divorced from questions about ideology and values.

And Surrealism, in all this? The first epigraph of the novel is a line of anagrammatic punning by the Surrealist poet Robert Desnos:

"Les lois de nos désirs sont les dés sans loisir"—literally, "The laws of our desires are dice without leisure." The laws of desire, of Desiderio, require ceaseless movement, the perpetual motion of "dice without leisure." But the movement of dice (note that *dés* can also be read as a short name for Desiderio) is by definition the opposite of the predictable and the mechanical. It is in order to maintain this movement, and hence the laws of desire, his laws, that Desiderio kills the would-be Master of desires—who, in true Master fashion, always remains unmoved—and his daughter.

It may be interesting to speculate on the relation of Surrealist ideas about desire to the "desiring machines" dreamed up by Deleuze and Guattari in their *Anti-Oedipus*, published the same year as Carter's novel. At first glance, the *machines désirantes* may appear close to Dr. Hoffman's desire machines (such is the power of the signifier); but in fact, they are far from them and close to Surrealism. For Deleuze and Guattari, as for the Surrealists, desire is "in its essence revolutionary" and implies ceaseless movement—that is why their ideal subject is the bachelor, "nomad and vagabond" (a kind of Desiderio, perhaps). The "fixed subject" is the repressed subject. In their terms as well, Dr. Hoffman's love pens would have to be considered the very opposite of liberation, or revolution.[16]

What, then, is the fate of the Surrealist imagination in the society of the spectacle? Not good. At best, "la révolution surréaliste" becomes a private passion, not a means to change the world. Desiderio, the public smiling man with a hero's statue in the town square, dreams every night of his lost Albertina, and writes his delirious memoirs in dedication to her. Meanwhile, life goes on as usual, dominated by the Minister's computers and clocks that all run on time.

"What It Is To Be a Woman"

If the "Surrealist imagination" founders on the shoals of the society of the spectacle, then one of the reasons for this foundering is related not to technology or postmodern capitalism, but to sexual politics. Technology and capitalism change with the times—modern/postmodern, industrial/postindustrial, mechanical/digital. Sexual politics, by contrast, is timeless, transcultural, international—or so Carter implies, in my reading of her novel. Here is one place where the gap between technology and ideology becomes apparent: even the most revolutionary technological advances do not necessarily change the relations between men and women. Desiderio, in his various travels, observes a number of societies: the society of the Amerindian River People, that of the African tribe, and that of the centaurs. In all of these, especially in the last two, women are in a horrifyingly subordinate position. In the African tribe, women are raised to be soulless soldiers by having all feeling, including maternal feeling, literally excised out of them. Among the centaurs, women do all the work while the men pray—and women are "tattooed all over, even in their faces, in order to cause them more suffering, for [the centaurs] believed women were born only to suffer" (p. 172).

This sexual politics of inequality not only characterizes the primitive or fantastic societies, but also characterizes every other world that Desiderio visits or inhabits. The city he lived in, before the onslaught of Dr. Hoffman's images, was "thickly, obtusely masculine" (p. 15), as is the Minister of Determination. But so, in its own way, is the insubstantial dream-world of Dr. Hoffman. The peepshow displays that Desiderio describes at several points are like Surrealist paintings, to be sure; but they are also unmistakably male voyeuristic fantasies (as Surrealist paintings often are), representing female orifices and body parts, and scenes of extreme sexual violence perpetrated on the bodies of women. One of them, bearing the suggestive title "Everyone Knows What the Night is For," shows a three-dimensional model of a mutilated woman with a knife in her belly (p. 45). Its description evoked for me, by an immediate association, Duchamp's famous installation at the Philadelphia Museum of Art, *Etant donné* (*Given That*), which shows a similarly mutilated female figure; installed in its own dark room, *Etant donné* requires that the viewer glue an eye to a peephole in order to see the scene. Carter's peep-show as a whole may be an allusion to this work, which literally makes every viewer into a voyeur.

Continuing the voyeur theme, the "Erotic Traveller" chapter (Chapter 5) has Desiderio and the Count visit a Sadean brothel, the "House of Anonymity," which features live prostitutes staged in the most degraded and violated poses. In a sense, the violation spills over to the two men, who are dressed for the occasion in special costumes, which mask their faces while leaving their genitals fully exposed: "the garb grossly emphasized our manhoods while utterly denying our humanity" (p. 130).

Desiderio's own position in the novel is ambiguous. As a man, he generally enjoys the male privileges. (This is most emphasized in the episode with the centaurs: Albertina is raped by every male in the group and, when she heals, is sent into the fields to work with the women; Desiderio, as befits a man, is allowed to study and roam, learning the centaurs' customs and mythology.) At the same time, he clearly has an unusually sharp view of and sympathy for women's roles, and on at least one occasion is made to find out "what it is to be a woman" in a more violent way, when he is gang-raped by nine Moroccan acrobats in the traveling circus he accompanies disguised as the peep-show proprietor's nephew. This experience, he later tells us, allows him to understand what Albertina goes through when she is raped by the centaurs, and to "suffer with her" in the process. Finally, Desiderio is physically a mirror image of Albertina, who herself takes the shape of a young man on several occasions. They are "exactly the same height" (p. 136), and by the end of their adventures they look like twins: seeing himself in a mirror in Dr. Hoffman's castle, Desiderio remarks, "Time and travel had changed me almost beyond my own recognition. Now I was entirely Albertina in the male aspect. That is why I know I was beautiful when i was a young man. Because I know I looked like Albertina" (p. 199).

Here, in the sexual ambiguities of the lovers, may lie the most politically radical aspect of *The Infernal Desire Machines of Dr. Hoffman*. But Carter did not develop those radical possibilities in this novel, as she was to do in her next one, *The Passion of New Eve* (which, perhaps not by chance, accorded more attention to the figure of the mother than to that of the father), and in yet another way in the novel after that, *Nights at the Circus*.[17] The new twist brought by *Nights at the Circus* (in the meantime, Carter had remarried and had become a mother herself) is that the radical possibilities of fluid gender roles are given a happy ending. Similarly, the mood of her last published novel, *Wise Children*, is magnificently comic, with a self-consciously Shakespearean cast (in both senses of that word). In *Dr. Hoffman*, however, the ending is quite dark, if ironic: the social status quo is maintained and, despite the son's heroization, the Father wins. It doesn't matter which Father, the Minister or Dr. Hoffman, for they both want to lay down the law—and even if it is not the same law, women's place remains identical in both. Albertina, like countless other daughters in literature (and life), loves her Daddy above all other men, even to the point of self-sacrifice. Desiderio, like countless other males in Western literature and life, "kills the thing he loves" and spends the rest of his days dreaming about her.

From all of which one may conclude that if the world is really to change, it will have to start by imagining differently "what it is to be a woman"—and a man. Differently from the Minister, differently from Dr. Hoffman, differently even from the Surrealists, whose imaginative faculties faltered on the threshold of sexual roles.

That, at least, was the necessary conclusion in 1972, when *The Infernal Desire Machines of Dr. Hoffman* was published and the women's movement in the United States and England was gathering steam. And in 1993? I wish I could say that the problem has become historical, in other words passé, in the United States if not elsewhere. But time passes slowly in these parts. Although "what it is to be a woman" is not the same now as it was then (some women today even get to teach Angela Carter and other feminist postmodernists at major universities, and obtain tenure), there is (as my mother used to say) plenty of room for improvement.[18]

8

I have tried to express the terrible passions of humanity by means of red and green.

—Vincent Van Gogh,
Letter to his brother Theo,
1888

My objective is to say what I believe about my world, about my time, about what I live, about the things that surround me.

—Maria Magdalena
Compos-Pons, Interview
with Lillian Mansour,
1988

The only thing that is different from one time to another is what is seen.

—Gertrude Stein,
"Composition as
Explanation," 1926

Is beauty the goal of art? Do artists pursue beauty? These are not questions that normally preoccupy my waking hours. But they were thrust upon me when I was invited, recently, to speak at a conference of artists and critics titled, somewhat plaintively I thought, "Whatever Happened to Beauty? Aesthetics in a Culture of Signs." The program of the conference included a short descriptive blurb that ran as follows:

"Whatever happened to beauty? Artists used to debate how to capture nature's eternal beauty, or how to present a newly created beauty. But beauty has often been excluded from recent discussion, with some artists even disavowing it. Many contemporary artists concentrate instead on representing society and its politics; their concern for conveying a message may shift art toward semiotics, away from aesthetics. Does the pursuit of beauty interfere with reflection on social conditions? Or is the aesthetic always the social, and the social always aesthetic? Join our group of distinguished artists, scholars, and critics to explore these issues from the multiple viewpoints of the 1990's."

Being basically a "literature person," my first impulse was to analyze the blurb. This gesture, I was aware, elevated a humble piece of publicity prose (composed, for all I knew, by a committee rather than a person) to the status of a "text." But it was a good lead, and still is, so I shall retain it. I should note, however, that the heart of this essay (in more ways than one) is in the second half, where I discuss a number of works by contemporary Latino artists who have not had much exposure or commentary in the United States.

Questioning Beauty

"Whatever happened to beauty? Aesthetics in a Culture of Signs." From the start, we are on slippery ground. Our text has slipped awfully quickly from "beauty" to "aesthetics," as if the two terms were unproblematically synonymous; and it also seems to have established, almost without noticing, an opposition between beauty and aesthetics on the hand, and "signs" on the other. After stating that many contemporary artists are, unlike their predecessors, no longer concerned about beauty but "concentrate instead on representing society and its politics," the text suggests that "their concern for conveying a message may shift art toward semiotics, away from aesthetics." I find this presumed opposition between the aesthetic and the semiotic troubling. Like all human activity, art participates in semiosis, the process of signification. It is not always clear how a work of art signifies or what it signifies to different viewers (or even to a single viewer at different times), or what it was intended to signify; in some cases, perhaps all it says, or was meant to say, is "I am a work of art and you should look at me that way." But whatever the case may be, I think it is wrong to suggest that the aesthetic is in an essential way opposed to the semiotic, for that would suggest that art participates in no process of signification. And *that*, in turn, would suggest that art is not a human activity.

In fact, reading the text carefully, one realizes that semiotics is not what its question is really about. The opposition that worries this text is not between the aesthetic and the semiotic, but between the aesthetic and the social or political: "Does the pursuit of beauty interfere with reflection on social conditions?" That is certainly a legitimate question, especially given what we know about the fate of artists in some totalitarian societies, but I think it begs a more fundamental one: Is the pursuit of beauty what art has traditionally been about? We are back to the slippage between the aesthetic and the beautiful. One cannot really blame the text here, for this slippage seems to be built in to the very word and concept of the "aesthetic." If we look up "aesthetic" in the dictionary (in this case, the *American Heritage Dictionary*), what do we find? "1. Of or pertaining to the criticism of taste. 2.a. Of or pertaining to the sense of the beautiful. b. Artistic." The plural noun "aesthetics" is defined as "the branch of philosophy that provides a theory of the beautiful and of the fine arts." The assumption that the artistic and the beautiful are one and the same seems not even to be noticed, in these definitions, *as* an assumption: rather, it appears to be part of the order of language and of the order of things. What is even more curious is that etymologically, again according to my dictionary, the word "aesthetic" implies neither beauty nor art: *aesthetikos,* in Greek, means "pertaining to sense perception," from *aestheta,* "perceptible things," and *aisthenasthai,* "to perceive." So we have this seamless and apparently originary slippage from perception to beauty to art, all in the space of a single word. No wonder we're in a conceptual muddle!

Are all things perceived, or all perceptible things, beautiful? Certainly not—not even if one allows for widely divergent historical and cultural notions of beauty. Are all things perceived, or all perceptible things, art? Clearly not—not even if one allows for widely divergent definitions of art. Are all beautiful things art? Obviously not—flowers, people, and other natural things can be beautiful but are not art. Is all art beautiful? Ah, there's the question. Perhaps all great art is beautiful, or all good art is beautiful? That, too, is a question. Perhaps all artists—prior to those contemporary artists who are the exception, that is—have wanted to produce beauty? That claim has been made; our blurb makes it: "Artists used to debate how to capture nature's eternal beauty, or how to present a newly created beauty. But beauty has often been excluded from recent discussion, with some artists even disavowing it." Well, how recent is "recent"? Here is what Vincent Van Gogh wrote to his brother Theo in 1888 about his newly finished painting, *The Night Café:* "The picture is one of the ugliest I have done. It is the equivalent, though different, of the 'Potato Eaters.'" And then he added this stunning sentence: "I have tried to express the terrible passions of humanity by means of red and green."[1]

I think it is safe to assume that Van Gogh, although he called them ugly, did not consider either *The Night Café* or *The Potato Eaters* failed paintings. But it appears that he was less concerned with creating something beautiful than with expressing something terrible and true. And if one looks at the statements of dozens of other artists belonging to dozens of schools and movements from Cézanne to Francis Bacon, all of them trying to explain what they are doing and why, it is quite astonishing to see how *rarely* the word "beauty" appears. Instead, it is words like "see" (or "vision") and "express" and "truth" that strike one by their frequency. Here is Gauguin, writing a letter in 1898 about his just finished painting, *Whence Do We Come? What Are We? Where Are We Going?*: "They will say that it is careless . . . not finished . . . I believe that this canvas not only surpasses all the preceding ones, but also that I will never do anything better or even similar to it. Before dying I put into it all my energy, such a painful passion under terrible circumstances, and a vision so clear without corrections, that the haste disappears and the life surges up" (Chipp, pp. 71–72). And here is Picasso in an interview in 1935: "When we invented Cubism we had no intention whatever of inventing Cubism. We wanted simply to express what was in us . . . Academic training in beauty is a sham . . . The beauties of the Parthenon, Venuses, Nymphs, Narcissus are so many lies. Art is not the application of a canon of beauty but what the instinct and the brain can conceive beyond any canon" (p. 271).

Even Matisse, who now seems to us so very much a painter concerned with harmony and pleasing forms and colors, even Matisse said he was less interested in the beautiful than in the true. In his "Notes of a Painter" of 1908, he criticized the Impressionists for relying too much on the fleeting moment: "A rapid rendering of a landscape represents only one moment of its appearance. I prefer, by insisting upon its essentials, to discover its more enduring character and content, even at the risk of sacrificing some of its pleasing qualities" (p. 133).

Of course, one could claim that all of this is already part of the recent contesting of beauty, part of the "antiaesthetic." But that claim would not hold, because no one would accuse the so-called high modernists of being "antiaesthetic," and the artists I have quoted are all part of modernism, not of the antiaesthetic avant-garde or of postmodernism. If I had quoted the Futurist Marinetti or the Dada Duchamp, or the Surrealists or the Pop artists, then we could speak of the antiaesthetic (even though those artists and movements are no longer recent but have become historical). The same is true of contemporary politically self-conscious artists like Hans Haacke, who has focused his work on subjects ranging from the New York real estate market to the connections between art patronage and the politics of apartheid, or David Wojnarowicz, whose work is concerned almost exclusively with AIDS and with gay male existence in America, or feminist postmodernists like Barbara Kruger, Cindy Sherman, and Kiki Smith, whose diverse works often focus on sexual politics and the female body. I purposely chose more "classic" modernist artists in order to avoid that confusion. Nor is going far back in time liable to change the argument, because for the greatest part of the history of Western art, artists explicitly placed their art in the service of what many would now call extra-artistic exigencies or truths: religious, political, social, spiritual, ideological. A visit to the historic churches, palaces, and public buildings of any Italian city is extremely instructive in that regard.

What I am suggesting, in short, is that a certain indifference, or even skepticism, by artists with regard to beauty is not simply a recent phenomenon; and correlatively, that the pursuit of beauty has been far from the exclusive, or even the primary, concern of artists throughout history. Alternatives to beauty, chief among them the pursuit of personal or collective truth, freshness of vision and authenticity of expression, have occupied an important place in artists' own conception of their activity and its aims. Of course, one could claim that the successful pursuit and rendering of truth, vision, and expression by an individual artist is precisely what constitutes beauty—but that would simply close down the argument, for if everything positive in art is beauty, or if all good or great art is beautiful by definition, then clearly no one would want to contest beauty or disavow it and there would be no reason for conferences wondering "Whatever Happened to Beauty?"

Still, I know of at least one truly interesting, if paradoxical, formulation about the necessary link between great art and beauty—

and since it is by Gertrude Stein, I am going to call it Stein's paradox. Basically, the paradox is this: certain works of art pass almost overnight from the status of ugly to beautiful, and in that process they become classics. A classic work of art, says Stein, is one that its first or contemporary viewers considered ugly but that suddenly, after a certain amount of time has passed, everyone considers beautiful. What makes Stein's observation of this paradox so interesting is that she does not stop there, at what might be called a celebration of the classic or the great work of art. She goes further, to put into question the very idea of beauty. Let me quote her at some length here—from her essay "Composition as Explanation":

> For a very long time everybody refuses and then almost without a pause almost everybody accepts . . . The rapidity of the change is always startling. Now the only difficulty with the *volte-face* concerning the arts is this. When the acceptance comes, by that acceptance the thing created becomes a classic. And what is the characteristic of a classic. The characteristic quality of a classic is that it is beautiful. Now of course it is perfectly true that a more or less first rate work of art is beautiful but the trouble is that when that first rate work of art becomes a classic because it is accepted the only thing that is important from then on to the majority of the acceptors . . . is that it is so wonderfully beautiful. Of course it is wonderfully beautiful, only when it is still a thing irritating, annoying, stimulating then all quality of beauty is denied to it . . . If every one were not so indolent they would realise that beauty is beauty even when it is irritating and stimulating not only when it is accepted and classic. Of course it is extremely difficult nothing more so than to remember back to its not being beautiful once it has become beautiful.[2]

At first glance, Stein seems to be claiming a certain permanent quality of beauty that all great art possesses, even when no one recognizes it yet. But the really interesting thing is that she redefines the beautiful; she laments the fact that the classic work, in being found beautiful, is no longer felt to be irritating, annoying, or stimulating. The exclusive insistence on beauty, she suggests—and she means here the viewer's insistence, not the artist's—does away with precisely those qualities of the work that made it exciting and new. As if, paradoxically, the beauty of the work when it has become a classic somehow eradicated the beauty it had when it was a "contemporary." But *that* beauty consisted in its ability to irritate and annoy and stimulate, which is the very opposite of the notion of beauty that has dominated Western thinking since Kant: beauty as something that pleases not by arousing the passions but by putting them at a distance. For Kant, the beautiful is what produces a perfectly disinterested pleasure, purged of both disgust and desire.

For Stein, the ideal would be to be able to look at a classic as if it were a contemporary—that is, remembering "back to its not being beautiful once it has become beautiful." Correlatively, she would want one to see, and seek out, the beauty of contemporaries *before* they become classics, while they are still ugly. "For the enjoyer . . . really would enjoy the created so much better just after it has been made than when it is a classic" (p. 514), and "it is so very much more exciting and satisfactory for everybody if one can have contemporaries, if all one's contemporaries could be one's contemporaries" (p. 515).

As I read her, Stein suggests that beauty is less in the object than in the eyes of the beholder; and furthermore, that there are at least two ways to look at (or for) beauty in a work of art. One way is restful and classicizing and uses beauty as a *passe-partout,* a reassuring passkey with which to shut out the messiness of an ambivalent or negative response. The other is restless and contemporary, and struggles with and against the work over what constitutes (its) beauty. Although I think Stein prefers the second kind of looking, I would not want to claim that she completely disavows the first kind. She obviously recognizes that there is something comforting, and good, about looking at a work one finds immediately, unambivalently beautiful, especially if one knows that it is the work of a great artist, understood and classified as such in the history books—a classic. But she also obviously values the other kind of looking, which appreciates not comfort but irritation and stimulation—or, to use a more "antiaesthetic" word, shock.

At this point, I had better leave Stein behind and speak for myself. I want to suggest that the second kind of looking is not looking for beauty (however you define it), but for alternatives to beauty: invention, expression, wit, humor, or even aggression and pain and rage. Beauty, of course, may also be there, and be perceived, even if it is not looked for. In that case, one oscillates between beauty and its alternatives, in a kind of "bifocal" vision. For me personally at the present time, the most interesting (though not necessarily the most comforting) experiences of looking involve looking at contemporary works that elicit, or at least allow for, such bifocal vision.

The bifocal aspect does not necessarily correspond to the restful versus the restless, or the beautiful versus its alternatives. But it always involves a revision of some sort, or, if you will, a double take: moving perhaps from the familiar to the strange, or from one kind of familiar to another, or from one degree of puzzlement to another. This kind of looking does not categorically disavow beauty, but it is open to the alternatives, and vice versa; it is willing to err, in every sense of that word—to deviate, to wander, to make mistakes. In short, it is willing to run the risk of being contemporary.

Looking at Contemporary Art; or, the Double Take

How does one look at the contemporary? Let me give you some examples. I have chosen them from an exhibition I saw in the fall of 1991 at the Institute of Contemporary Art in Boston, *The Bleeding Heart / El corazón sangrante*. The exhibition featured the work of contemporary Latino artists from Mexico, Cuba, and the United States, as well as some earlier work, including a piece of Aztec statuary, some religious paintings from the colonial period, and, from this century, three works by Frida Kahlo. After it left Boston, the show traveled to Houston and a number of other cities, to close in Mexico in August 1993.

Why did I choose this particular exhibition as the source of my examples? The simplest reason is that it intrigued me, enough to return to see it more than once. To use Stein's vocabulary, it irritated me and also stimulated me. Then there was the fact that with the exception of Kahlo and Ana Mendieta, the Cuban artist who died tragically in New York in 1985, every artist in the show was new to me. Again using Stein's vocabulary, they were all contemporaries, not classics, although one could argue that Kahlo is now a classic and that possibly Mendieta will soon be one, if she isn't one already. The others were completely new discoveries for me, and indeed many of them had been new even to the curators of the ICA, who worked closely with a co-curator in Mexico in selecting works for the show.[3] That meant that no body of critical wisdom—what Roland Barthes called the doxa—surrounded this work, at least not yet, not in the United States; at the same time, the work was not totally strange either, for one notable thing about Latino culture, in particular the art and culture of Mexico, is its mixed European and native American strains. Several of the artists in the show are living or have lived in the United States; several are Chicanos, born and raised and educated in the States; a few from Mexico and Cuba have studied at U.S. schools.

This adds an interesting new layer to the idea of the contemporary, for clearly the question of place—cultural as well as geographical—is at least as important, today, as the question of time in determining who one's contemporaries are. A contemporary is literally one who is "of the time," of our time and place. But on this small planet, and especially on these mixed American continents, what exactly does that notion—"our time and place"—mean? Are "we" all in the same place, even if we are all in Boston or New York—or Chicago, Los Angeles, or Austin—at the same time? What place do we call home, those of us who have moved around a lot between cities, cultures, languages, or who come from a culture that is itself a mixture, whether on one side of the border or the other?

These were among the general questions posed by the *Bleeding Heart* show, for me. Added to them was a personal question: How does a European-born American woman professor of literature with more than a casual interest in the historical avant-gardes look at the work of contemporaries who are of her culture (mixed as it is) in some respects, and outside it (or differently mixed) in others?

The first work one saw upon entering the exhibition was not by a contemporary: it was *The Allegory of the Sacrament* (1690), by Juan Correa. Speak of aesthetics and semiotics! Like so many Baroque paintings (but also Renaissance and medieval paintings), this one must be *read* in order to be (really) seen. Here is the Christian story of the sacred bleeding heart compressed into a single busy image: note the vine growing from Christ's wound and covering the cross; the grapes that Christ himself squeezes to convert into wine (they are the "product" of his bleeding heart, but they also *are* his bleeding heart), aided by the Church in the person of the bishop; and down below, the hungry sheep waiting for their sustenance—a bit of a

Juan Correa, *Allegory of the Sacrament*, 1690; oil on canvas.

David Avalos, *Hubcap Milagro—Junipero Serra's Next Miracle: Turning Blood into Thunderbird Wine*, 1989; hubcap; sawblades, wood, lead, acrylic paint, Thunderbird wine bottle, funnel.

mixed metaphor, since sheep don't much care for wine, whether holy or profane. But we get the point, for Christ the shepherd is but another version of Christ who nourishes. Note, too, the enormous grape/globe beneath Christ's knee: this painting pays homage to Christian dominance, in the New World as well as the Old.

Upstairs, among the first things one saw was an object by the contemporary San Diego artist David Avalos, *Hubcap Milagro— Junipero Serra's Next Miracle: Turning Blood into Thunderbird Wine* (1989). Again, a work that must be read, but this time one that is witheringly critical of the Christian mission in the New World. The title itself tells a whole story: a *milagro* is part of Latin Christian folk culture, a small ex-votive object offered to saints as a request for or acknowledgment of miracles.[4] Avalos "updates" the *milagro* by making it a hubcap, and he uses it to critique rather than to celebrate the power of Christianity—in this instance, the power of California's most famous priest, the founder of its first missions in the eighteenth century, Father Junipero Serra. In Avalos' version of one of Father Serra's miracles, the message seems to be one of profit taking: BINGO, we have found a way to convert the blood of the stigmata into an "American classic"! BINGO, we have struck it rich! (Note the letters BINGO on the fingers of the hand that bears the wound.) One does not need a translation to understand that this is an angry, sacrilegious, but also virulently humorous denunciation of the very thing celebrated by the Baroque painting downstairs: the Christian colonization of the New World. Incidentally, this work by Avalos was found to be extremely offensive when it was shown in 1990 in Ohio. An irate Catholic viewer said, "This is the sort of thing I would be against the National Endowment for the Arts supporting."[5]

I, on the other hand, loved it. At first, I connected it not to the Baroque painting below but rather to all the blasphemous or otherwise offensive or corrosive Dada and Surrealist objects I have seen over the years. Like its Dada and Surrealist predecessors, this object did not seem to me beautiful, certainly not in any ordinarily understood sense of "beauty"; nor was it meant, I thought, to seem so. However, it possessed qualities I valued just as much as beauty: humor, inventiveness, and a kind of biting, extremely aggressive irreverence.

My first association to it was Man Ray's *Gift* of 1921, a much simpler object but similarly memorable for its aggressiveness. Just as Man Ray's "gift" of a clothes iron studded with nails is a poisoned gift, designed to tear up rather than smooth out any fabric it touches (in German, *Gift* means poison), so Avalos' *milagro* seems designed to tear up the cultural myth of Christian missionary goodness, rather than work miraculous cures. Unless, of course, one considers the deconstruction of this cultural myth a kind of curing process of its own.

Another of my associations to Avalos' hubcap was Robert Rauschenberg's *Coca-Cola Plan,* a Surrealist-inspired combine made in 1958. Note the critical edge, here as in Avalos: Coca-Cola is America's new eagle, ready to take over the world. Rauschenberg,

Man Ray, *Gift,* 1921; flatiron with metal tacks.

Robert Rauschenberg, *Coca-Cola Plan*, 1958; combine painting.

too, is tearing up, in his own way, a cultural icon—that of the soaring American eagle, now replaced by Coke bottles of questionable cleanliness.

But Avalos' *Hubcap* was actually more interesting than these associations, for it was part of a complex total environment he called "Café Mestizo." The word *mestizo* refers to the mixed-race population of Mexico, and more recently it has referred as well to the cultural hybrids of Chicano life. Avalos, who—as I found out after starting to do research on his work—is an articulate theorist of *mestizaje* (the mixing of races) and a political activist and member of the Border Arts Workshop in San Diego, wrote in his introduction to the 1989 installation of Café Mestizo in a New York gallery: "For too many in the United States, *mestizo* means 'half-breed.' At Café Mestizo, the management refuses to serve the half-baked cultural notion that combining two races produces something less than a whole."[6]

But again, the interesting thing is how Avalos succeeds in being both political and artistically inventive, as if his political outrage fueled the outrageous and violent combinations he invents in his art. In the middle of Café Mestizo stands the proprietor, Mr. Chili, a parodic version of a macho Latin male, bristling with hot peppers and a very phallic head; he strikes me as a bit lovable and a bit pathetic, as well as perhaps somewhat self-ironic, in his posturing. On the left as you enter the café, you find the Thunderbird *milagro* in its complete setup, flanked by two jars of "Dolores" brand pig's feet and two "La mano poderosa" holy candles in jars. These candles further complicate the meaning of the *milagro*: What exactly does the "powerful hand," *mano poderosa*, accomplish? Is the Church in Latin culture even today part of a booming business rather than a spiritual agent? (Junipero Serra's "next" miracle suggests the present, not the historic past.)

Walking around the café, we see *Combination Platter 1: Niopales fronterizo,* consisting of a hubcap platter with a gun on it and flowers strewn around a barbed-wire roll (an allusion to the potentially fatal attraction, for illegal immigrants, of a border crossing on the Mexican American frontier); *Combination Platter 3: Straight-Razor Taco,* which I will get to in a moment; finally, on the extreme right of the café, *Combination Platter 2: The Manhattan Special,* featuring a woman's high-heeled shoe, a Manhattan glass, lipstick, and a knife. One of my associations to this particular work was once again a Surrealist object, which also features a woman's high-heeled shoes: Meret Oppenheim's *Ma Gouvernante, My Nurse, Mein Kindermädchen (My Governess, My Nurse, My Nanny)* of 1936. But Avalos' work is somewhat more complicated and more difficult to read. On Oppenheim's platter, the shoes are a metonymic substitute for the governess (she is the one who wears the shoes); and they also serve as a

David Avalos, *Café Mestizo,* 1989; installation photographed at the Institute of Contemporary Art, Boston, 1991.

David Avalos, *Hubcap Milagro—Junipero Serra's Next Miracle: Turning Blood into Thunderbird Wine,* 1989, installation in *Café Mestizo,* photographed at the Institute of Contemporary Art, Boston, 1991.

David Avalos, *Hubcap Milagro—Combination Platter 2: The Manhattan Special*, 1989; hubcap, sawblades, martini glass, high-heeled shoe, lead, wood, lipstick.

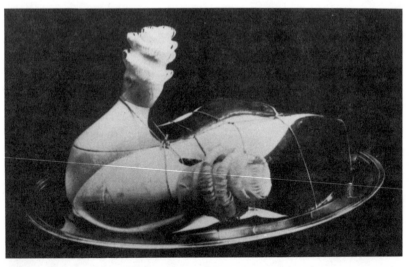

Meret Oppenheim, *Ma Gouvernante, My Nurse, Mein Kindermädchen (My Governess, My Nurse, My Nanny)*, 1936; high-heeled shoes, twine, paper, platter.

metaphor for the governess, since the shoes, like the woman, are "served up" (no doubt for the men in the family, in good Victorian fashion), trussed, unable to move. On Avalos' platter, the shoe is again both metonym (belonging to the woman) and metaphor for the woman, who is "served up" (this time for any paying customer?) and constructed as sexual by her lipstick and high-heeled pumps. But here, she is threatening as well as (perhaps) threatened. Inside the shoe is a heart-shaped object that could figure the female genitals, but there is something sharp in it—a striking configuration of the attraction as well as the danger of female sexuality in its cultural construction. One wonders: Is this construction of female sexuality specific to Latin culture, the culture of Mr. Chili? Or is it more general, characterizing American culture, or Western culture, or even a worldwide cultural imagination about femininity? It is not clear whether the woman in question—or in the shoe—is a Mexican *mestiza* or a Manhattan socialite. Perhaps she is both: a *mestiza* in Manhattan. But she could just as easily be a Parisian prostitute or a vamp from Hong Kong sipping her American drink.

One can ask, from a feminist perspective, whether Avalos' recurrent preoccupation with female genitals (another of his Hubcaps, the *Straight-Razor Taco,* figures a heart-shaped *vagina dentata,* razor in the middle) is simply one more sign of his Surrealist lineage; for we know how obsessively the male Surrealists (Man Ray, Hans Bellmer, Max Ernst, and others) lingered over this and other parts of the female anatomy. Although the Surrealist connection certainly provides one possible reading, I would suggest another one as well, specifically linked to the concept of *mestizaje.* It becomes clearer if we look at the cover photo of the exhibition catalogue for the New York version of *Café Mestizo,* in which the *Straight-Razor Taco* appears next to a copy of James Fenimore Cooper's *The Last of the Mohicans.*

In Avalos' reading, as developed in his catalogue essay, this novel is an ideological statement about racial purity: "In Cooper's value system, it is better that the Mohican nation perish than that Uncas and Cora live to produce *mestizos.*" In this perspective, we might see Avalos' preoccupation with the female genitals as linked to the biological origin of the *mestizo.* Historically, the "mother of the *mestizo*" in Mexican culture is La Malinche, the native woman who

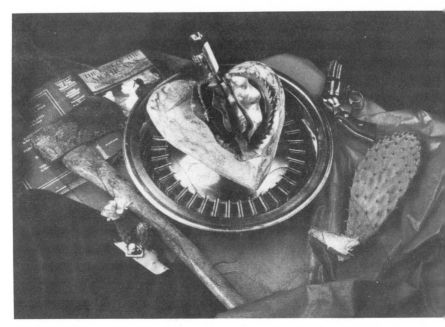

David Avalos, *Hubcap Milagro—Combination Platter 3: The Straight-Razor Taco*, 1989; photographed with axe, pistol, and *The Last of the Mohicans* for cover of exhibition catalogue, Intar Gallery, New York, 1989.

became Cortez's lover and interpreter, thus facilitating the Spanish conquest. This traditionally much-maligned figure is, however, someone that Avalos (along with a number of contemporary feminist critics and historians) has defended in his writings—not because she consorted with the conqueror but because she is the "mother of the *mestizo*." The picture of the *Straight-Razor Taco* next to *The Last of the Mohicans* turns out to be extremely complicated in its meanings, for what appears as the (universally) threatening *vagina dentata* seems to occupy a strongly positive place as the origin of "mixed bloods." This was precisely the place, Avalos maintains, that was destroyed in Cooper's novel in the name of racial purity.[7]

To sum up: Avalos delights me because I move with him from one set of known references (Dada, Surrealism, Rauschenberg) to an enlarged, expanded, differently politicized version of "that kind of art"—from one familiar thing to something that is different in its political scope and specifications but that gives a pleasure of the same, or at least a similar, kind. This two-step movement is what I earlier referred to as bifocal vision, or the double take. I emphasize that the pleasure it offers, although undeniably aesthetic, has very little—indeed, perhaps nothing at all—to do with beauty.

Now let's move on to something completely different, the work of three contemporary women artists in the *Bleeding Heart* show: the Cubans Ana Mendieta and Maria Magdalena Campos-Pons (who is currently living in Boston and attended the Massachusetts College of Art after art school in Cuba); and the Chilean-born Eugenia Vargas, who currently lives in Mexico City. In all three cases, my double take consisted in seeing the work from afar as formally beautiful, and discovering on closer inspection that it was also painful and unsettling.

Campos-Pons's work *I Am a Fountain* (1990), consisting of large three-dimensional forms, occupied a whole wall in one room (in the photograph, note Ana Mendieta's *Body Tracks* on the left, in the

Maria Magdalena Campos-Pons, *I Am a Fountain*, 1990; oil on board, clay tablets; installation photographed at the Institute of Contemporary Art, Boston, 1991.

adjoining room). Seen from afar, it appeared as an abstract arrangement of free forms in striking colors. From close up, its accompanying inscriptions became visible: "Soy una Fuente" ("I Am a Fountain"), and from left to right: *agua*, water; *lagrimas*, tears; *sangre*, blood; *leche*, milk; *vida*, life; *mierda*, shit; *pensiamentos*, thoughts (the curlicued figure). The apparently abstract forms that constitute the work are also female body parts: what we see is a fragmented body with all of its evacuations, disquieting and strange, yet not ceasing to be beautiful. Indeed, besides the fragmentation, it is the beauty of some of the forms representing substances like blood or shit that creates the sense of disquiet. The viewer sees the self-exposure of the artist, who turns her body into a series of objects at once beautiful and repulsive, to be viewed.

How does this kind of self-exposure differ from the way women's bodies are exhibited for viewing by male artists? I think it has to do with the pronoun "I" ("I am a fountain"). This is not a "she" offered to the viewer by a third party, as in the traditional nude, where—as John Berger has amply shown, in *Ways of Seeing*—both painter and viewer are coded as male; here, the woman is not only a subject in the sense of "subjected to the (male) gaze," but also the artist-subject who affirms herself as an artist in the very process of self-exposure.

The same layered process of looking and showing occurs in the case of Ana Mendieta. Her series of works titled *Body Tracks* (1982) may resemble minimalist works in the manner of, say, Morris Louis. But the effect is very different when one sees how those works were produced—as recorded, for example, in the photograph of Mendieta's performance at Franklin Furnace in New York City, where she is shown kneeling, applying blood and tempera directly from her hands to the paper on the wall. Once again, what starts out looking like a formal abstraction—shall we call it beautiful?—turns out to be a disquieting personal exploration in which the artist's own body is both exposed and made into art.

A similar thing occurs, though in a different medium and by different means, with the photographs of Eugenia Vargas. I have been unable to obtain installation shots. But imagine five large untitled photographs on a single white wall. On the left, you see a

Maria Magdalena Campos-Pons, *I am a Fountain*,
1990; close-up.

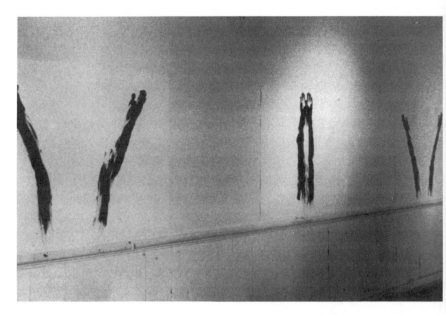

Ana Mendieta, *Body Tracks*, 1982; blood and tempera on paper.

Ana Mendieta, *Body Tracks*, 1982; photograph of performance at Franklin Furnace, New York City, 1982.

Eugenia Vargas, *Untitled 1*, 1991; color photograph.

highly ordered symmetrical composition chiefly in black and white, with an artful double-frame effect on both sides: black, then white. Looking more closely, however, you notice that the three images within the large white strip in the middle are pictures of a woman— in fact, of the artist—photographed in profile with her breast exposed and from the back, wearing a wooden saddle over her head. The saddle looks almost like a torture instrument, establishing a striking contrast between the unsaddled horses (which are in any case toy horses, too small for that saddle) and the woman encaged by the saddle. Viewers familiar with the photographs of Man Ray or Brassaï may be reminded of certain of their works of the 1930s, showing women with their heads caught in nets or metal cages.

The next picture by Vargas is a composition, again chiefly in black, playing variations on geometric shapes: the square and the cross. In the middle, something looks a bit like a crucifixion, al-

Eugenia Vargas, *Untitled 5*, 1991; color photograph.

though without Christ's body. The body in this work is once again the artist's, exposed in layers: on top, her face superimposed on what could be an X-ray, the outside on the inside; and taped over that, a childhood photo introducing yet another layer, this time temporal. In the small square below is a strangely distorted head shot taken from above, making her look almost grotesque; and on the two sides, taped to the photograph, are two spools from rolls of film. The effect produced is double: from one angle, the picture can be read as an ordered construction with a modernist self-referential designation ("this is a photograph, developed from film that was once on those spools or on spools like them"); from another, we see the disruptive, painful self-exposure and self-exploration that went into the creation of the formal composition.

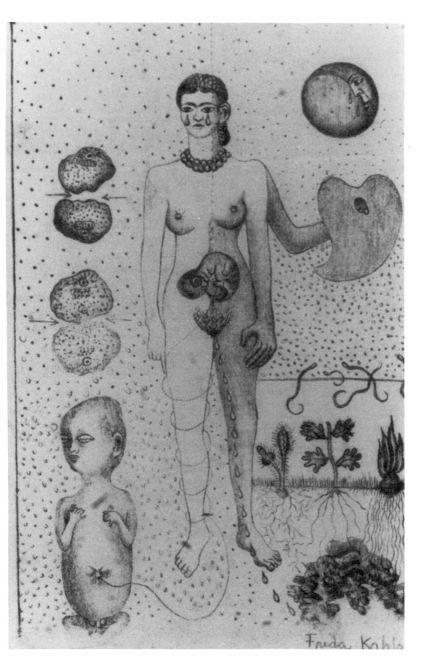

Frida Kahlo, *The Miscarriage*, 1936; lithograph on paper.

Frida Kahlo, *Self-Portrait with Cropped Hair*, 1940; oil on canvas.

This is, then, another form of the double take—going from the comforting to the unsettling, from the classicizing to the painfully contemporary.

Finally, I want to comment on two images by Frida Kahlo, who I have claimed has already passed into the realm of the classic in Stein's terms. I would suggest that Vargas, Mendieta, and Campos belong to a tradition that Kahlo inaugurated, certainly in Latin American art by women; and that we are able to *see* their work as contemporary at least partly because Kahlo's work, now classic, has prepared the way. Looking at Kahlo's pictures, what do we see? Something beautiful, but also something terrible. The 1936 lithograph *El aborto* (*The Miscarriage*) refers to Kahlo's miscarriage that year. The almost clinical anatomical drawing of the fetus adds a strangely dissociated quality to the sense of loss conveyed by this work. Dissociation is also suggested by the double self-image, one side dark, the other light (there exist a number of similarly doubled self-portraits in her work).

In the 1940 *Self-Portrait with Cropped Hair,* the artist, having cut off her long black hair and donned a heavy man's suit, sits looking out at the viewer with an almost defiant air. Above her, the words and music of a popular song:

Mira que si te quise, fué por el pelo,
Ahora que estás pelona, ya no te quiero.

Look, if I loved you it was for your hair,
So now that you're hairless, I don't love you any more.

Who is singing this song? Is this a case of self-hatred as well as automutilation? She herself is holding the scissors; it is she who has inflicted this punishment on herself. Symbolically, she has unsexed herself, cut off the traditional sign of female beauty and desirability. But this female mutilation is also, curiously, a kind of male castration—the scissors are held right between her thighs, with a limp lock of hair dangling in the middle; and note all the drooping phallic shapes strewn around her on the floor. This is a woman apparently possessing neither female desirability nor male potency. Yet she has painted this powerful picture. Her eyes, looking at us unflinchingly, indicate her strength.

This stunning painting allows us to practice, for once, exactly the rare kind of viewing that Gertrude Stein dreamed of: to look at a classic as if it were contemporary, seeing both its beauty and its ability to have been—indeed, still be—ugly. Ugly, like *The Potato Eaters*.

LIVING BETWEEN:
THE LO^N_VELINESS
OF THE
"ALONESTANDING
WOMAN"

9

When I first met Christine Brooke-Rose, in the fall of 1977, she was living in Paris and teaching at Vincennes, the new, revolutionary university that had been founded after the "events" of May 1968. In literary studies, Vincennes was a hotbed of structuralism and poststructuralism, often practiced by the same critic; in psychoanalysis, it was resolutely Lacanian; in linguistics, Chomskyan. It boasted among its faculty some of the best-known Parisian intellectuals—writers and philosophers such as Gilles Deleuze, Michel Foucault (before he moved on), Hélène Cixous. It was Cixous who had invited Brooke-Rose to join the faculty in 1968. Christine was living in London at the time, an up-and-coming author who, after publishing four sturdy realist novels, had started writing "experimental" fictions with one-word titles: *Out* (1964), *Such* (1966), *Between* (1968). Since she had recently separated from her husband of many years and needed a change of air, and since she had childhood ties to the French language (her mother was Swiss, her father English; she grew up in Belgium and Switzerland, speaking French, English, and German with equal ease), she packed up her books and crossed the Channel.

Then acquires alles a broken-up quality, die hat der charm of my clever sweet, my deutsche Mädchen-goddess.

—Christine Brooke-Rose,
Between

She is always translating from one language to another and never quite knows to which language she belongs.

—Christine Brooke-Rose,
"A Conversation with Christine Brooke-Rose"

Traditionally, men belong to groups, to society (the matrix, the canon). Women belong to men.

—Christine Brooke-Rose,
"Illiterations"

Nine years later, when we met and became friends, I was living in Paris for a year with my husband and two young sons (the younger one was a baby, four months old), working on a scholarly book—a structural study of the ideological novel, sometimes called the "thesis" novel, whose French name is *le roman à thèse*. Christine, ever punning, inscribed a copy of her latest novel, *Thru*, with the dedication: "For Susan, this roman à syn-thèse, pro-thèse (foutaise)"—synthesis, prosthesis, thing-a-ma-jesis. The pun can be translated (badly), but loses all flavor in translation. To "get it," to love it, you have to know both French and English.

I have often thought about that year we spent as near neighbors, Christine and I. Much water has flowed under the bridge (it must be the Pont Mirabeau, for we were in Paris and had read Apollinaire) since then. Christine no longer lives in Paris and has retired from Vincennes (which is no longer in Vincennes, but in the working-class suburb of St. Denis). She has settled in Provence, but is thinking of moving to London. I no longer have young sons (happily, they have grown up) and am no longer married. I am now approaching the age Christine was when we first met, more than fifteen years ago. Like the heroine of her novel *Between* (which I read for the first time in the 1980s) and like Christine herself, I am now an "alonestanding woman." That last phrase is another piece of wordplay, this time mine, for which, if you are to get it, you need to know a language besides English: not French, but German.[1]

Roland Barthes spoke of the modern text—what he called the "writerly text," the text of "bliss" (*jouissance*)—as a "happy Babel." Contrary to the Old Testament, where Babel stands as an emblem of God's jealous wrath, in the modern text "the confusion of tongues is no longer a punishment, the subject gains access to bliss by the cohabitation of languages *working side by side*."[2]

Barthes's erotic innuendo about linguistic cohabitation calls to mind the Surrealist ideal of poetry as "words making love." To the reader of Christine Brooke-Rose's novel *Between*, it calls to mind a passage that not only states but wittily exemplifies that same cohabitation: "As if languages loved each other behind their own façades, despite alles was man denkt darüber davon dazu. As if words fraternised silently beneath the syntax, finding each other funny and delicious in a Misch-Masch of tender fornication, inside the bombed out hallowed structures and the rigid steel glass modern edifices of the brain. Du, do you love me?"[3] The brain in which words fraternize in this novel is that of a woman ("A woman of uncertain age uncertain loyalties"—p. 445) whose life history situates her on an imaginary frontier between France, Germany, and England: French mother (dead), German father (disappeared before her birth), English husband (divorced). Her profession reinforces and multiplies this transitional status, for she is a simultaneous translator (French to German) who is literally always "between conferences": from the International Conference of Demographers in Copenhagen to the Congress on the Writer and Communication in Prague, by way of archeologists in Istanbul, semiologists in Dubrovnik, acupuncturists somewhere in Italy, and sundry other conventioneers in Budapest, Sofia, Moscow, Amsterdam, Paris, London, New York, und so weiter weiter gehen, the unnamed woman travels.

Her body afloat in the bellies of countless airplanes where "travel talk ensues," or curled between the sheets in countless hotel rooms each with its bottle of mineral water wasser aqua agua eau minérale on the nightstand, or else squeezed into a glass booth above the meeting rooms of countless "conventions where no communication ever occurs," she is a crossroad where more than four languages meet. Her consciousness, floating between sleep and waking, irony and nostalgia, anticipation and memory, is a jumble of natural languages (English, French, Italian, und so weiter), professional jargons picked up at congresses ("Oh, archeology, medicine, irrigation, economic aid for the under-developed areas and so forth"— p. 468), the global currencies of advertising slogans, guidebooks, phrasebooks for foreigners (the meaning of "foreigner" varying, of course, according to the country one is in), public notices in airports, televised news broadcasts, lines of half-remembered poems (Shakespeare, Goethe, Cavalcanti, Auden, Eliot, e tutti quanti), as well as the voices of past (and some present) lovers, friends, neighbors, and interrogators of diverse classes, countries, sexes. Like this:

—Un cottage? Que voulez-vous dire, un cottage?—Hé bien, mon père, une toute petite maison, à la campagne. A box a refuge a still small centre within the village within the wooded countryside within the alien land, where Mr. Jones the builder who converts the bathroom says bee-day? Oh you mean a biddy. Yes I can get a biddy for you but you aven't got much room ave you? Ah sì! Un cottage. The pale fat priest-interpreter looks over his half-spectacles made for reading the sheafs of notes before him. Un piccolo chalet. Va bene così? Un piccolo chalet?

—Va bene.

Or this:

In fondo a sinistra the men in the café sit transfixed by the flickering local variation in the presentation of opposite viewpoints on every aspect of an instant world through faceless men who have no doubt acquired faces for them as their arch-priests of actualità that zooms flashcuts explodes to OMO! Da oggi con Perboral! Lava ancora più bianco! Gut-gut. Più bianco than what? We live in an age of transition, perpetually between white and whiter than white. Very tiring. Zoom. (pp. 418–419)

In the first passage, the interrogators are Italian priests taking a deposition from our heroine, who has petitioned the Vatican for an annulment in addition to her civil divorce. (Because she wants to remarry? No. Because she is a practicing Catholic? No. Because . . .? Just because.) In the second passage—which occurs a few lines after the first, part of what Richard Martin has called Brooke-Rose's "interest in vocal collage"[4]—the priests have been replaced by TV newscasters, "arch-priests of actualità," celebrants of instant news in an instant world. Their words are in turn interrupted by the explosive celebration of OMO—not a new brand of humanity, but an improved (or so we are told) brand of detergent that "washes even whiter."

Is this world of zooming juxtapositions the happy Babel dreamed of by Barthes? Or is it closer to the nightmare of Jean Baudrillard, a world of simulacra where all real distinctions are abolished and we are left only with "the simulated generation of difference"?[5]

"What difference does it make?" This question recurs like a refrain in *Between*. And the answer, it would seem, is: Not much. Un piccolo chalet or a box cottage, a bee-day or a biddy, a real priest or an "arch-priest," a deutsche Mädchen-goddess or a French girl (the woman has been both, depending on who named her), a Signor Ingegnere Giovanni-Battista di Qualcosa or a Comrade Pan Bogumil Somethingski, a nightstand with aqua minerale or mineralwasser, a room in Sofia, Belgrade, or Oslo—they are all, in the end, mere flickering local variations on a single theme: "We live in an age of transition wouldn't you agree and must cope as best we can" (p. 476).

An unnamed woman (or, as the case may be, multiply, ambiguously named, which comes down to the same thing—or does it?), a woman of uncertain age, standing on her own (no children as "traces" of marriage), eine alleinstehende Frau: this figure occupies the center not only of *Between* but of the two novels that followed it: *Thru* (1975) and *Amalgamemnon* (1984). She is an ambiguous figure, this alonestanding woman—on the one hand, close to being submerged by sadness, as by the detritus of a civilization whose broken-up quality she both registers and exemplifies (the woman of *Between* speaks of "this great loss at the centre of things almost from the beginning if beginning we can call it sub specie aeternitatis"—p. 463); on the other hand, *playing* with that very sense of loss, that same detritus, and producing (sometimes) an exhilarating laughter. Like this: "What story? Oh you know as the Holy Ghost said that scandal spread by St. Peter about me and the Virgin Mary. He likes ready-made stories the schmutziger the witziger with a burst of crude laughter tout de suite and the tooter the sweeter"[6] (p. 423).

When asked, in a recent interview, about the joyful tone and playfulness in her late novels, Christine Brooke-Rose spoke about serenity: "Humor is one of the ways to achieve that serenity and the bubbling result of it. Almost out of disillusion, if you like, that you don't expect anything else. It gives me, at any rate, a tremendous . . . how shall I put it . . . self-reliance."[7] No doubt one has to have lived between languages, like the alleinstehende Frau and like Christine Brooke-Rose herself—and furthermore, or pahr dessue le marshy, as she says about the foolish fond old man who is bald on top of it all (p. 427), one has to have lived between the *same* languages, which were those of Hitler, Mussolini, Chamberlain, and Pétain as well as of Goethe, Cavalcanti, Shakespeare, and Baudelaire—in order to fully appreciate the inventiveness and humor, as well as the utterly disabused worldliness, of a novel like *Between*.

It helps, in addition, if one has some personal involvement (not necessarily experience, but a sense of involvement) with the history of Europe before 1945. For this woman's "broken-up quality" is due not only to her intermediate state between languages, as Brooke-Rose has suggested ("She just doesn't know who she is, she is always translating from one language to another and never quite knows to which language she belongs",)[8] but also, surely, to the historical conditions that created her interlinguistic status. As we find out in the course of the novel, this alleinstehende Frau was a French girl whose mother sent her to Nuremberg for a year in 1938 to perfect her German while she lived with her paternal aunt, a baroness and a convinced Nazi. Trapped in Germany at the outbreak of the war, the girl ends up working for the German censorship office as a translator of Allied documents, thus viewing the war through the the point of view of the "enemy." Immediately after the war, she is "taken under the wings" of an Allied officer and gets a job as a translator with the occupying forces in Germany, who are looking at German documents. Thus, she again views the war, this time in retrospect, "from the enemy point of view" (p. 487). But it is not the same enemy: "we" and the enemy have traded places.

Who the enemy is depends on where one stands, and when. "You must forgive these questions Fräulein but in view of your French upbringing we must make sure of your undivided loyalty," says the German interrogator about to hire her for the censorship office around 1941 (p. 444). "You will excuse these questions Fräulein but in view of your nationality we must make sure of your undivided loyalty," says the British interrogator about to hire her in 1945 (p. 486). Is it surprising that in this world "acquires alles a broken-up quality"? And that the notion of "undivided loyalty" appears comically grotesque?

Why does the woman seek an annulment, even though she wants neither to remarry nor to reenter the Church? I would hazard a speculation related to history: to annul a marriage is to decree, with all the authority invested in the Church, that a certain event never happened. In other words, it is to do away with history—or no, not do away with it, but return it to an earlier time, a time of wholeness, prior to the breaking (of the hymen). When she was a young girl, before the war, the woman visited, with her German boyfriend, the church in Munich that holds the remains of the "frail skeletal nun in a glass case, Heilige Munditia. Patronin der alleinstehenden Frauen" (p. 491). During the war, she visited it again, with a different boyfriend—but the church was damaged, and the nun gone (p. 530). Much later, now, when she herself has become a "desiccated skeletal alleinstehende Frau" (p. 547), she visits the church again, this time unaccompanied: the church has been "totally rebuilt" and the frail skeletal nun once more lies in her glass case (p. 567).

The annulment of her marriage restores the heroine, we might say, to her glass case. But it is not the original case, merely a copy—a simulation. The reason the Church gives for annulling the marriage is itself, interestingly, a reason of simulation: "mulieris simulationis contra bona indissolubilitatis et prolis" (p. 473). Or as the priest had put it earlier: "So you decided in advance madame, to divorce if it didn't work, thus annulling the contract in the eyes of God?" (p. 458). By entering the marriage as a simulator, without total commitment, she was living a lie; that lie in turn justified the fiction of annulment. Do two simulations make a real? Or just more lies?

Traveling down the page where the Latin quotation stating the reason for the annulment appears, my eye stops; the words jump out unannounced, as if suddenly turning a corner: "I hated all that interrogation Liebes why, quite like the end of the war trying to get a job and a Persil-Schein certificate denazifying us whiter than white." Whose voice is this? Was the denazification certificate like today's OMO, which "washes even whiter" but whose virtues are doubtless highly exaggerated? Who is speaking? Not all the perfumes of Araby will get these hands clean.

The peculiar link between history, memory, repetition-with-difference, and a consciousness I want to call postmodern (postmodern *because* it is concerned with its relation to history, memory, and repetition-with-difference) is one of the constant underlying themes in *Between*, and in much of Christine Brooke-Rose's fiction since then. But what is the connection between this enduring preoccupation and the figure of the middle-aged "alonestanding woman"?

The woman interpreter of *Between*, who has seen from both sides the war that brought us Dachau and Auschwitz (after which, according to Adorno's well-known claim, there can be no more poetry—or at the very least, no more poetry as we knew it), says about a much younger colleague: "Sandra chatters happily on in un amour de soutien-gorge, belonging apparently to a different species altogether undamaged unconcerned doing the same work with ease and careless poise from the start unretarded by wars national prejudices bilingualism fraternisation sex . . ." (p. 532). Apparently, unlike her innocent young colleague, the alleinstehende Frau is not undamaged, not unconcerned, not unretarded by wars, national prejudices, und so weiter, ever weiter and more knee-deep in the detritus. Why? One of the recurring phrases in *Between* is "in this our masculine-dominated civilization" (pp. 510, 533), alternating with "masculine upward myths" and "man-dominated myth" (pp. 505, 553). Is Brooke-Rose suggesting that the historical mess we have gotten ourselves into "in this supposedly rationalistic age so dominated by masculine upward myths" is the work of men? And that, just perhaps, getting us out of it will be the work of women who are able to stand up by (and for) themselves? She would probably demur, if asked: novels should never "suggest" anything as unambiguous as that (unless they are *romans à thèse*, but that's not a respectable genre). Still . . . Zygmunt Bauman, a Polish Jewish sociologist living in England, claims that the role of intellectuals in the postmodern age has shifted from that of legislator (telling a culture what it needs to know and think) to that of interpreter, translator, a shuttler between cultures, between languages. Rosi Braidotti, an Italian philosopher living in Holland, claims that the quintessential shuttler between cultures and languages, *la polyglotte*, is a woman.[9] The unnamed simultaneous interpreter of *Between*, who happens to be a woman constantly shuttling, not undamaged or unconcerned, may stand as one emblem of our ambiguous present, and (with a bit of luck) of our still uncertain future.

HISTORY/MEMORY

PART FOUR

LIFE-STORY, HISTORY, FICTION: SIMONE DE BEAUVOIR'S WARTIME WRITINGS

10

In the spring of 1990, my fancy often turned to thoughts of Simone de Beauvoir. Forced to stay home for a week to recover from an eye operation, I spent my time alternating between the rare luxury of daytime sleep and the equally rare luxury, in a teaching year, of long hours of reading in bed. One eye was bandaged, but the other one raced down the pages of Deirdre Bair's massive biography of Beauvoir.[1] More than seven hundred pages of life-story, told in scrupulous detail from beginning to end: I read the book conscientiously, in the prepublication proofs I had been sent by the *Atlantic*, which had asked me to review it. But mingled with the professional obligation was a deep sense of personal pleasure, as memories of when I first read Simone de Beauvoir's life-story kept surfacing and crisscrossing with this reading. *Memoirs of a Dutiful Daughter, The Prime of Life*—I had read those books in Paris (the second had not even been translated yet), during the year I spent there after graduating from college. Propped up on pillows on the bed in my room at the Cité Universitaire, I would dream about Beauvoir and Sartre, the Sorbonne during the twenties, Paris during the Occupa-

It is when one has been able to reach the moment of opening oneself completely to the other that the scene of the other, which is more specifically the scene of History, will be able to take place in a very vast way.

—Hélène Cixous, "From the Scene of the Unconscious to the Scene of History"

I think it is good for thoughts to be shaped by experience; at any rate, that is the path I have always followed.

—Simone de Beauvoir, "Foreword" to Alice Schwarzer, *After the Second Sex*

tion, the Resistance. That was the spring of 1961, a season of crisis over the Algerian war. The newly founded terrorist group O.A.S., as a last-ditch effort to maintain "l'Algérie française," was planting bombs in strategic places associated with opposition to the war and support for Algerian independence. Naturally, the offices of Sartre and Beauvoir's journal, *Les Temps modernes,* were on their list, as was Sartre's apartment. The previous fall, Sartre and Beauvoir had both signed the *Déclaration des 121,* the intellectuals' manifesto calling for active resistance to the war, including military insubordination.

For a number of years, Sartre and Beauvoir had been associated with left-wing causes: anticolonialism, support for Castro, goodwill trips to China and the Soviet Union. Although new intellectual movements such as structuralism would soon be challenging their dominance, in 1961 they were still (at least, they appeared to me to be) at the height of their celebrity and influence. They were *engagé* writers, taking the weight of the world on their shoulders. They were my idols, individually and as a couple.

A few years earlier, Simone de Beauvoir had won France's most prestigious literary prize, the Prix Goncourt, with her autobiographical novel about postwar French intellectuals, *The Mandarins* (1954); some years before that, she had earned both local notoriety and a permanent place in modern intellectual history by publishing *The Second Sex* (1949), a work of immense erudition and passion that would become one of the founding works of contemporary feminism. To me, however, during that year in Paris, she was most important as an autobiographer. She had just published *La Force de l'âge (The Prime of Life),* the fat book I was reading, whose second half covered the years of the war and the beginning of her career as a writer. Projecting backward, I endowed the story she told there, about her life during the 1930s and 1940s, with all of her political and intellectual prestige of the 1950s and 1960s. "My life would be a beautiful story, which would become true as I told it to myself," she had written in *Memoirs of a Dutiful Daughter,* describing her first dreams of becoming a writer.[2] In *The Prime of Life,* she recounted how her personal "belle histoire" had collided with, and been forever changed by, the collective history of France during the war. "Not only had the war changed my relations to everything, but it had changed everything . . . After June 1940, I no longer recognized things, or people, or moments, or places, or myself."[3] The only thing that hadn't changed, and wouldn't change, she implied, was her relation of mutual love and commitment to Sartre.

The heroine of her autobiography, she was also my heroine—a character I felt close to and would have liked to emulate. "That was almost thirty years ago," I told myself as I read Deirdre Bair's biography. "You were naive then." In fact, I had gone through quite a few stages in my understanding of Beauvoir since those heady days of reading at the Cité Universitaire; nowadays, my appreciation of her life and work was a great deal more realistic. I knew about her evasiveness and her self-deceptions, especially where her personal relation to Sartre was concerned; about her complicated intellectual and emotional relation, over the years, to feminism and to "other women." I had even written about some of the contradictions in her self-conception as a (woman) writer (see Chapter 4). My days of idealizing identification were long past.

Considering all this, it would be inaccurate to say that I was disillusioned by the cold light brought to bear on some aspects of Beauvoir's life in Bair's carefully documented narrative. No, it was not disillusionment but a curious sense of separation I experienced when I learned that in October 1940 Simone de Beauvoir had signed the oath required by the Vichy government from all teachers, attesting to the fact that she was neither Jewish nor a Freemason; and that in 1943, after being dismissed from her teaching post because of an official complaint from the mother of her young friend Nathalie Sorokine (Lise in *The Prime of Life*), she accepted a job at the German-controlled radio station, Radio-Paris. Bair goes into great detail about this, explaining that Beauvoir's job was in no way political but consisted merely of selecting material for a cultural program on "historical music," and also explaining Beauvoir's own position that she had done nothing wrong but merely bowed to the necessity of earning a living. And yet, Bair notes, "No matter how she explained it away, she was uneasy about this work. She glossed over it in her memoirs, always resented being questioned about it, and was furious whenever she learned of a scholar or journalist who wrote about it" (p. 307).

For me, reading Bair's account, it was not a matter of judging Simone de Beauvoir. She did no worse than many others at the time, and certainly did better than many; although she later omitted some facts or glossed over them in *The Prime of Life,* she told no outright lies; to judge her for not having been heroic would have been sheer hypocrisy. The sense of separation I felt, however, was a different matter; it came, quite simply, from my realization that had I been in her place, I would not have had the choice of signing the oath or working for Radio-Paris. Nor could I have frequented the Café de Flore, whether it was a favorite hangout of German officers (as Bair says historians claim) or whether it was shunned by them (as Beauvoir claimed in *The Prime of Life*). My choices, as a Jewish woman, even if I had been a self-identified *French* Jewish woman, would have been very very different.

Just as I was mulling this over, the French publishing scene brought me more food for thought. Almost at the same time as the Bair biography appeared in the United States, Beauvoir's war diary, *Journal de guerre* (covering the period between September 1939 and January 1941) and her supposedly "lost" but suddenly "found" letters to Sartre (two volumes covering the years 1930 to 1963) were published in Paris.[4] I threw myself at them, looking for I knew not exactly what (perhaps there would be a diary entry in October 1940, mentioning the oath?). Concentrating only on the war years, what I found were not revelations—unless one considers the confirmation of Beauvoir's bisexuality, which she long denied, a revelation—but rather a network of paths leading to other texts, which now demanded to be reread, or read for the first time. These hitherto private works, then, provided a way of opening up, or a new way of entering, a whole series of other, public works: Sartre's letters to her, for example, published several years earlier, as well as Sartre's own war notebooks (symmetry *oblige*); *The Prime of Life,* indeed all of Beauvoir's autobiographical writings, including interviews about herself; and most obviously, the published works that she conceived and wrote entirely during the war years. These include her second novel, *The Blood of Others,* about which she began jotting notes in her diary in January 1941 and which she finished in 1943; her only play, *Les Bouches inutiles (Who Shall Die?),* staged in Paris in November 1944; and her first philosophical essay, *Pyrrhus et Cinéas,* which she wrote at the invitation of Jean Grenier (who was an editor at Gallimard) in 1943.

I cannot follow all of these paths here, but I will try to gesture toward a few. The one that especially interests me is the path that leads through the diary to *The Blood of Others,* a novel that had a huge success at the time of its publication but is rarely discussed today, and that Beauvoir herself belittled in her autobiography.[5] Following this path allows one to see how Beauvoir negotiated the complicated interactions between life-story, history, and fiction; and it obliges one (I should say, in this case, me) to experience in a particularly vivid way what otherwise might remain only in the realm of theory: the increasingly vexed issue, in current feminist thought, regarding the relative importance of gender, race, ethnicity, and class as analytical and critical categories.

Facts

Sartre to the Castor ("Beaver," his term of endearment for Beauvoir), somewhere in Alsace, January 6, 1940:

> I've just read Heine's biography, and it inspired some curious thoughts in me. Since I praised him to myself for having succeeded in assuming his identity as a Jew, and saw with brilliant clarity that Jewish rationalists like Pieter or Brunschvick [two fellow soldiers] were inauthentic by thinking of themselves as men first, not as Jews, I was forced to conclude, logically, that I had to assume my own identity as a Frenchman; I did so without enthusiasm, and above all it had no meaning for me. Nothing more than an inevitable and obvious conclusion. I wonder where it all leads, and I'm going to put my mind to it tomorrow.[6]

Castor to Sartre, Paris, January 8, 1940:

> I don't know whether we have to assume ourselves as French, I'll think about it until tomorrow; in part yes, certainly . . . Didn't we talk about that at the "Rey" once, how we couldn't feel as much solidarity with the persecuted Jews in Germany as we would with Jews in France, and that the fact of being "in situation" necessarily involved the sense of frontiers? I'll think about it (but it seems to me that this assuming doesn't lead to patriotism any more than assuming the war leads to

warmongering); in that case it's a matter (or not?) of attaining universals, ideas, works, etc., through a singular historical position.[7]

Note Beauvoir's use of the contrary-to-fact conditional ("as we would with Jews in France") to talk about the persecution of French Jews: the Vichy anti-Jewish decrees were still in the future. Note also that she seeks to allay Sartre's worries about what it would mean for him to assume his identity (the French word they use is "*condition*") as a Frenchman. It would not entail "patriotism," a value they don't hold high; it would still allow one to reach the level of universals, albeit from a singular historical position. Clearly, at this point she (like Sartre himself, it would appear) is interested in transcendence not as a movement toward other human subjects but as a direct accession to universals, "ideas, works, etc."

The day after his letter to her, Sartre tells her he has written thirty-nine pages in his "dark blue notebook" on his relation to France.[8] I rush to his war diary, the *Carnets de la drôle de guerre:* alas, that notebook was lost. The day after her letter to him, Beauvoir celebrates her thirty-second birthday (a fact she mentions to Sartre but fails to note in her diary for that day); she will not return to the question of frontiers, France/Germany, or to the question of the relation between singular and universal, or the question of Jews versus non-Jews, until much later—after June 1940. Instead, on January 9 she tells Sartre, among other details, about her latest potential "conquest" at the *lycée:* "the brunette from H[enry] IV [another *lycée*] who sent me a letter at the beginning of the year; I contemplated cheating on Sorokine with her, but she put on a red wig after speaking to me and some people warned me that she was a rotten apple."[9]

The liberty, one might even say the locker-room quality, of Beauvoir's amorous confidences to Sartre, as well as the details of her sexual encounters with Nathalie Sorokine and another ex-student, Louise Védrine, as told to him and in her diary, are among the revelations, after all, of these volumes. (Louise Védrine, whose real name was Bianca Bienenfeld, has in the meantime written her own memoirs about those times—they do not make either Beauvoir or Sartre look good.)[10] All references to this aspect of her life were carefully edited out of the diary passages reproduced in *The Prime of Life.* Beauvoir told Alice Schwarzer in 1978 that she wished she had given, in her autobiography, a "frank and balanced account of [her] own sexuality. A truly sincere one."[11] But she seems to have been unable to give a frank account even after that admission; when, in a later interview (1982), Schwarzer asked her point blank, "Have you never had a sexual relationship with a woman?" Beauvoir lied: "No. I have had some very important friendships with women, of course, some very close relationships, sometimes close in a physical sense. But they never aroused erotic passion on my part."[12] One could, I suppose, construe this to mean, casuistically, that her sexual relationships with women "didn't count" since there was never any real erotic passion, and therefore conclude that she was not lying. I mention this because, as we shall see, Beauvoir was not above a certain casuistry when dealing with embarrassing questions. The fact is that passionate or not, she did have sexual relations with women, and she wrote about them frankly and in detail both to Sartre and in her diary.

Some of the critical reactions to these volumes, when they were published in Paris, were extremely negative—almost as if the critic felt betrayed, like a jilted lover: "How is one to read these *Lettres* and this *Journal?* What do we learn from them?" asked Marianne Alphant in a long review in *Libération.* "That *The Prime of Life* is a trumped-up story? That we have been duped . . .? Undoubtedly. But also that the philosopher didn't have time to think . . . That the pioneer of feminism only liked women who were submissive to her domination. That this austere muse had the fantasies of a shopgirl [*des états d'âme de midinette*]."[13] As one reads Marianne Alphant's pitiless accumulation of quotations to support her claim (in the style of "She told me I was very beautiful to look at, which flattered me, I like the way I look these days, it's because of my earrings and the turban, they look as beautiful to me as if they were on someone else"—p. 167), one has to admit that she may be right about the "états d'âme de midinette." Bianca Bienenfeld Lamblin's memoir confirms some of Alphant's other intuitions as well, such as Beauvoir's need to dominate or her lack of scruples about lying to people who felt close to her.

My own feeling, as I read the *Journal,* floated somewhere between admiration and disbelief. Was it really possible—especially for an intellectual, a teacher of philosophy who read the newspapers and listened to the radio—to live in Paris from September 1939 to June 1940 *as if nothing had changed?* Evidently, it was. Not for nothing was this later called the "phony war"—it was as if it did not exist at all. Beauvoir's days, reported in all their "chronological banality" (Marianne Alphant's phrase), consisted of working on her novel (*She Came To Stay,* her first published work) in a café in the morning, usually at Le Dôme or La Coupole; writing to her soldiers, Sartre and "le petit Bost" (Jacques-Laurent Bost, Sartre's former student, who had become her lover on an outing they took in the Alps the previous year) in another café, lunching in a third, teaching in two different *lycées,* occasionally correcting student papers, reading a lot, doing her nails, going to concerts, movies, and the opera with various young women friends, mediating the disputes that arose (often over who got to see her and for how long) among those friends—and, of course, writing in her diary. There is an entry for every single day, without fail, from September 1, 1939, to February 23, 1940. If she misses a day, she makes up for it the next day, or even several days later—never by quickly summarizing what has happened, but always by writing what looks like that day's account, usually in the present tense.

In early September, she spends a few difficult days getting used to Sartre's absence—she saw him off at the train, with other draftees, on September 2. On September 7, she is still feeling sad: "I go to the hairdresser, he makes me a beautiful *coiffure,* I feel sad at not having anyone to show myself to" (p. 31). By September 26, on a trip to visit Louise Védrine in Brittany, she feels better. She spends a day by herself exploring the Pointe du Raz: "It's as beautiful as every-thing I'd been told about it . . . [Despite the war] I feel an immense joy in the present, no matter what the future will bring" (p. 62).

Reading this, I am filled with a kind of admiration: she's a spunky woman—nothing can faze her for long. In early November, she manages to wangle a travel permit to visit Sartre in Alsace for a few days, pretending she has to visit a sick relative. He skips out of his barracks to see her several times a day; waiting for him in her room, she feels "plunged into the world of war, it fills me up—I feel poetic and happy" (p. 121). Twice on the preceding days, she uses the word "adventure" to describe how this trip feels: "I'm beginning to have a real feeling of adventure" (p. 116); "The feeling of adventure continues" (p. 117). A few weeks earlier, when Sartre had been suddenly transferred and she had had to cancel her trip to visit him, she had cried, but soon felt better: "I have another good cry and fix my make-up as well as I can. Then I go and eat some fries and crêpes at the *crêperie* while finishing Agatha Christie" (p. 80).

Is this spunkiness or blind egotism? Is she indomitable or unconscionable? For her, the question never arises; the possibility that others might find the life she is leading smug or self-centered never crosses her mind. To condemn Beauvoir for her apparent blindness during this period, as one may be tempted to do (and as some critics obviously did), is understandable; but it is an anachronistic judgment, based on what we know now to have happened later. If one tries to imagine what it was actually like to live as a civilian in Paris during the winter of 1939–1940, *without knowing what was in store,* it becomes easier to understand Beauvoir's apparent insensitivity, her selfish pursuit of pleasure even as catastrophe is about to strike. At New Year's, she goes skiing and loves it—she takes private lessons and makes good progress. In late January, Sartre arrives in Paris on a ten-day leave and she is happy. A few days after he leaves, it's Bost's turn.

Then, after the entry of February 23, a sudden break. The next notebook, number 6, is dated "9 June–18 July."[14] Unlike the previous notebooks, this one is fragmented, irregular, with great gaps between entries. The first twenty-seven pages consist of a retrospective account, written in Paris at the end of June, of Beauvoir's exit from Paris on June 9, shortly before the Germans entered the city; her stay at La Pouèze, near Le Mans, with her and Sartre's friend Mme Morel; and her return to the capital after the armistice, first in a car with other returning Parisians and then, after the car ran out of gas, in a German truck. The trip back to Paris took two days: "Rarely have I spent more interesting and heady days [*jours plus intéressants et forts*] than those two"(p. 315). In Le Mans, while they were waiting for gas, she had a chance to look closely at the German soldiers:

> Many were young and looked appealing . . . There were many soldiers all smiling and happy and young and often quite handsome . . . and I could feel what a wonderful adventure it must be for a young German

to find himself in France as a conqueror . . .—it was crushing to see them with their beautiful ambulance wagons, their neat appearance, their confidently polite manners, whereas France was represented by hundreds of fearful and ragged refugees who had only those handsome soldiers to rely on for food, gas, transportation, a remedy to their current misery. (pp. 317–318)

At this point, my attempt at historical empathy begins to fade. I cannot but feel my *difference* from Beauvoir, and judge her. Does she still see only the adventure, is she still finding her days "interesting"? Those "handsome soldiers" she saw in Le Mans, and with whose superiority she clearly identified rather than with the "fearful and ragged French refugees," will soon be rounding up Jews and hunting down Resistants. Has this woman no soul? (I am suddenly reminded of the despicable pharmacist in Marcel Ophuls' film about that period, *The Sorrow and the Pity.* "You understand, one had to look out for oneself," he tells Ophuls with his cynical smile, explaining that his family managed quite well by "not getting involved.")

One thing in her favor: in the middle of the paragraph describing her feelings in Le Mans, she inserts a sentence about the writing present, which I omitted in quoting that paragraph above: "All those [soldiers] I see right now in Paris with their cameras and rosy faces look like such imbeciles that I hesitate—but the day before yesterday, at Le Mans, they looked totally different to me and I felt what a wonderful adventure . . ." At least she is no longer charmed by them. But my discomfort persists: what if the German soldiers in Paris had looked intelligent?

The rest of this notebook produces a mixed effect. Life starts again, with Sorokine and other friends. She buys a bicycle and proudly learns to ride it, using it to get to the *lycée* and to take pleasure rides. Things still "interest" her—but she no longer identifies with the German soldiers. She even notes scornfully, on July 2: "The newspapers are loathsome, exhorting the French to be moral, to be more like the Germans, etc." (p. 334). On July 11, listening to the radio, she hears good music—but it is interspersed with dreadful German homilies (vilifying foreigners and Jews, praising work, and so on). She has begun seriously reading Hegel at the

Bibliothèque Nationale, and finds that comforting—it reminds her of her student days. Around this time, she writes a letter to Sartre (he was in a military prison camp in southern France) in which she finally returns to the question of universals and the individual, left in abeyance since January:

> I remember a conversation at the "Louis XV," where we discussed whether we thought of ourselves in terms of the limits of a human life, and wondered whether it made any sense to speak from the point of view of universal life . . . It seemed to us then that that point of view reduced everything to a kind of absurd indifference. But I no longer believe that: in the end, that point of view is *real* and the joint influence of Hegel and what's happening now [*les événements*] are making me adopt from the inside, for the first time in my life, that attitude close to Spinozism which had always been so foreign to me. (p. 182)

The joint influence of Hegel and "les événements." Does the war seem real to her at last?

The notebook for this period stops on July 19, interrupted after the dateline as if she could not bear to continue. The next notebook begins on September 20: "This is a letter I am beginning for you—maybe you'll receive it in a year" (p. 355). She doesn't know where Sartre is, where she can write to him. He has been transferred to a prison camp in Germany, but she doesn't know that yet. Finally, she is beginning to suffer. The second entry, quite short, is dated October 1, a big gap: "My sweet darling—I haven't kept up this little notebook—I didn't have the morale—each time I stop to speak to you, I begin to cry. I'm moody [*instable*], with a great many moments of anguish and agitation. And even when I'm calm, when a few days pass that feel rich and peaceful, it's always against a background of nothingness (*néant*); it's soul-wrenching. As if my whole life were between parentheses" (p. 357). On October 17 she is able to start writing to him again for real, to Germany, and regains some of her optimism: "All is going very well for me." October 18: "People, concerts, a lot of work—you see, it's an honest life."[15] Not a word, to Sartre or in her diary, about having signed the Vichy oath; it evidently caused no crisis of conscience.

Still, something is not quite right. Her diary remains fragmentary, with rare entries: November, January. On January 9, 1941, she reads the current issue of the literary journal *La Nouvelle Revue Française* (the first one to appear since the Occupation, under the new collaborationist editorship of Pierre Drieu La Rochelle) and finds it "ridicule et odieux"; she thinks about how fascism reduces the human to its animal, biological aspect, and realizes that since she, too, is human, "it's really *I* who am involved [*en jeu*]. I feel that to the point of anguish." She no longer derives comfort from Hegel, from "that historical infinite in which Hegel optimistically dilutes everything. Anguish . . . solitude, as complete as in the face of death. Last year, I was still with Sartre—now I live in a world in which Sartre is absent, muzzled. Psychologically, I was stupidly proud sometimes to feel myself so solid and to manage so well. But today, those superficial defenses are no longer a help. I feel dazed" (pp. 361–362). Then, suddenly, a metaphor:

> To make oneself an ant among ants, or a free consciousness before others. A *metaphysical* solidarity that is a new discovery for me, I who was a solipsist. I cannot be a consciousness, a mind, among ants. I realize in what ways our antihumanism fell short. To admire man as a given [as in the "classic" humanism she and Sartre scorned] is stupid; but there is no other reality than human reality—all values are founded on it. And it's the "that toward which it transcends itself" which has always moved us and which orients our individual destiny, each one of us. (p. 362)

Reading this passage on one of the last pages of the *Journal de guerre,* my pulse quickens: What is happening here? Deprived of Sartre's presence, alone in front of death, she seems to be discovering, *for the first time,* the historical and ethical existence of others. Sartre had never been an "other" for her; he had been her second self. With him, she could still be a solipsist, living a "solipsisme à deux." To see the other (not Sartre, but a "real" other) no longer as a consciousness to be annihilated (recall the epigraph, from Hegel, placed at the head of *She Came To Stay:* "Each consciousness seeks the death of the other"), but as "that toward which human reality transcends itself," is nothing less than a major philosophical leap—one that, by an extraordinary coincidence, Sartre was making at the same time in his German stalag. "His experience as a prisoner marked him deeply: it taught him solidarity," wrote Beauvoir about him in *The Force of Circumstance*.[16]

But she, too, discovered solidarity, in her own way, while he was in prison. January 21, 1941: "How short-sighted my old idea of happiness seems to me! It dominated ten years of my life, but I think I'm almost completely through with it . . . My novel [*She Came To Stay*]. Rushing to finish it. Rests on a philosophical position that is no longer mine. The next one will be about the *situation of the individual,* its ethical significance and its relation to the social" (p. 363). Eight days later: "I would like my next novel to illustrate the relation to others in its existential complexity. It's a fine subject. *To suppress* the consciousness of the other is a bit puerile. The problem attains the social, etc., but it must exist starting from an individual case. I must find a relationship of subject-object, probably an unrequited love, simply" (p. 365). With that entry, the *Journal* proper ends, followed by a few pages of notes devoted to the new novel she is planning.[17] It is a matter of finding the right "individual case" to illustrate her point:

> Possible scene: the exodus [the flight of refugees in June 1940], seen through the woman's eyes, with the temptation to give up on herself; she would have lost her love at that point, feeling injured. And then she recovers, maintains her value as an individual—a destiny linked to that of the world. Throws herself into antifascist activity. (But what an ungrateful task, to deal with the social, and how to avoid the appearance of preaching?) [*Comment éviter que ça ne fasse édifiant et moralisateur?*] (p. 368)

Fiction

The Blood of Others, finished in the spring of 1943, had to wait until 1945 to be published because of its antifascist theme. Read as a "novel of the Resistance," it was an immediate and huge success. Later, Beauvoir judged it harshly, accepting Maurice Blanchot's assessment that it was too illustrative, too much of a *roman à thèse.* (Her discomfort was already indicated by the parenthetical remark about "preaching" I quoted above.) The *thèse* it illustrates, she explains in *The Prime of Life,* is not so much political as existential:

the main subject is not the Resistance, but the relation of individuals linked by free choice in a common project.[18]

Still, the public of 1945 was not wrong to see in *The Blood of Others* a novel about the Resistance. The hero, Jean Blomart, is a bourgeois who has joined the working class and become a union organizer. Once the war breaks out, his problem is whether to engage as a leader in terrorist activities against the Nazis, knowing that his actions will inevitably cause the death both of his own comrades and of innocent civilians whom the Nazis will kill in retaliation. Whence the title of the book, indicating Blomart's ethical dilemma. The more interesting protagonist of this novel, however, especially in my present perspective, is Hélène, the young woman who falls in love with Jean before the war and manages, by the sheer force of her own love, to convince him that he "should" marry her. (The war breaks out before they can get married.)

For the greater part of the story, Hélène recalls the two main female characters of *She Came To Stay:* her youthfulness and her unabashed pursuit of the man she loves are traits she shares with Xavière; with Françoise, the heroine of *She Came to Stay,* she shares a determination to find individual happiness and to let nothing stop her, certainly not any ethical considerations about community or solidarity. Hélène is a solipsist, and unashamed of it. Even after the war breaks out, she does not change: after Jean is mobilized, and contrary to his express wishes, she manages to take advantage of his family connections and have him transferred to a "safe" job in Paris. When Jean tries to dissuade her by evoking his solidarity with his buddies, "les copains," she answers "with desperation": "I don't give a damn about the others . . . I don't owe anything to anybody . . . I'll kill myself if you die, and I don't want to die."[19] His response is to break off with her and reenlist as a soldier.

Clearly, Beauvoir put a lot of herself into Hélène (one example among many: in several places in the *Journal,* Beauvoir mentions that she will not continue living if Sartre is killed). But the really interesting thing is what she left out, or on the contrary exaggerated; and now that we have the *Journal de guerre* and the letters to Sartre, it is possible to offer some hypotheses about that—hypotheses of more than merely anecdotal interest.

The chief thing Beauvoir left out is intellect, or more exactly intellectualism. Hélène is not an intellectual; she is not interested in ideas and she does not write. She is the manager of a candy store who paints and draws in her spare time (perhaps an allusion to Beauvoir's sister, an artist whose name is also Hélène). Her chief preoccupation is her love for Jean, who provides her with a sense of purpose and being. Although Hélène is not a full-fledged version of "the woman in love" as painted in *The Second Sex*—a figure Beauvoir found both fascinating and repulsive—she comes close to it.

If Beauvoir deprived Hélène of her own intellectual drive, she compensated in other ways. The most important of these is that in the end Hélène not only discovers her solidarity with other human beings, including persecuted Jews, but becomes an active member of the Resistance. Her change is shown as occurring gradually, in stages: first, during the exodus and then the return to Paris, she gives up her seat in the car to a woman and her child while she herself finds a place in a German truck (Beauvoir did no such thing—she abandoned the car out of impatience, since they had run out of gas). Then, even though she has the chance to advance her career as a designer and become rich by doing business in Germany, she changes her mind at the last minute and decides to remain with her fellow countrymen. Finally, one day when her Jewish friend Yvonne is about to be arrested by the Vichy police, she helps her escape. That same day, crossing the Place de la Contrescarpe, she sees some parked police buses and women and children being herded toward them. One of the policemen forcibly separates a little girl from her mother, who cries out after her as Hélène stands by, horrified and helpless. No date is given for this incident, but "la rafle du Vél d'hiv" of July 16, 1942, in which thousands of Jews were rounded up and turned over to the Nazis, seems to be the historical reference.

This is the experience which definitively tips the balance for Hélène. "I was watching History pass by! It was my story [*mon histoire*]. All of this is happening to me" (p. 215). (I think here of Beauvoir's journal entry of January 1941: "it's really *I* who am involved.") Hélène goes to find Jean, asking for his help in getting Yvonne to safety and offering to join his group. Beauvoir makes a point of emphasizing, here, that love is no longer the motive for

Hélène's actions—she earns Jean's real love this time, but it is a "bonus." What is foremost is their common action of resistance.

Shall we call this a compensatory fantasy on Beauvoir's part—she who signed the Vichy oath in 1940 with so few qualms that she didn't even bother to mention it in her diary? She who never, in fact, participated in any Resistance activity during the war and who accepted, a few months after finishing *The Blood of Others,* to work for the German-controlled Radio-Paris? Perhaps. It is worth emphasizing, then, that Hélène pays for her heroism and her personal fulfillment with her life—indeed, from the opening page of the novel she is on her deathbed. The story is told entirely in flashbacks, as Jean sits by her bedside. On the previous night's mission, she was shot by the Nazis; in the morning, as the novel ends, she dies.

Was this ending Beauvoir's way of settling the score with her own compensatory fantasy? One of her last notes for the novel in 1941 reads: "(Something moralizing and asshole-ish [*con*] about this subject.)"[20] If her heroine went so far in her sense of solidarity with others as to actually risk her life, she only got what she asked for. As for Beauvoir, she writes to Sartre from the Alps, where she is on a skiing vacation with "le petit Bost" in January 1944:

> Here I am, sore all over and very happy. I've already got a long day [of skiing] behind me and I had a fantastic time. I'll tell you all about it in order. First, on Monday I went to the radio station . . .—it was a lot of fun to see a program [being made], and what's especially interesting to me is that Jacques Armand offered me a job as a technical producer [*metteuse en ondes*]. He'll teach me the job, and after that I'll record my programs myself. It must pay quite well, and if it takes a lot of time I'll leave more of the other work [gathering the material] to Bost.[21]

Curious, isn't it? She told Deirdre Bair that her job consisted exclusively of gathering material, not actually working at the radio station. In *The Prime of Life,* she had written: "The writers in our circle had tacitly adopted certain rules. One must not write in the newspapers and magazines of the Occupied Zone, nor speak on Radio-Paris."[22] Less than twenty pages after this passage, when she has to deal with the unpleasant subject of her dismissal from the *lycée,* she writes: "My only problem was, how to earn a living. I don't know by what connection I got a job as 'metteuse en ondes' at the national radio; I have already said that, according to our code, it was all right to work there: everything depended on what one did."[23] In fact, she had not said earlier that "it was all right to work there"; she had said that it was *not* all right to speak on the air. Technically, she did not speak on the air: the job of *metteuse en ondes* evidently involved everything *but* speaking on the air. Here is a case of Beauvoir's casuistry, if ever there was one. Her letter to Sartre speaks of "mes émissions"—"my programs" or "my broadcasts." The idea for the program was hers ("a colorless program: reconstitutions, spoken, sung, and with sound effects, of ancient festivals from the Middle Ages to our own day");[24] presumably, her name was mentioned on the air, but it was not her voice that mentioned it. Could it be that she referred to "radio nationale" in the second passage instead of "Radio-Paris" so as to make the casuistry less glaring?

Gender Identity and Historical Experience

We have come full circle, back to the personal issues raised by my reading and rereading of Beauvoir. But in fact we have never left them, for this whole essay has been an attempt to give an account of (and to account, at least in part, for) the conflicting responses elicited in me by that experience. How does one think again about an author who has played a significant role in one's life? Beauvoir's private writings not only cast a new light on her other works, especially on her autobiography, which turns out so obviously to have been "edited" (as if we didn't know that all aubobiographies are public self-portraits, carefully posed). They have also forced me to consider from a personal perspective the importance of differences, rather than similarities, among individuals belonging to the same broad category. Potentially, every genuine reading experience is a life-changing encounter, even though few individual books can be said to have truly transformed one's life. The transforming effects are cumulative, each new work contributing its own small parcel. Reading Beauvoir's war diaries, rereading some of her other works, I find myself confronting issues of personal identity: What really determines the shape and texture of a life?

For a long time, feminists assumed that gender is by far the most important determining factor in a person's life. This may in fact be true, in a general way; and as a founding assumption, it can lead to a positive sense of solidarity among women, over and above other divisions. But as the recent emphasis on differences, both in feminist thought and in cultural theorizing in general, has made clear, such an assumption can also lead to a mythical universalism—or, in more hostile terms, to the hegemony of a single dominant group which seeks, even if unconsciously, to assimilate all others. Many white middle-class feminists in the United States have learned, over the past few years, that the designation of their race and class can serve as a marker of separation and even, occasionally, of hostility and conflict in their relation to other women, even though they may all consider themselves feminists.[25] As Joan Scott has remarked, "it becomes clear that in certain circumstances gender is far less central than race, ethnicity, or class in the construction of personal identity."[26] (It may not be merely coincidental that this observation occurs à propos of the war diaries of Anne Frank and Ettie Hillesum, two young Jewish women who did not survive the war.) The issue for feminist theorists is not only methodological or analytic; it is also, in a very real and sometimes painful sense, personal and existential. If gender is a category that unites women, will the others have the effect of driving them apart? On an even more general level, one can ask the same question about the category "human being." Is it, like its onetime synonym, "man," a mythologizing universal that elides significant differences and their political consequences? That argument has been made more than once, and persuasively. Yet in some circumstances, for example in cases of torture and other violations of what are correctly called "human rights," one wants to affirm the general category.

Although the question about the primacy of gender has surfaced only recently *within* feminism, it was for a long time thrown *at* feminism by orthodox Marxists. Beauvoir refused to call herself a feminist for a long time because she believed that gender as an analytic category was less central than class. As she explained to Alice Schwarzer in 1972:

> At the end of *The Second Sex* I said that I was not a feminist because
> I believed that the problems of women would resolve themselves

automatically in the context of socialist development. By feminist, I meant fighting on specifically feminine issues independently of the class struggle . . . I am a feminist today, because I realized that we must fight for the situation of women, here and now, before our dreams of socialism come true.[27]

By contrast, whether because of another change of mind or because she considered History as transcending both class and gender, in 1984 Beauvoir insisted that certain collective experiences took precedence over gender in the patterning of a life. When asked, by Hélène Wenzel, whether she found that "there are well-marked stages in a woman's life that are different from those in a man's," Beauvoir answered: "No, I don't think so. I don't think it's due to sex, it's due obviously to politics, events; . . . the Resistance, Liberation, the war in Algeria . . . That's what marked the big epochs in our lives, it's the historical events, the historical involvements one has in these larger events. It's much more important than any other kind of difference."[28]

This statement, especially when read after the *Journal de guerre* and its associated texts, elicits a whole series of responses. Surely, the emphatic "No" is wrong. There *are* well-marked stages in a woman's life that are different from a man's. She is right about the importance of collective events. But collective events are experienced in very different ways, depending on who one is. Her insistence on the shared experience of "Resistance, Liberation" among French people is dishonest, for it elides the differences in the way those events were experienced, not only between Jews and non-Jews but between, say, women intellectuals who actively participated in the Resistance and those who did not.[29] On the other hand, to deny a certain bedrock of shared historical experience leads to ever greater fragmentation and to its own kind of dishonesty. How does one define exactly who one is? Where do the significant differences begin, or end?

More questions than answers, as I conclude these reflections. Still, of one thing I am certain. It took courage and a gritty honesty for Beauvoir to authorize the publication, even posthumously, of writings that she surely knew would cast her in a less than heroic light. There is its own kind of heroism in daring to reveal one's human weaknesses and imperfections. Beauvoir's wartime writings contain no revelations nearly as troubling as those that have come to light about other intellectual heroes like Martin Heidegger or Paul de Man. Maybe it was because her "imperfections" were relatively minor that she found it easier to save for publication the private writings that document them. (Heidegger and de Man, significantly, kept silent to the end, and it does not appear that they left behind any diaries for posthumous publication.) Still, Beauvoir made a choice that could not have been a simple or easy one. She could have tossed these manuscripts into the fire. Without glossing over her failings or eliding our differences, as a reader I cannot but feel grateful for her generosity.

WAR MEMORIES: ON AUTOBIOGRAPHICAL READING

11

A few years ago, I realized with a jolt that I belong to a diminishing segment of the world's population: men and women who have personal memories of the Second World War in Europe. I don't have many, since I was only five years old when the war ended. But I have some, particularly from the last year of the war. Whereas for friends who are only a few years younger than I, the war is at best a transmitted memory, for me it is a lived one.

Does this fact make a difference in the way I read other people's accounts of wartime experiences? Do I read them differently from, say, someone similar to me in temperament but born in the United States around 1950, or even 1945? I don't know. What I do know is this: I read certain kinds of war memories with a breathless attention few other kinds of writing elicit in me, and that has no real correlation with the "literary quality" of the writing; the war memories that most affect me are those in which I recognize aspects of my own; and finally, reading other people's war memories has become indissociable, for me, from the desire (and recently, the act) of writing my own.

"All individuals have at least one book in

I have no childhood memories.
—Georges Perec, *W ou le souvenir d'enfance*

Write then, I must.
—Saul Friedländer, *When Memory Comes*

them: their autobiography." Among people I know—writers, academics—that is a truism: call it the autobiographical imperative, whether acted on or not. The idea I want to pursue here is that the autobiographical imperative applies not only to writing about one's life but to reading about it; reading *for* it; reading, perhaps, *in order to* write about it. That is what I call autobiographical reading, or more emphatically, "strong" autobiographical reading.

"Strong," because in one sense the notion of autobiographical reading is banal and familiar. We all project ourselves into what we read, especially into narrative. Just as it has been claimed that all writing, even the driest of critical studies, is in some way autobiographical, so it can be claimed that all reading is. Another truism—but insofar as it is only that, a very wide generality, the observation loses its interest. What makes it interesting is its enactment in, and implications for, specific cases. One might say, then, that "strong" applies not only to a particular kind of autobiographical reading, but to a particular kind of account of such reading. To explore this double possibility, I want to discuss the autobiographical reading of war memories, using first the case of an other, then my own.

An Exemplary Case: Wiesel's *Day*

"I never spoke about it; I never made notes; I only read. I read every single book that appeared on the Holocaust. I still do. I'm a voracious reader of Holocaust Literature and World War II Literature. I still want to understand what happened." The person speaking here is Elie Wiesel, around 1974.[1] By then he was internationally known and celebrated, the author of more than a dozen books translated into many languages. The time he is speaking about, however, is the ten-year period 1945–1955, the time between his liberation from the Buchenwald concentration camp and the writing of his autobiographical account of the last year of the war. *Night (La Nuit)*, first written in Yiddish in 1955 and published in Argentina in 1956, appeared in French in 1958. Over the next decade, Wiesel published eleven books—more than one per year. He has stated that only *Night* is autobiographical; yet "all the stories are one story . . . [built] in concentric circles. The center is the same and is in *Night*. What happened during that Night I'm afraid will not be revealed."[2]

So much writing, at whose heart is an absence. Will "what happened during that Night" not be revealed because the author is willfully withholding it from his reader? Or because he himself is in the position of a reader confronted with a text he does not understand—a text that, for precisely that reason, he must continue to read and to write over and over? Probably it is a little of both. One cannot discount the cynicism, or more exactly the lack of hope in being understood, that might prevent a witness from revealing all he knows. In his third book, *Day* (*Le Jour,* 1961), which despite its hopeful title strikes me as extremely dark and despairing, Wiesel invents a scene in which the narrator, Eliezer, a survivor of Auschwitz, decides very consciously *not* to tell what he knows. He realizes that his listener, although insistent in asking him the right question ("Answer me! Why don't you want to live? Why?"), would not be able to bear hearing the answer: "I felt like telling him: go. Paul Russell, you are a straightforward and courageous man. Your duty is to leave me. Don't ask me to talk. Don't try to know . . . The heroes of my legends are cruel and without pity. They are capable of strangling you."[3] In the end, when his listener—the doctor who operated on him after an accident and saved his life—persists with his questioning, Eliezer lies to him: "I began to persuade him he was wrong so he would go away, so he would leave me alone. Of course I wanted to live. Obviously I wanted to live, create, do lasting things." The doctor leaves, satisfied: "I admit my mistake. I'm glad. Really." Eliezer mockingly echoes him: "I too. I was glad to have convinced him. Really" (pp. 273–274).

This example of narrative withholding is complicated, of course, by the fact that the reader is given more information than the well-meaning doctor, who remains in ignorance. But even while sharing the narrator's inner thoughts, the reader receives no revelation—unless it be that for Eliezer there can be neither a forgetting of the past nor a final, redemptive telling of it. There can only be retellings, each one a failure in its own way. "In all of my books, I think, I indicate the impossibility of communicating a story," Wiesel states in one of his conversatons with Harry James Cargas (p. 85). *Day* can be read as an extended parable, or set of parables, of just that impossibility. Besides the scene with the doctor, there are at least three other scenes of failed communication about "what happened during that Night," including one in which the narrator himself becomes the unwilling listener of another victim's story. When confronted with the horror of what a young woman who has invited him to her room endured as a twelve-year-old child prostitute in Auschwitz ("'Did you ever sleep with a twelve-year-old woman?' she asked me"—p. 290), Eliezer runs away. Her story, like his, has the power to strangle its listeners: "I listened . . . my clenched fingers were like a vise around my throat" (p. 289). After he runs away from her, incapable of listening to one more word, he realizes that his hands are still clutching his throat.

The most significant thing about this failed encounter is that even though he, too, was at Auschwitz, and even though the young woman's name, Sarah, is that of his dead mother who perished there, Eliezer is unable to respond adequately to her story. "You are a saint. A saint: that's what you are," he tells her, provoking her sarcastic laughter (p. 293). Just how inadequate this response is is clear to the reader who remembers a previous scene (told earlier, though occurring later in the fictional time) where a young American woman with no experience of the camps calls Eliezer a saint, provoking *his* sarcastic laughter. Unlike him as listener, she stays after hearing his story and even falls in love with him. But their communication fails, too, in the end, because she demands that he "forget the past" and think only of their love. The day after he promises her to do just that, Eliezer purposely steps in front of an onrushing taxi. He survives, but does not forget the past. Quite the contrary: "I think if I were able to forget I would hate myself. Our stay there planted time bombs within us. From time to time one of them explodes . . . It's inevitable. Anyone who has been there has brought back some of humanity's madness" (p. 303).

By its repeated stagings of "the impossibility of communicating [the] story," *Day* paradoxically demonstrates, at the same time, the absolute necessity, for the survivors, of telling their story. Wiesel speaks of the "obsession to tell the tale,"[4] which according to him is the obsession of all those who remained alive—even though, as he shows in *Day*, this obsession may be accompanied by the equally strong feeling that any attempt to communicate their experience will ultimately fail. The earliest of the narrative stagings in *Day* is instructive in that regard. Recounted in a flashback that interrupts the scene where Eliezer tells his story to the American woman, Kathleen, this is literally the "primal scene" of narration: Standing with a stranger on the deck of a ship in the middle of the ocean, Eliezer, who has been thinking of throwing himself into the water, listens as the stranger tells him about a similar incident in his own life. Then, suddenly, he too begins to tell his story: "I told him what I had never told anyone. My childhood, my mystic dreams, my religious passions, my memories of German concentration camps, my belief that I was now just a messenger of the dead among the living" (p. 243). The stranger listens to Eliezer's narrative in complete silence, asking for neither explanations nor clarifications; then, just before dawn, he speaks: "'You must know this,' he finally said. 'I think I'm going to hate you'" (p. 244).

I call this the primal scene of narration not only because it is the first such scene in the fictional time of the novel, and not only because we are told that it is the first time Eliezer tells the story to anyone, but because it clearly refers back to Wiesel's own first work, the autobiographical narrative of *Night*. We don't actually hear what Eliezer tells the stranger, but its summary ("my childhood, my mystic dreams," and so on) corresponds almost exactly to the story told in *Night*. The fact that the listener never interrupts but listens in silence suggests that he could also figure as a reader. The paradox is this: insofar as the communication of the story is successful, it compels the listener/reader to hear it to the end, but also makes him hate the one who tells it, and thereby makes further communication impossible. Indeed, after listening to Eliezer's story, the stranger flees; and although Eliezer returns to the deck several more times in an effort to find him, he never sees him again.

Far from fulfilling its apparent promise of an edifying tale (although it has been read as such by some),[5] *Day* exemplifies what Alvin Rosenfeld has called the "revisionary and antithetical nature of so much of Holocaust writing, which not only mimics and parodies but finally refutes and rejects its direct literary antecedents."[6] Whereas the sequence of titles, *Night, Dawn* (*L'Aube*, 1960), *Day* (in some countries, they have been published in a single volume), seems to promise an edifying upward arc, the actual movement in this trilogy is from night to a day whose most salient characteristic is that it is bearable only to the extent it refuses to put the night behind it.

"I never spoke about it; I never made notes; I only read. I read every single book that appeared on the Holocaust." Before writing about his own experience, Wiesel waited ten years, during which he read. It would seem that the obsession to tell the tale is doubled by the obsession to read the tale. His, then, is an exemplary case of "strong" autobiographical reading.

Stories That Could Have Been My Own

My own case is more modest, but may also offer some insights; for I, too, am an avid reader of a certain kind of Holocaust literature.

Whose writings, whose memories elicit my most breathless attention? Those of concentration camp survivors, whether Jewish or not—ranging in literary artistry from Primo Levi or Charlotte Delbo (or Elie Wiesel, in *Night*), to Lise Lesèvre, whose only published work so far as I am aware is the memoir she published a few years ago, at age eighty-six;[7] and those of European Jews who were children during the war. Necessarily, very few of the latter are camp survivors, and none were very young at the time, because all young children—say, under ten years old—who were deported were immediately sent to their deaths, whether alone or with their mothers.[8]

So far as autobiographical reading is concerned, there is a discrepancy here—for although I was a very young child during the war, neither I nor my immediate family (father, mother, aunts, uncles, grandparents) experienced the camps. The memories of camp survivors are as incommensurable with my memories or experience as with those of any other reader, contemporary or not, who did not experience the camps. This is not, therefore, autobiographical reading in the most literal (or "strongest") sense of the term. But I think it would be a mistake to insist on a narrowly construed, strictly experience-based self-definition as the basis of autobiographical reading. To recognize aspects of one's own life-story in another's is no doubt easier for one who has undergone some of the same experiences, in the same time and place; but it would be far too restrictive, and wrong-headed, to suggest that *only* one who has undergone a certain experience can respond to another's story, and to its telling, "properly"—or, in my terms, autobiographically. For one thing, no individual's experience of an event, even of the same event, is fully identical to another's; even in such a case, it requires an imaginative leap to read the other's story "as if it were one's own." The willingness or ability to make that imaginative leap may be stronger in one who has firsthand experience of the time and place; but paradoxically, the closeness to the experience may also provoke a reverse reaction, a refusal to read autobiographically, or to read at all (think of Eliezer's reaction to the story of the girl who had been at Auschwitz). Such refusal is not unusual among Holocaust survivors, and is the other side of the compulsion to read: the avoidance of reading.[9] I will content myself with the somewhat lame conclusion, therefore, that "it all depends": the ways of the imagination and its relation to the experience of self are too complicated for categorical pronouncements.

My own reading of the memories of camp survivors, independently of any appreciation for the author's style or depth of vision, is shamelessly, unsophisticatedly, referential: What happened? When? Where? How did it feel? The more straightforward the telling, the more hooked I am. I am unable to read *novels* about the camps—what I want, and need, are events that are remembered, even if distorted or blurred. In this domain, I am a firm believer in Philippe Lejeune's "autobiographical pact"—which does not mean that I believe everything remembered is "objectively true."[10] I assess the quality of my response not only by its breathlessness, but also by what makes me cry. In Lise Lesèvre's book, which I find astonishingly "upbeat" for such a work, I cried in two places: first when she describes meeting her fifteen-year-old son in the courtyard of the Montluc prison, both of them about to board the train that will take him to his death: "Suddenly, my Jean-Pierre appears in a group. He looks very tall to me, very pale, very thin seen thus in broad daylight. I rush toward him: the soldiers bar the way with guns. I break through the barricade and I'm in the arms of that big boy. The soldiers try to separate us, but without brutality. The trucks arrive, it's all push and shove. I lose Jean-Pierre"[11] (p. 75). The second place was at the very end, when she arrives at the Hotel Lutetia in May 1945 with other deportees and is met by her sole surviving family member, her older son Georges: "Soon, a group of *maquisards* [Resistance fighters] makes its joyful entry. They race toward me: Georges arrives the first. What joy! I must have lost consciousness for some time. The first, Georges! And the last as well. I found that out a few weeks later" (p. 153). The fact that I myself am the mother of two sons, one of whom just turned fifteen and is a "big boy," does not escape me as I think about this.

Charlotte Delbo, a survivor of Auschwitz who wrote several books about her experience (like Lise Lesèvre, she was not Jewish and was deported as a member of the Resistance), suggests an important distinction between remembering and recounting past events from "deep memory, the memory of the senses," and remembering from "external memory, the memory of thought."[12] Readers of Proust may be reminded of his distinction between "voluntary" memory, which recalls the past only partially, distanced by rational ordering, and "involuntary" memory, which comes unbidden and renders the past in all its richness of sensory detail, all its pleasure and pain. Possibly, the "upbeat" quality of Lise Lesèvre's book may be due to its having been written chiefly from "external memory." (I would say the same about another recent war memoir, Lucie Aubrac's triumphal account of "outwitting the Gestapo," *Ils partiront dans l'ivresse.*)[13] Yet Lesèvre's book made me cry. Did I cry when reading Charlotte Delbo's first book about Auschwitz, *Aucun de nous ne reviendra?*[14] I don't think so, even though Delbo is a true writer who succeeds in recreating Auschwitz in its full horror, from "deep memory." My crying has nothing to do with the quality of the writing or with my ultimate literary experience of the work, which can be very powerful without causing tears; rather, it has to do with its autobiographical resonance. In Lesèvre's book, the resonance was with/to my life as a mother; in *Night,* I cried when reading Wiesel's description of his father's death in Buchenwald, during the last days before liberation. There the resonance was with/to my life as a daughter whose father died young—my father, having survived the war, died fourteen years later of a heart attack at age forty-nine. Note that gender is not the most relevant category here; the loss of a father affects sons and daughters if not identically, no doubt equally deeply.

But I want to come, finally, to the kind of autobiographical reading that is most intimately linked, as prelude or as accompaniment, to autobiographical writing. In my case, it is reading the war memories of Jews who were young children in Europe during the war. As before, the question of literary quality (or perhaps I should say literary self-consciousness, crafting, complexity) plays only a secondary role in my response to these works, which range from Georges Perec's highly crafted *W ou le souvenir d'enfance* (1975), recognized by critics as one of that great writer's most important books, through Saul Friedländer's only "literary" work (besides his numerous publications as a historian), *When Memory Comes* (*Quand vient le souvenir*, 1978), to the short reminiscences written by the psychoanalyst Claudine Vegh in the voices of the fifteen men and women to whose recollections she listened, *I Didn't Say Goodbye* (*Je ne lui ai pas dit au revoir*, 1979). All of these narratives, written many years after the events they tell, are narratives of loss—and, as the other side of loss if you survive it, of autonomy and self-reliance. Perec, born in 1936, lost his father to the French army in 1940 and his mother to the Nazis in 1942; Friedländer, born in 1932, said a wrenching good-bye to his parents, Czech refugees living in France, when he was ten years old, and never saw them again. The men and women Claudine Vegh listened to (for a "mémoire de psychiatrie" at the end of her medical training) were all, like herself—she includes her own reminiscence in the book—children who lost at least one parent, and in two cases their whole family, to deportation. I read these books for the first time years ago, usually at one sitting (the "breathlessness test"). I reread them all in preparing to write this essay: their effect has not worn off. I still cry in places, which turn out upon reflection to be exactly the places I would expect, given who I am.

What exactly am I looking for, and finding, in these works? I did not lose a parent during the war—yet I recognize the stories all too well. They could have been my own.

Luck

"The arrival at A. There were many buses . . . the children declared as French must hold a green slip of paper (I still don't understand why I was declared as French, and my brothers and sisters who were much younger, were not). We are separated."[15] This is Robert, in *I Didn't Say Goodbye*—the only surviving member of his family. They were rounded up by French gendarmes in 1942 in the Dordogne, southwestern France, where they were hiding. His father, mother, sister, and two brothers were deported and did not return; he was left behind. Spared.

Here is Saul (at that time, still Paul) Friedländer, sent by his parents to a summer camp for Jewish children in the Massif Central in July 1942: "A terrible din woke us up about two or three o'clock the next morning . . . Downstairs in the entrance hall gendarmes in helmets were bustling about . . . Someone read out a list: those whose names were called had to get dressed immediately . . . All the children over ten were being taken away."[16] Paul was just ten. Lucky. And here is Georges Perec, newly baptized in 1942, in his boarding school run by nuns in a small town near Grenoble: "Once, the Germans came to the school. It was one morning. From very far away, we saw two of them—officers—crossing the courtyard accompanied by the principals. We went to class as usual, but we didn't see them again."[17]

The other day, I came across an astonishing statistic; literally, it dumbfounded me. Deborah Dwork, in her study of Jewish children in Nazi Europe, writes: "Only eleven percent of Jewish children alive at the beginning of the war survived to its conclusion . . . The very fact that they survived at all makes them exceptions to the general rule of death. There is absolutely no evidence to indicate that survival was due to anything more—or anything less—than luck and fortuitous circumstances."[18] I am part of the lucky ninth. I am especially lucky, since my parents, too, survived.

Separation/Self-Reliance

"My mother accompanied me to the gare de Lyon. I was six years old. She entrusted me to a Red Cross convoy that was leaving for Grenoble, in the Free Zone. She bought me a picture magazine, a Charlie Chaplin, whose cover showed Charlie with his cane, his hat, his shoes, his small mustache, jumping with a parachute" (p. 76). For years, Perec remembered himself in this scene—the last time he saw his mother—with his arm in a sling; yet his aunts, who survived and remember, assure him that both his arms were just fine—no sling. They disagreed, for a while, on the question of whether he wore a hernia brace, but after some checking he determined that he did wear such a brace. He concludes this section as follows: "A triple trait runs through this memory: parachute, arm in a sling, hernia brace: it involves suspension, support, prosthesis almost. In order to be, you had to be propped. Sixteen years later, in 1958, when the haphazard fate of military service made me into a short-lived parachutist, I was able to read, at the very instant of jumping, the decoded text of that memory: I was thrown into the void; all the threads were broken; I was falling, alone and without support." Free-fall. Then the parachute opened: "The corolla unfolded, a fragile but sure prop before the mastered fall" (p. 77).

Separation, a feeling of absolute abandonment, followed by mastery: two sides of a single, terrifying experience. In order to be, you had to be propped. When the external prop disappears, one either sinks . . . or not. All of these children managed not to sink—at a price, however. "I was ten when they were deported; I think it's my mother's absence that has marked me most, even more than the deportation . . . I feel that I have struggled so much during my life, and now I don't even understand the meaning of that struggle. It's as though there is an immense vacuum around me, a vacuum which, in spite of all my efforts, I cannot fill" (Vegh, p. 146–147). This is Colette, who lost her whole family. When she spoke these words, she was married, the mother of four children; a successful professional, like all the other people who told Claudine Vegh their story. Like Saul Friedländer, who writes about his experiences as a young man: "since I could not forget the facts, I made up my mind to view everything with indifference; every sort of resonance within me was stifled" (p. 102).

Self-reliance was bought at the price of numbness, then or later. Sometimes, the lucky ones found their mother in dreams, or heard her from beyond the grave. Ten-year-old Saul Friedländer, ill from his loss and ready to let himself die, dreamed of an incident that had happened four years earlier: On the train carrying his family from Prague to Paris, he had wandered away from their compartment and couldn't find his way back. Then, just when he was totally panicked, he saw his mother: she had gone searching for him. He threw himself into her arms, sobbing (p. 97–98). After that dream, he recovered from his illness. Robert tells a similar story, in *I Didn't Say Goodbye*: "From the train that took them to Auschwitz, my mother dropped a card; it reached me, when I was ill, at the priests' home. There were just a few words: 'Boubele' (a Yiddish endearment), 'look after yourself. We are on our way to Auschwitz. I love you, Mummy.' . . . It was fortunate that I received that message, otherwise I wouldn't have fought to survive" (Vegh, p. 158).

Until very recently, I was unaware that my most characteristic response to a threatened loss—of a friend, a lover, anyone or anything that meant something to me—was to cut loose. *Do it now, before the pain begins. If you do it now, there will be no pain. You don't need this person, this thing. You are self-reliant.*

Split Selves

"I had passed over to Catholicism, body and soul . . . Thus, in my own way, I had become a renegade: though conscious of my origins, I nevertheless felt at ease within a community of those who had nothing but scorn for Jews . . . Paul Friedländer had disappeared; Paul-Henri Ferland was someone else" (pp. 121–122). Different name, different religion, different self. Simulation, dissimulation: How does one know who one is? Friedländer changed his name again after the war, this time voluntarily: he became Saul. Now he wonders: "perhaps I am the one who has become totally different, perhaps I am the one who now preserves, in the very depths of myself, certain disparate, incompatible fragments of existence, cut off from all reality, with no continuity whatsoever, like those shards of steel that survivors of great battles sometimes carry about inside their bodies" (p. 110).

Perec, too, was baptized while he was being hidden by the nuns; for a while he became very devout, finding special comfort in a picture of the Virgin and Child he had hung above his bed.

These are more than the ordinary "split subjects" known to psychoanalysts. These are the walking wounded, the survivors of great battles.

Memory/Delay

"It took me a long, long time to find the way back to my own past," writes Friedländer (p. 102). The first autobiographical section of

Perec's *W ou le souvenir d'enfance* begins with the contradictory sentence: "Je n'ai pas de souvenirs d'enfance," "I have no childhood memories" (p. 13); and all of Claudine Vegh's subjects insist that they are speaking about their war memories for the first time since the war. It is as if the rule of forgetting, and its corollary, the rule of silence, necessary at first in order to make life bearable, had eventually to be broken—but not for many years. Claudine Vegh recounts how, the summer after the war, she was sent to a vacation camp with other Jewish children, many of them orphans, all of whom had suffered the trauma of loss. The rule of the camp, she recalls, was "oblivion at all costs or, at least, never to talk 'about it'" (p. 27). Bruno Bettelheim, in his postface to Vegh's book, focuses on how one remembers after years of willed forgetfulness: "It seems that it requires a distance of twenty years or more, to understand how much a particular tragedy suffered in childhood can transform your whole sense of life."[19] Analysts who are doing current work on trauma have suggested that a "latency" period is part of the very structure of trauma: "events, in so far as they are traumatic, assume their force precisely in their temporal delay."[20] It follows from this that war memories, even more than ordinary memories, are layered: they "bring back" the past, but a past perhaps truly experienced *for the first time* through the prism of the delayed present.

Writing

The road to one's past does not necessarily pass through writing—or, for that matter, reading. But for some people, it does. And for them, it is an absence at the heart of the past that makes writing necessary. It is because his parents have no burial place that Saul Friedländer feels he must write: "Writing . . . does at least preserve a presence" (p. 135). Perec is less optimistic about the link between writing and presence: "I know that what I say is blank, is neutral, is the sign once and for all of an annihilation once and for all . . . I will never rediscover, even in my constant retelling, anything but the last reflection of a word absent to writing, the scandal of their silence and of my silence." Yet the very annihilation that he feels compelled to signal over and over ("what I say is blank") produces something tangible, an affirmation: "I write because we lived together, because I was one among them, a shadow amid their shadows, a body near their body; I write because they left in me their indelible mark, and the trace of it is writing: their memory is dead to writing; writing is the memory of their death and the affirmation of my life" (p. 59).

This kind of writing can only exist layered: the W sections of *W ou le souvenir d'enfance,* constituting a kind of science fiction fantasy, compensate with fiction for the memories annihilated by the disappearance of the mother. The autobiographical sections, alternating with the W sections, string together the memories that remain; but those memories exist and can be told only in a dissociated, fragmentary form, of which the alternation of chapters (always involving interruption, a cutting off) is but one indication: "From then on [after the mother's disappearance], memories exist, . . . but nothing links them together. They are like that noncursive writing, composed of isolated letters incapable of joining with others to form a word, which was my characteristic mode until I was seventeen or eighteen years old" (p. 93).

No smooth linkages, no grand syntheses are possible in this writing; it is fragmentary and incomplete *in its essence.* Claudine Vegh writes her subjects' stories, like her own, with abrupt beginnings and endings, short paragraphs, clipped sentences. Saul Friedländer, although allowing himself a more lyrical, reflective style, nevertheless insists on a certain lack of pattern and completion: "For it is not a matter here of simplifying the image and presenting, in an exemplary mode, the story of a descent and a rising again. Those who have descended never completely rise again."[21]

Toward Autobiography

Those who have descended never completely rise again. Why, then, write? Why tell the tale? With these questions, we come full circle, back to the dilemma, and the paradox, explored by Wiesel in *Day.* But although the double bind of "having to tell, having to fail" belongs most excruciatingly to those whose tales are the most painful, the most unrepresentable, perhaps it is inherent in all autobiographical writing. No one will ever experience my life as I have, no one will ever fully understand my story. Will *I* ever fully understand my story?

A few months ago, I told a friend that I was working on this essay and that I was particularly interested in the memories of Jews who had been children during the war. "Would you like to meet some?" he asked me. "I can put you in touch." He then told me that he belonged to a group which met monthly at the home of different members. Some of the people in the group had been in the camps, others not; some were young children when the war broke out, others already teenagers; some had lost parents, others not. They had come to the United States from Germany, Austria, Poland, Hungary, Belgium, Holland, France—some directly, others via Israel. The group had existed for around nine years. I expressed surprise that such a group existed around Boston without my having heard about it, even though I had lived here for more than ten years. My friend told me to come to the next meeting.

As I walked up the path of the neat suburban home on a May afternoon, carrying my bowl of pasta salad (for the potluck meal following the formal part of the meeting), I asked myself what I had in common with the person I saw ahead of me: an elderly man, short and balding, wearing a short-sleeved open-necked shirt and walking with a slight stoop, who reminded me of the vague friends my mother would introduce me to when I visited her in Miami Beach. Inside, the first person I saw was a woman I had met at graduate student parties in Cambridge in the 1960s and had bumped into once or twice in Harvard Square more recently. When she saw me, her jaw dropped. "What are you doing here?" she asked. "I am like you," I answered. Her surprise was no greater than mine.

As the meeting got underway and I looked around the room, I had to admit to myself that I felt little in common with most of the people there. They appeared to be quite a bit older than I was, and many spoke with heavy accents. They were all "professionals" (as the friend who had invited me had proudly told me), but they still seemed to me to belong to another world. It now occurs to me that two of the women were professors of French—where exactly was my "difference"?

One of the Hungarian women (evidently a long-standing member of the group, for she spoke easily and a lot) reminded me of a favorite aunt from my childhood, my father's sister: besides the unmistakable accent, which signals a Hungarian to me anywhere, in elevators, restaurants, or the most crowded noisy room, this woman had the sparkling humor and the bossy but pleasant manner I had always associated with my aunt, from the time I first knew her when I was a little girl in Budapest. After the meeting ended and we broke up into informal groups around the table laden with food, I spoke to her and discovered she was only a few years older than I. She told me she had spent the last year of the war in one of the special houses set aside for Jews in Budapest, as some other people I knew had done. We spoke in Hungarian, a language I rarely speak, now that most of the people with whom I was used to speaking it—my mother, her sister, her brother, that whole generation of her family—are dead. Later, as I left the house carrying my empty bowl, I wondered whether I would go to the group's next meeting. I'm still not sure, but I think perhaps I will.

Those who feel compelled, at some time in their life, to embark on autobiographical writing do so because they have no choice: they must do it, whatever the consequences. Some, especially blessed, find readers others than themselves, some of whom may in turn one day become writers of their own lives, their own losses. For as may have been clear to you from the start, the only kind of autobiography I find truly essential, to read *or* write—and this, I admit, may be a prejudice on my part—is the kind that tries to recover, through writing, an irrecoverable absence.

MY WAR IN
FOUR
EPISODES

12

Some years back, I returned to Hungary after a thirty-five-year absence. I had left as a child with my parents, crossing on foot into Czecho-slovakia (the Communist government had stopped granting exit visas) in August 1949. I returned with my two sons aged fourteen and seven, as a tourist, in August 1984. I was spending that summer in Paris, doing research at the Bibliothèque Nationale and working on various writing projects. The trip to Hungary, planned for a while, came as a welcome interruption. My children, who were in the countryside with their father, took the train to Paris and the next day we flew to Budapest. As we got off the plane after an ordinary two-hour flight, I realized with a shock that the journey it had taken me thirty-five years to embark on was shorter in actual time than one of my frequent flights from Boston to Miami, which I had been making for years to visit my mother.

A few months earlier it was my mother who had come to visit us, flying north to consult a specialist at Massachusetts General Hospital. She was suffering from an old-age disease, temporal arteritis, for which the only effective medication was cortisone. But the drug was killing her, psychologically if not physically. Her fine, beautiful face had become coarse and bloated, her hair had started falling out, soon her skin would become so thin that the slightest bruise would draw blood and create ugly scabs over her arms and legs. She had always been proud of her good looks; she viewed these changes in her body not as a disease to be coped with but as a death sentence.

The only thing that still cheered her up (later, even that would go) was being around her grandchildren. On that visit in particular, they had a grand time. My older son, in an elated mood, got her to teach him some dirty words in Hungarian, and he and his brother went around the house singing them with glee, mispronouncing all the words. "Csirkeszar, csirkeszar, edd meg csirkeszar." "Chicken shit, chicken shit, go eat chicken shit." My mother, a thing rare for her now, laughed and laughed.

Watching her play Rummi-Kub one night with the boys (she loved the game—it was a version of the gin rummy she and my father had played with friends during summer evenings in Hungary), I suddenly *saw*, as clearly as if projected on a screen, my mother as a young woman, holding my hand as we walked down a boulevard in winter, setting our faces against the wind and playing the Multiplication Game. What's eight times seven? What's seven times four? What's three times nine? The questions came faster and faster, until we were both tripping over our tongues and laughing. How I had loved her, my beautiful mother who knew how to play!

I decided before the end of my mother's visit that I had to take my children to the place where I had known that young woman. I told myself that I expected no great revelations from Budapest; but I desired to see again and to let my sons see the city of my childhood, which had suddenly become for me, now that she was dying, also the city of my mother's youth.

To a large degree, my desire was satisfied. We spent several days of a two-week stay (some of it outside Budapest) roaming the city, visiting the house and neighborhood where I had lived, taking many rolls of photographs. My sons shot pictures of me in the large cobblestoned courtyard where I had played as a child—quite shabby now, surrounded by pockmarked walls, with tufts of grass growing between the cobblestones; they snapped me on the fourth floor, leaning over the wrought-iron banister in front of the apartment where I had lived with my parents and grandmother; they took snapshots of me on the steps of the *chupah,* the wedding canopy, in the courtyard of the synagogue where my parents were married (the synagogue itself was closed and boarded up). That same courtyard had been the recreation yard of my old religious school, now empty of children (it had become a kosher canteen for the elderly). In a curious way, I felt as if I had occupied all those places of my childhood so that I could return many years later and be photographed there by my children. I became, for a few days, a tour guide of my own life.

I told my sons about some of the memories stirred up by those stones and streets: the long Sunday walks with my mother and friends in the hills of Buda, the scurrying to ballet lessons along crowded avenues in Pest during weekdays, accompanied by the Viennese lady I called "Madame" who taught me French, the visits to the pastry shop where they sold sugar cones filled with whipped chestnut cream in winter, thick and sweet and so smooth to the tongue. My sons listened, mildly interested; but I realized that for them this was a vacation, not a nostalgia trip. I had better not indulge too much in reminiscences.

One thing I didn't tell them about were my memories (which presented themselves to me chiefly as a series of images) of the last year of the Second World War. I didn't consciously remain silent on that score; simply, it did not occur to me to talk about that year of my life, far back in early childhood, while we were in Budapest. It was only after returning to Paris, emptied of Parisians in the late August heat (my children, too, had returned to the country), that I decided to write down the episodes I still carried with me from that year—fragmentary, incomplete, but possessing a vividness that surprised me. The experience of seeing again the places of my childhood had restored the sharpness of those images, as well as revealed the desire, long suppressed, to put them into words.

Running

They began rounding up the Jews in Budapest quite late in the war. Spring 1944. I was four and a half years old.

We lived in an apartment building in a busy part of the city, not far from the Opera House. On the corner of our street stood a large yellow church; a few streets further, the Orthodox synagogue and the Jewish Community Bureau, where my father worked as an administrator. In their courtyard, on an upper story, was the elementary school for girls in which I started first grade after the war. The word for "school," ISKOLA, was proudly chiseled into the stone wall. It never occurred to me that one day the school might cease to exist, that one day there might not be enough Jewish girls in Budapest to fill it.

Our apartment building had four stories, with a large inner courtyard bordered on each floor by a gallery with wrought-iron railings. I would run up and down the gallery on our floor, and whenever I stopped and looked down into the courtyard, I felt dizzy. I held on to the wrought iron, my heart pounding with excitement and fear, knowing all the while that I was safe. Then my grandmother would call me in for a snack of buttered bread, thickly sliced rye with a heavy crust, topped by a piece of salted green pepper. ("Oh, gross!" say my children—but they love green pepper, it must be in the blood.)

To the left as you entered the building was the staircase, of noble proportions, with its own wrought-iron railings of complex design. The steps were of smooth whitish stone, worn down in the middle. We lived three flights up, in an apartment with tall windows and a stone balcony overlooking the street. The main room was the dining room: huge square table in the middle, flanked on one side by two shiny pot-bellied buffets; on the other side, a grand piano under which I liked to sit and play. On the same side as the piano, but near the opposite corner, stood a ceramic stove with light green tiles, used for heating, not cooking; facing each other on opposite walls, two double doors opened onto my parents' bedroom on the right, my grandmother's room on the left. At that time, I still slept in my parents' room. After the war, when my grandmother flew off to join my uncle in New York, I inherited her room.

The night the Nazis came, around three or four in the morning, my mother woke me up and dressed me. She and my father and grandmother spoke in whispers, hurrying. After I was dressed, still half asleep, my mother took me by the hand and ran down the stairs with me. Or maybe she picked me up and ran, carrying me. She had torn the yellow star off her coat. At the bottom of the stairs, we slowed down. There were soldiers on both sides of the street door, the concierge standing next to them—a plump youngish woman, dressed in a heavy coat and felt slippers. It appeared that her job was to identify the Jewish tenants so that none would leave the building on their own.

My mother and I walked past the concierge and the soldiers, out into the street where day was dawning. She held me tightly. We walked up the street toward the church, keeping a steady pace. *Don't look as if you didn't belong here.* After we had turned the corner, we started to run. A mad, panicked dash to the next corner, then a stop, out of breath. Saved.

I have never understood why the concierge let us go. Was she moved by the sight of the woman and child, or had my parents paid her off? Probably they had, for my father succeeded in slipping out a few minutes later. My grandmother stayed behind and was put into a place they called the ghetto, where she lived until the war was over. Later, when I told this story to my friends (everyone in first grade had a story, recounted with melodramatic flourishes on the way home from school), I found it miraculous that she was not taken to Auschwitz, or lined up and shot into the Danube like the people another girl told about. It was at that time, I believe, that I began to conceive of history as a form of luck.

The next scene takes place a few weeks after our escape from the house, on a farm far from Budapest. My parents had decided to leave me with the Christian farmers for my safety, as many other Jewish families were doing with their children. My mother probably explained this to me, although I have no recollection of it. Nor do I remember actually arriving at the farm. I remember being there, scared.

The kitchen of the farmhouse had an earthen floor, a long wooden table in the middle; in one corner stood a massive butter churn. I am standing next to the table with my mother and the farmer's wife. My mother has dressed me in a frilly dress and white leather shoes, like the ones I wear on afternoon visits in town. She kisses me and says it won't be for long. Then she leaves. I cry.

Now I am running across the large dust-covered yard, chased by geese. They are immense, honking furiously, wings aflutter. They're on my heels, stretching their necks to bite me. I run into the kitchen, screaming. The farmer's children laugh and call me a city girl. I can't stop crying, and feel as if I will burn up with shame. As the tears stream down and smear my face, I make a promise to myself: they won't see me cry again.

How long did I stay on the farm? I don't know. It felt like a long time. Since it was summer, I must have turned five while I was there. Meanwhile, back in Budapest, my father managed to get false papers for all three of us. He and my mother decided to take me back, danger or no.

By the time they came for me, I was used to the farm. My mother found me crouching in the dust with the other children, dressed only in a pair of panties, barefooted, busy playing with some broken bits of pottery. I hardly looked up when she ran to me and hugged me.

Snow

Thanks to our false papers, my parents found a job as caretakers on an estate in Buda. The owner of the estate was an old noblewoman, a sculptress. I have no visual memory of her, but I imagine her as a tall, thin, kindly lady with white hair—like the Old Lady in the story of Babar, which I read a few years later. According to my mother, the old lady became very fond of me, even invited my mother to give me an occasional bath in her bathtub. On most days, my mother washed me while I stood in a small enameled basin on the floor next to the stove in our room. The room was so small that I would bump into the stove and burn myself if I wasn't careful. We had to make fires in the stove by then; it was autumn, turning cold.

My name was Mary. My mother whispered to me every morning not to forget it, never to say my real name, no matter who asked. I told her not to worry, I wouldn't tell. I felt grown-up and superior, carrying a secret like that.

Besides the old lady and us, four other people lived in the house: the lady's young nephew, recently married, with his wife, and an older couple who were also caretakers of some kind. They had been with the lady for many years, and were suspicious of us. One day they asked me what my mother's maiden name was. I said I didn't know, and told my mother. She told them not to ask me questions like that: Couldn't they see I was just a baby? Her maiden name was Stern, a Jewish name. I knew that name—it was my grandmother's. Luckily for us, I didn't know what "maiden name" meant.

When winter came, more people arrived, relatives of the old lady. We all lived in one wing of the house to save heat. During the day, the warmest place was the kitchen or a glass-enclosed veranda that received a great deal of sun. The lady's nephew and his wife spent all day on the veranda in wicker armchairs, reading or playing cards. I liked to watch them. The young man especially had a languid, almost petulant air that fascinated me. I recall him as tall and handsome. My mother said he was an "aristocrat," which I under-stood from her intonation to mean something like "beautiful but weak." Watching him turn the pages of a book or run his fingers through his long wavy hair, I felt totally infatuated with him; at the same time, perhaps because of my mother's tone of voice as she said the word "aristocrat," his gracefulness filled me with a kind of scorn.

For Christmas, we decorated a tree. I sang "Holy Night" and received presents. My mother had taught me the song during the whole month of December. There was a Christ-child in a cradle beneath the tree. I was fascinated by the lifelike figure of the holy baby and by his mother's golden hair, but most of all I loved the shining colored globes and the streams of glittering silver on the tree. Sometimes I felt sorry that we weren't really Christians—we could have had a tree like that every year.

In January, it turned bitter cold and snow fell. There were air raids at night, and we all started sleeping on cots in the basement. It soon became clear that my father was the man of the house. He made sure that we all gathered in the basement during air raids, even during the day. He listened to the short-wave radio and told us when the Germans began retreating. When the pipes froze and we had no water, he organized our noctural expeditions to gather snow.

How can I describe those winter nights? For years they remained in my memory as an emblem of the war, of the immense adventure that, with hindsight and retelling, the war became for me. Picture a dozen shadows covered by white sheets, flitting across a snow-covered landscape. The sheets prevented us from being seen from the air, blended with the white ground and trees. Mounds of soft snow, darkness and silence—and with all that hushed beauty, a tingling sense of conspiracy. We carried pots and pans, scooping the cleanest snow into them with a spoon. When a pot was full, we took it inside, emptied it into a kettle on the stove, then went back to gather more. Three kettlefuls, my father said, would give us enough water for two days.

I don't know how many times we gathered snow, in fact. Maybe only twice, or once. No matter. I see myself, triumphant, smug, impatient for the boiled snow to cool so that I can drink it. As I bring the glass to my lips, I meet my father's eyes. We exchange a look of pleasure.

I am five years old and I am drinking snow. Outside, bombs are falling. Here in the steamy kitchen, nothing can hurt me.

Liberation

The Russians arrived in spring. But first, we had German guests. A detachment in retreat invaded the house and set up radio equipment in our kitchen. They were distant, polite, ordinary. I had imagined monsters, like Hitler. (Hitler had horns, he was a giant.) My mother prepared meals for them, listening to their talk—they had no idea that she understood them. She would report their conversations to my father, but there was nothing new. Defeated or not, to us they were still a menace. After a few days, they left. I felt extremely pleased with us, clever Davids outwitting Goliath.

A few nights later, a bomb fell in our backyard. It made a terrific noise, and for a moment we thought it was the end. But when it turned out to have missed the house, we became quite jovial. As soon as there was enough daylight, we trooped out to inspect it. Whose bomb it was, we did not know; but there it sat, less than fifty meters from the house, in the middle of a crater it had made in landing, round and dark green like a watermelon. Somehow it all seemed like a joke, even though we kept repeating how lucky we were, how tragically ironic and ironically tragic it would have been to get killed when the war was almost over.

The Russians arrived huge and smiling, wrapped in large coats with fur on their heads. They were our Liberators—we welcomed them. When they saw my father's gold watch, they laughed delightedly and asked him for it. We didn't understand their words, but their gestures were clear. My father took off the watch and gave it to them. Then they asked my mother to go to their camp and cook for them. They put their arms around her, laughing. She pointed to me, laughing back and shaking her head. Who would take care of the little girl? They insisted, but she held fast. I felt frightened. Finally they let her go.

After that, everything becomes a blur. How much longer did we stay in the house? Did we ever tell the old lady who we were? She was sick, according to my mother's story, and died during the last days of the war. But I have no memory of that.

Home

In 1945, sometime between March and May, we walked back to our house, crossing the Danube on a makeshift bridge. (All of Budapest's beautiful bridges were bombed by the Germans during the last weeks of fighting, I recently found out.) Walking between my parents, holding each one's hand, I felt madly lucky and absolutely victorious, as if our survival had been wholly our doing and at the same time due entirely to chance. I was not aware of the paradox then, or if I was aware of it, could certainly not have expressed it. But as I grow older, it occurs to me that I have often felt that way about my life: seeing it, for better or worse, as my own creation, and at the same time, contradictorily, as the product of blind luck.

That day, I mostly stared and tried to register everything—storing it for future use, though I knew not exactly what. I saw a dead horse lying on its side in the street, its legs stretched out; someone had cut a square hole in its flank for meat. From time to time, a bombed-out wall showed where a house had been. We passed empty stores, their doors wide open—looted, said my mother. Inside one, on the floor in front of the counter, a white-haired woman lay dead. I could not take my eyes from her, despite my mother's pulling me away. Who had killed her? Had they done it for money? What did her skin feel like, now that she was dead? Was it cold and leathery? After a while, I stopped thinking and even looking. I concentrated on putting one foot in front of the other.

On our street, all the houses were intact. We walked into ours, through the downstairs door where the soldiers had stood a year before. The courtyard was covered with debris, and there were holes that looked like bulletholes in the walls; otherwise it looked the same. Up the stairs to the third landing: the lock on our apartment door was broken. Inside, the windows were all shattered. Dust lay over everything, stirred occasionally by a breeze. The sky through the glassless windowframes looked so near you could almost touch it. I was no longer Mary, but for a moment I could not remember my name.

EPILOGUE: THE POLITICS OF POSTMODERNISM AFTER THE WALL; OR, WHAT DO WE DO WHEN THE "ETHNIC CLEANSING" STARTS?

Budapest, May 1993: Every day the newspapers talk about Bosnia. Will aerial bombings stop the Serbian aggression? Will sending in ground troops start another Vietnam? Will the Serbs, if attacked, turn on the Vojvodina, a region in Serbia inhabited mostly by Hungarians? But not to intervene is unconscionable, like passively witnessing another Holocaust. Should the West send arms to the Muslims? Are the Bosnian Croats, too, killing Muslims? And in the background, the common knowledge which, once put into words, flares like an accusation: "The West has failed to protect Sarajevo, where Muslims, Croats, and Serbs lived together in peace for centuries."[1]

I am living for a few months in my native city, at the center of the center of Europe, two hundred kilometers from the border of what was once Yugoslavia, thinking again about the politics of postmodernism. The last time I wrote about this question was in Paris, spring 1989: Khomeini had just put a price on Salman Rushdie's head for writing a novel. Since then, more radical changes have occurred in Europe—which also means in the rest of the world—

All over the world today identity politics (that is to say, a separation in the name of undifferentiated identity of religion, nation or subnation) is big news and almost everywhere bad news.

—Gayatri Chakravorty Spivak, "Acting Bits / Identity Talk"

And yet there is something going on between poetry and power, something almost paradoxical. In some way, power is afraid of poetry, of what has no strength, only the power of words.

—Hélène Cixous, "We Who Are Free, Are We Free?"

than could have been foreseen by the most farsighted of political analysts. A cause for rejoicing? Yes, most say. A cause for worry? Yes, most say. (The current joke in Budapest: "What is the worst thing about Communism?" "What comes after it.") Some things have not changed, however; there is still a price on Rushdie's head.

In certain inner-city neighborhoods in the United States, those in which the greatest poverty and hopelessness reign, young men have killed each other for not showing respect: "He dissed me" ("He showed me disrespect") is considered sufficient cause. Up to today, the Iranian government continues to claim that Rushdie "dissed" the Prophet with his fiction. The price of "dissing" is death.

When is the price of "dissing" death? When is the self so fragile that the mere perception of a slight (not a physical threat—a slight, a symbolic act) provokes it to murder? Are these questions about the politics of postmodernism? I recently came across an essay by Hélène Cixous, just published:

> In our grating and jarring present . . . a phobia of nonidentity has spread, and individuals, and nations like individuals, are infected with this neurosis, this pain, this fear of nonrecognition, where each constructs, erects his self-identification, less out of intimate reflection than out of a system of rejection and hatred. The Serb says: I am not Croatian; to be Croatian is to be non-Serb. And each affirms him- or herself as distinct, as unique and nonother, as though there were room only for one and not for two . . .
>
> Who is afraid of nonidentity, of nonrecognition?[2]

I would ask, rather, who is not afraid? And how can those who are not afraid persuade those who are to stop dreaming of murder? Can they persuade them to stop being afraid? And what can those who are not afraid do when the dream of murder becomes the reality of murder, when "each side's paranoia [feeds] upon the other's"?[3]

Yes, these are definitely questions about the politics of postmodernism.

The "Postmodernism Debate" Seen through the Telescope

Why ask about the politics of postmodernism in 1993? To answer that question (for those who came in in the middle of the movie), I offer a brief bedtime story:

Once upon a time, not so long ago, there existed in the world of intellectuals a "debate over postmodernism." Although it was carried out in the pages of learned books and journals chiefly in the United States and England, some of its best-known participants came from other countries, such as France, Germany, or India, and its fame spread far and wide. The debate concerned the definition and evaluation of a wide range of philosophical ideas and cultural practices, lumped under the heading "postmodernism." One of the chief questions asked about these ideas and practices was: "Does postmodernism have a politics?" Which meant, in fact: "Does it have a positive political 'edge'?"

In philosophy, postmodernism was identified as a self-styled mode of "weak thought," prizing playfulness above logic, irony above absolutes, paradoxes above resolutions, doubt above demonstration. Some intellectuals found this dance of ideas liberating; to others, it appeared irresponsible, a dangerous nihilism. In the arts—literature, photography, architecture, film, performance, painting—postmodernism was identified with a freewheeling use of pastiche, quotation, and collage, methods that some intellectuals saw as innovative and critical, having the potential to undo (or at least put into question) received ideas and established ideologies. Other intellectuals voiced their disapproval or despair: for them, the loose eclecticism of postmodernist art, mixing up historical styles, ignoring boundaries between genres, scrambling distinctions between "high" art and low, between original and copy, was of a piece with the laxness of postmodernist philosophizing, a sign of the cultural exhaustion of late capitalism, or of the decay produced by the proliferation of mass culture.

The first group (let's call them pro-postmodernists) sought at times to distinguish the "postmodernism of resistance" from the postmodernism of "anything goes," and invoked the experimental work of feminists, people of color, and other traditionally silenced subjects as examples. (According to them, postmodernism did have a politics, and it was good—that is, progressive.) For the second group (let's call them pro-modernists), such a distinction was useless. In order to resist, they argued, one has to have firmly held values and principles; postmodernism, whether as an artistic practice or as a philosophy, lacked the necessary firmness, and therefore represented an unfortunate falling away from the positive, largely still unfulfilled project of modernity. Finally, there was a third group, which we may call the cultural pessimists. They, too, denied the possibility of a postmodernism of resistance; to that extent, they shared the negative analysis of the pro-modernists. However, they also refused to envisage a "better" (modernist) alternative, because in their view postmodernism was here to stay.

The attitude of the first group toward postmodernism was, on the whole, celebratory; that of the second, disapproving; that of the third ranged from the resigned to the cynical. If I were asked to name names, I would not. Let everybody recognize his or her own kin.[4] I will simply simply mention, for the record, that I consider Jean Baudrillard a member of group three, not group one; and that almost everyone in the first two groups has, so far as I can see, on occasion dipped one foot, or at least a couple of toes, in group three. That is what is known as the ambivalence of (and toward) postmodernism.

But enough play; let's be serious. Four years ago, in an essay concerned chiefly with the salutary conjunction of feminism (as politics) and postmodernism (as artistic practice), I spent many pages worrying about the political status of postmodernist irony and postmodernist intertextuality (the use of quotation, parody, pastiche, and other kinds of textual *mélanges*), arguing that political effects reside not in texts but in the way they are read—not in what a work "is" but in what it "does" for a given reader or community of readers in a particular place and time. I still hold to that idea, and would provide further evidence for it by citing the controversy over some photographs by Robert Mapplethorpe that broke out in the United States in the summer of 1989. The controversy, which concerned the definition of obscenity in art and the use of public funds to support unpopular art—and which almost led to the dismantling of the National Endowment for the Arts, the government organization that had provided some funding for the Mapplethorpe exhibit and was therefore considered too "political" by its right-wing critics—contributed to the self-conscious politicization of many American artists and museum officials; this in turn fostered a climate of political readings for contemporary art. Another contributing factor of politicization was the ongoing problem of AIDS, which affected many members of the artistic community and produced some powerful works of criticism and protest, as well as expressions of personal anguish. The mixed-media collages of David Wojnarowicz (who has since died of AIDS) are one example—in 1990 Wojnarowicz, too, got into trouble with right-wing critics of the NEA.

The question of political reading of works of art, whether visual or verbal, continues to interest me; but the question I really struggle with today, and which I now think I treated too lightly four years ago, concerns the political status of the plural self rather than of the plural text—not postmodernist intertextuality, but postmodernist subjectivity. Conceptions of the text and conceptions of the self are, of course, not unrelated: unity, coherence, stability are all categories that apply to the one as well as to the other. But how much higher the stakes are where the self is concerned, and how much more urgent the dilemmas it poses, are illustrated all too tragically in the current Bosnian conflict and have been dramatized elsewhere as well in the post-Wall world.

In my earlier discussion, I formulated the question primarily in terms of gender identity, because at that time (and, indeed, since then) the postmodernist theory of the "decentered" subject—as opposed to some form of feminine specificity—was vigorously debated among feminist theorists. The "decentered" subject, evading all stable categorizations, including that of gender, was seen by some feminists (including myself) as a great point of alliance between postmodernism and feminism. Other theorists, no less "sophisticated" and no less adept at deconstructive moves in literary criticism, were less sanguine about this alliance and cautioned against giving up what women had struggled so long to obtain: a female signature, the recognition of a female self. The feminist discussion is continuing, and over the past few years we have seen increasingly subtle defenses of both the (so-called) essentialist and the (so-called) postmodernist positions.[5] Personally, I continue to maintain that the ability to put the self "into play"—into what D. W. Winnicott called an "unintegrated state of the personality"—is essential to creativity, whether in women or men; nor would I recant the statement, made on the last page of *Subversive Intent,* that "I feel much drawn to [Julia Kristeva's] evocation of the 'happy cosmopolitan,' foreign not only to others but to him- or herself, harboring not an essence but a 'pulverized origin.'"[6]

What has changed for me, after the Wall, is that I have lost my innocence about the "happy cosmopolitan." Things are not so simple; the idea of a postmodernist paradise in which one can try on identities like costumes in a shopping mall ("I'm a happy cosmopolitan; you can be a happy essentialist; they can be happy ironists or defenders of the one and only Faith") appears to me now as not only naive, but intolerably thoughtless in a world where—once again—whole populations are murdered in the name of (ethnic) identity.

Does this statement make me into a "modernist" defender of Reason and universal values? Some would argue that that is the only way to counter the irrationalism, the racism, the xenophobia that have resurfaced or grown stronger, in the East and in the West, since the fall of the Wall. Christopher Norris makes this argument, and it is interesting that he states it most impassionedly in the context of a war—but not "my" war. His most recent attack on postmodernism—which he simply and, in my opinion, unreflectively equates with the writings solely of Jean Baudrillard—is prompted by his indignation at the Gulf War, which he considers to have been a cynical, imperialist, unjust attack on Iraqi civilians.[7] As a matter of fact, I, too, was opposed to that war and to the outbursts of "yellow-ribbon" patriotism it provoked in the United States, and I agree that a great deal of hypocrisy was involved in the rhetoric used to justify it (covering up naked oil interests with a discourse of democratic indignation); but none of that seems to me a sufficient basis on which to launch a blitzkrieg against Baudrillard-cum-postmodernism. "My war," the Bosnian war (but also, I suddenly realize, my other war, the war of my early childhood, World War II) prompts an altogether different set of reflections: Is it possible to theorize an *ethical* postmodernist subjectivity without recourse to universal values, but also without the innocent thoughtlessness of the "happy cosmopolitan"? Is it possible to argue that such an ethical postmodernist subjectivity has *political* (collective, relating to the public good) import and relevance? Finally, is it possible to argue for a political postmodernist praxis? In plainer words, what do we do if words fail and the shooting starts?

Ethical Postmodernism

It appears to be a truth universally accepted, by the modernist critics of postmodernism, that postmodernist theory is incapable of furnishing either an ethics or a politics. By arguing against a unified (rational) subject and (his) universal values, this theory, according to its critics, is unable "to take any principled oppositional stand," be it as concerns individual action or "local or world politics."[8] Irremediably compromised by its own relativism (so the argument continues), postmodernist thought has no moral foundation, just as, for similar reasons, it occupies no firm epistemological ground.

I find it astonishing that this argument is still current (witness its being made, in 1992, by Norris), despite the fact that it has been answered again and again by postmodernist theorists of contingency—who argue, in brief, that values are not universal but context-bound, not discovered in some Platonic sky but fashioned by historically situated human beings, and are for that reason subject to change. Barbara Herrnstein Smith and Richard Rorty, who are among the most articulate of these theorists, have explicitly (and, to my mind, persuasively) countered the notion that a belief in the contingency of values implies moral paralysis. "The fundamental premise of [this] book," writes Rorty at the end of his *Contingency, Irony, and Solidarity,* "is that a belief can still regulate action, can still be thought worth dying for, among people who are quite aware that this belief is caused by nothing deeper than contingent historical circumstances."[9] And Smith, in a similar vein, writes:

> Someone's distaste for or inability to grasp notions such as "absolute value" and "objective truth" does not in itself deprive her of such other human characteristics, relevant to moral action, as memory, imagination, early training and example, conditioned loyalties, instinctive sympathies and antipathies, and so forth. Nor does it deprive her of all interest in the subtler, more diffuse, and longer-range consequences of her actions and the actions of others.[10]

The universalist (or, if you will, modernist) claim is that only by ascribing universal validity to one's ethical beliefs is one able to act ethically. A postmodernist ethics refuses to take that step, arguing that such ascriptions merely elevate one set of contingent beliefs to "universal" status and that too many horrors have been inflicted by some human beings on others in the name of *their* universal values. As Smith's and Rorty's arguments show, however, this does not mean that there can be no such thing as a postmodernist ethics. The accusation that a refusal of universalism leads to a paralyzing, immoral relativism seems to me just that—an accusation, not a demonstration. And since we are in the realm of intellectual debate (as opposed to, say, physical conflict), the only way to counter the accusation is by replying to it as often and as forcefully, as persuasively, as one can.

But have we not strayed somewhat from the question of postmodernist subjectivity? I think not. What I am calling postmodernist subjectivity seeks, first and foremost, to undo a unitary and essentialist conception of the self that would allow for statements of the type: "I am only, unconditionally X" or "He is, she is, only, unconditionally Y." Does that mean that Serbs should not think of themselves as Serbs, and Croats not think of themselves as Croats? No, it means that Serbs should not think of themselves as "only, unconditionally Serbs" unto the death; nor (remember, this is before the shooting starts) should they think of their Croat neighbors as "only, unconditionally Croats." For besides being Serbs and Croats, they are also sons or daughters, parents, students, teachers, doctors, plumbers, apartment dwellers or village neighbors, TV watchers and sports fans, and many other things as well. If you don't put all your identity eggs in one basket, the chances are less likely that you will kill anyone who looks at them (or who you think looks at them) as if he wanted to break them. If you don't put all the identity eggs of people who are different from you in one basket, the chances are less likely that you will want to break theirs (or look as if you did).

The universalist/modernist argument would be that in order not to feel "only, unconditionally" Serb or Croat or Arab or a woman or anything else, one would need to replace such specific identifications with the general category of "the human race." But I am persuaded by Rorty's argument that it is not by identifying with an imaginary community of "fellow human beings" that people engage in humane interaction with their fellow human beings; rather, they forge the bonds of community by "smaller and more local" links, and by "imaginative identification with the details of others' lives" (pp. 190, 191). "You don't have to be Jewish to love Levy's Jewish Rye," proclaimed subway advertising posters in New York City around twenty years ago. You don't have to be a universalist to love your neighbors enough not to kill them or wish them harm—even if they occasionally "diss" you, wittingly or not.

But I may be taking things too lightly again, as indeed I think (and will shortly argue) Rorty tends to do. Is it because we are both middle-class white Americans, occupying good jobs with lifetime security, that we lack a real sense of tragedy—and, I suspect, of irony as well? I ask myself this in Budapest, my native city, where even the street names speak of tragedy and irony. (A Hungarian acquaintance tells me, a few minutes after we are introduced: "Our Champs-Elysées, Andrássy Avenue [Andrássy was a late nineteenth-century statesman, from the period of Hungary's greatest prosperity] became Stalin Avenue in 1945, Young Guard Avenue after 1956, People's Republic Avenue under the Kádár regime, and is now once again Andrássy Avenue. Back to zero: a perfect image of our history over the past half-century!" And he laughs.) I must have left this city too early in life; I have become too light. Let me therefore call on a more tragically aware Central European to comment on the consequences of divorcing ethics from universalism. Zygmunt Bauman, a sociologist and a Polish Jewish exile living in England, writes: "The ethical paradox of the postmodern condition is that it restores to agents the fulness of moral choice and responsibility while simultaneously depriving them of the comfort of the universal guidance that modern self-confidence once promised. Ethical tasks of individuals grow while the socially produced resources to fulfil them shrink. Moral responsibility comes together with the loneliness of moral choice."[11]

You don't have to be a universalist to make humane ethical choices, or even to die for them—but you can feel a certain loss (ironically aware of your own nostalgia) at the thought of a time when you might have been.

Political Postmodernism

"This book tries to show how things look if we drop the demand for a theory which unifies the public and the private," writes Rorty in his introduction to *Contingency, Irony, and Solidarity* (p. xv). I, on the other hand, want to argue that it is essential to think about the continuity between the private and the public; and that without claiming anything as grand as a general unifying theory, one must consider a postmodernist conception of the self to have public relevance. In other words, that one can and should establish a continuity between postmodernist subjectivity, postmodernist ethics, and postmodernist politics.

Rorty's book is a good place to start in making this argument, because it presents an unusually clear and compelling case for what I am calling postmodernist subjectivity—and then stops short and claims that this subjectivity has no relevance at all for public discourse and the public good. I would like to push his argument further, to what I think is its proper conclusion.[12]

Theorists of the postmodern subject have a penchant for allegory, or more exactly for emblematic figures: Derrida's dancer, Haraway's cyborg, Scarpetta's cosmopolitan, Kristeva's happy cosmopolitan, Cixous' Jewoman, Spivak's feminist internationalist, my laughing mother—all of these are allegorical figures (some more poetic than others), standing for a set of ideas. But they are not only allegorical or emblematic; they are also utopian, offered as idealized models or myths. Haraway calls the cyborg an "ironic political myth," thus insisting on the continuity between the personal and the political.[13] Rorty, in an apparently similar move, offers the ironist as his emblematic figure—but he refuses to accord this figure political status.

The ironist makes her appearance in Rorty's book (all of his descriptions of this figure *as allegory* use feminine pronouns, although the actual philosophers he discusses as ironists are all male) in a chapter entitled "Private Irony and Liberal Hope." Here is his capsule description:

> I shall define an "ironist" as someone who fulfills three conditions: (1) She has radical and continuing doubt about the final vocabulary she currently uses [final vocabulary is the "set of words people employ to justify their actions, their beliefs, and their lives"], because she has beeen impressed by other vocabularies, vocabularies taken as final by people or books she has encountered; (2) she realizes that argument phrased in her present vocabulary can neither underwrite nor dissolve these doubts; (3) insofar as she philosophizes about her situation, she

does not think that her vocabulary is closer to reality than others, that it is in touch with a power not herself. (p. 73)

Moving from the singular to the plural, Rorty notes that ironists are "never quite able to take themselves seriously because always aware that the terms in which they describe themselves are subject to change, always aware of the contingency and fragility of their final vocabularies and thus of their selves" (73–74). The opposite of the ironist is the metaphysician, who must found his beliefs on proof and argumentation, and on values he claims as universal (Rorty consistently describes the metaphysician as "he").

So far, so good. (A minor disagreement: "fragility" is not the word I would use in describing the ironist's sense of self; "in process," a term proposed by Julia Kristeva some years ago, seems to me stronger, more positive, as well as less "feminine" in the traditional sense.) As I have already noted, Rorty counters the notion—put forth by metaphysicians, in his terms—that ironists are relativists unable to make ethical choices. He even gestures, occasionally, in the direction of claiming that ironists can constitute a *collective* force ("One of my aims in this book is to suggest the possibility of a liberal utopia: one in which ironism, in the relevant sense, is universal"—p. xv). At a crucial moment, however, he abandons that line of thought and never returns to it. In his chapter on the "liberal community," he confronts Habermas' critique of Foucault and other philosophers—Nietzsche, Heidegger, Derrida—whom Habermas considers as having dangerously veered from the project of the Enlightenment but whom Rorty admires as great ironists. Rorty concedes: "I agree with Habermas that as *public* philosophers they are at best useless and at worst dangerous, but I want to insist on the role they and others like them can play in accommodating the ironist's *private* sense of identity to her liberal hopes" (p. 68).

Even this attempt at an "accommodation" between private and public (Rorty evidently considers "accommodation" a weak link, nothing so ambitious or theoretically viable as a synthesis) is abandoned in his next chapter: "Ironist theorists like Hegel, Nietzsche, Derrida, and Foucault seem to me invaluable in our attempt to form a private self-image, but pretty much useless when it comes to politics" (p. 83). In the end, Rorty finds himself in a strange position: he concedes everything to the Habermasian critique of Foucault and Derrida as anti-Enlightenment philosophers—everything except the notions of universality and rationality, on which the Habermasian position is founded. He is therefore left, theoretically speaking, with neither the strength of Habermas nor the strength of "Foucault and the others." Rorty, like Habermas, makes little attempt to distinguish among his "ironist theorists" insofar as their political ideas are concerned—he seems to lump them all, as Habermas polemically did, into the "antiliberal" category without asking what each one is (or can be construed to be, on the basis of his philosophical positions) "for." In the end, he reduces them to a status approaching the trivial: "I tried to show how ironist theory can be privatized, and thus prevented from becoming a threat to political liberalism" (p. 190).

In what I read as a highly dramatic moment, Rorty makes the claim that "literary criticism does for ironists what the search for universal moral principles is supposed to do for metaphysicians"— that is, allow us to "revise our own moral identity" (p. 83). If, however, this high calling for ironist theory is merely a way of preventing it from "becoming a threat to political liberalism," that is—to say the least—an anticlimax.[14]

I believe that a much stronger case than Rorty is (or was, in 1989) willing to make can and should be made (and already has been made, by some) for the political relevance of postmodernist views of the self. As Anthony Appiah and Henry Louis Gates, Jr., note in their editors' introduction to a recent special issue of *Critical Inquiry* devoted to "Identities," "The calls for a 'post-essentialist' reconception of notions of identity have become increasingly common. The powerful resurgence of nationalisms in Eastern Europe provides just one example of the catalysts for such theorizing."[15] Already in 1981, the French cultural critic Guy Scarpetta noted that what had been a positive outcome of May 1968, the coming to voice of suppressed minorities, threatened a decade later to degenerate into new theories of "racial" or "biological" purity. Scarpetta, for that reason, proposed "cosmopolitanism" as his political myth: "to try the untenable position of a systematic crossing-over, of an essential exile, of an endlessly recommended diaspora, of movement, of a tearing away from everything that keeps you rooted, that fixes and freezes, to perceive that no value is fixed, no language is all—that, in the end, is cosmopolitanism."[16] The question that confronts today's "postessentialist" critics is how to get away from the negative consequences of identity politics without simply returning to notions of universalism, Reason, and the unified subject.

I suggest that one way to do this is to take the step Rorty refuses to take: accord to "ironism" (or to the same thing by a different name) a public stature. Rorty actually goes more than halfway toward that position when he claims that "a liberal culture whose public rhetoric is nominalist and historicist [that is, recogizing contingency, not claiming universal principles as a basis for values] is both possible and desirable." However, he concludes that he "cannot go on to claim that there could or ought to be a culture whose public rhetoric is *ironist.*" He "cannot imagine a culture which socialized its youth in such a way as to make them continually dubious about their own process of socialization. Irony seems inherently a private matter" (p. 87). But if a culture—or more precisely, a community—recognizes the contingency of its values and vocabularies, as Rorty claims is possible in public rhetoric, then why is it unimaginable that its public rhetoric should go one step further and become ironist *according to his own definition?* Rorty suggests that a culture that socialized its youth in an atmosphere of doubt is not viable. Yet his figure of the individual ironist, who is characterized by "radical and continuing doubt about the final vocabulary she uses," is not only viable but can act as an agent of ethical choice. Why, then, can't a community aim for a similar combination of self-doubt and responsible action? Since public rhetorics of certainty, whether of the historicist or the universalist variety, don't seem to have worked all that well in preventing war, genocide, and other forms of political murder in the past two thousand years, why not try a public rhetoric of doubt?

No sooner have I written these words, than I already hear, in my own inner ear as well, the "realist" response: "Can you seriously claim that politicians and statesmen should engage in a rhetoric of doubt? That's really a flaky idea!" Etcetera. Yes, I know it sounds flaky—or to put it more kindly, utopian. So what? I can only repeat: the other kind of rhetoric hasn't done too well; why not envisage an alternative?

A few years ago, my colleague Barbara Johnson told the following story: After one of her lectures in a large course on deconstruction (or maybe it was another occasion of public speech, I no longer remember exactly), a young woman came up to her and asked, intrigued: "Are you a feminist, or are you just hesitant?" The female student wanted to know whether the female professor's lack of certainty (Rorty would call it her irony) was a failure of character, or on the contrary an ideological and rhetorical choice. It suddenly occurs to me that the question about a rhetoric of doubt is really a question about the place of women in the public sphere. The emblematic ironist, as Rorty portrays her, is a woman. Could it be that by insisting that irony is "inherently a private matter," Rorty was reiterating (even if unwittingly) the dictum that a woman's place is in the home?

But what if *women's* place were in the center of the public sphere? That, too, has not been tried in the last few millennia.

Postmodernist Praxis?

I said earlier that I thought Rorty, like me, lacked a sufficient sense of tragedy and even of irony (whose fiercest form is tragic, as Aristotle showed). An insufficient sense of tragedy and irony dulls one's awareness of the intractability of things. "Rough reality," "la réalité rugueuse" that Rimbaud said he wanted to embrace, has a way of eluding you—until it punches you in the face.

June 2, 1993: I'm back in the States for a few days. In the *New York Times*, Bosnia is still front-page news. "MORTAR FIRE KILLS TWELVE AT SOCCER GAME IN BOSNIAN CAPITAL. Sarajevo, June 1: Mortar shells exploded today amid a neighborhood soccer tournament, killing at least a dozen people and wounding 80 . . . The attack came on a day of chaotic violence . . . that was shocking even by local standards." The war is getting worse, now that it is clear the West will not rearm the Muslims, not bomb the Serbian artillery positions, not intervene. The so-called safe zones lack all safety, as well as fresh water. Three United Nations aid workers were killed yesterday in a region pounded by Bosnian Serb artillery over the past two weeks. "However, the Bosnian Serbs' leader, Radovan Karadzic, denied today that his forces were responsible for the attack."

The idea underlying *Contingency, Irony, and Solidarity* is that human beings are, on the whole, nice. To put it in philosophically less inane terms, Rorty believes that everyone in the world has the potential to be a liberal, borrowing Judith Shklar's definition of liberals as "the people who think that cruelty is the worst thing we can do" (p. xv). The liberal's desire to avoid inflicting pain constitutes, for Rorty, the modest but significant basis for human solidarity. The "liberal ironist," who refuses to invoke universals and lives in a constant (private) condition of self-doubt, nevertheless subscribes to the idea that not inflicting pain on others is the minimal, sufficient condition for a just and moral world. We are now living, Rorty concludes, in "the first epoch in human history in which large numbers of people have become able to separate the question 'Do you believe and desire what we believe and desire?' from the question 'Are you suffering?'" (p. 198). The first question, he says, is private; the second, public.

The Central European ironist laughs and reads the newspaper. The French literary critic asks herself: Has Rorty read Sade? Has he read Genet, or Bataille? Of course he must have, but his separation of private irony from public hope allows him to sweep them—along with Nietzsche and Heidegger, whom he mentions, plus Kafka, Gombrowicz, and a few others he does not—into the realm of the private. Philosophy in the boudoir, transgression in the closet, perversion in the prison cell? Sure, why not? But keep them private. They have nothing to do with politics.

No, he has not read Sade or Bataille or Genet. Or, for that matter, Duras, author of *La Douleur (War)*, a political book.

But do let's be serious, now that the end is near. I claim that, although it might be convenient, it is not possible, in a postmodernist discourse about politics, to separate considerations about private irony—or private obsessions and fears and hatreds, or private sadisms—from considerations about public action and the public good. Obviously, I don't mean by this that a postmodernist theory of politics should envisage legislation controlling private fantasies. But neither should it try to pretend that public action can be cordoned off from private fears.

Recently, I learned that Radovan Karadzic, the leader of the Bosnian Serbs—thus, presumably, one of the architects of the policy of systematic rape and murder of Muslim women by Serb "ethnic cleansing" squads—is a psychiatrist. This news shocked me almost as much as learning that the head of the Serb "interrogation bureau" in Pale is a one-time professor of literature. He is reputed to be merciless.[17] Did he teach postmodernist fiction? How would he interpret Salman Rushdie's statement that "the novel should be a celebration of impurity"?[18]

The Central European ironist would laugh at me this time, for sure. Yet I cannot help thinking that postmodernist intellectuals may have a social role other than that of torturer. Zygmunt Bauman has theorized that, succeeding to the modernist view of intellectuals as legislators ("collective owners of knowledge of direct and crucial relevance to the maintenance and perfection of the social order"), has come the postmodernist view of intellectuals as interpreters:

> With pluralism irreversible, a world-scale consensus on world-views and values unlikely, and all extant *Weltanschauungen* firmly grounded in their respective cultural traditions (more correctly: their respective autonomous institutionalizations of power), communication across traditions becomes the major problem of our time . . . The problem, therefore, calls urgently for specialists in translation between cultural traditions.[19]

Bauman, Central European ironist that he is, concludes on a pseudo-comic note: "In a nutshell, the proposed specialism [for intellectuals] boils down to the art of civilized conversation" (p. 143). But why not take seriously, just long enough to try it, the view propounded by Lonnie Kliever, quoted by Bauman, that "relativism, far from being a problem, is . . . a solution to the pluralist world's problem; moreover, its promotion is, so to speak, a moral duty of contemporary intellectuals"? In the absence of such relativism, Kliever suggests, "old authoritarian habits would soon reassert themselves and the pluralist world would turn into one of 'multiple absolutisms.'"[20] The bloody clash of multiple absolutisms is no longer in the conditional: it is what we are seeing today in Bosnia, and potentially in any number of other "border conflicts" between cultures, religions, and ethnic groups in Europe, the Middle East, and India (to name a few).

But that introduces (or brings us back to) the old, vexed question of the relation between action and theory: can the discourse of intellectuals, whether modernist or postmodernist or other, have any effect on "rough reality"? And what, in particular, can intellectual discourse accomplish once the shooting starts? "Today," wrote the ex-Yugoslav writer Vladimir Pistalo in 1992, "words have nothing in common with the atrocities committed." He felt that the witnesses' testimonies regarding the atrocities committed in Bosnia had not been heard, that their words had been stifled. Today (June 1993), the testimonies have been heard; yet, Pistalo's next question remains timely: "And if we got our words back . . . What would we cry out? That it's not right to destroy centuries-old monuments? That it's not right to slit other people's throats? That it's not right to mistreat women and children? That to destroy all values by means of oblivion, by instructions renewed each day, has no sense?"[21]

In this perspective, the "debate over postmodernism" appears grotesque; for in this perspective, the problem is not choosing between "modernist" or "postmodernist" views of subjectivity and ethics—Norris wasted his time writing a whole book attacking Baudrillard: The problem is deciding what to do when it becomes obvious that conversation, dialogue, translation have failed. In the absence of any possible debate, what relation can exist between intellectuals modernist or postmodernist, and butchers or would-be butchers? This question appears all the more agonizing when one realizes that some of the butchers and would-be butchers are themselves intellectuals.[22]

Wayne Booth, worrying in a recent essay about very similar questions concerning torture, asks: "How . . . could one ever persuade a regime and its hired torturers to listen to arguments as elusive and as non-utilitarian as those I've offered here?"[23] He then comes up with "an argument that ought to work, if listened to, even with the most self-centered, non-altruistic of would-be torturers." It runs like this: "You—you loyalist torturer—are actually destroying your own self. Since selves overlap—not just metaphorically but literally—it is clear that you are destroying not just the life drama of the tortured one but of your own soul as well" (p. 97). Note that Booth's notion of "overlapping selves" could qualify as postmodernist. Note, too (as I have, in the margin of my copy of the book in which Booth's essay appears), that the likely response of a torturer to this argument will be: "Oh, yeah?" Or, like the torturer in J. M. Coetzee's *Waiting for the Barbarians* (which Booth quotes), he might respond with "one more brutal blow." It is not the elusive or nonelusive, utilitarian or nonutilitarian nature of the argument that is in doubt, but the very nature of argumentation: words versus blows.

Finally, for me, the only question about the politics of postmodernism that really matters is this—and I offer it with fully ironic awareness of its inadequacy: How can one help create a world in which butchers and would-be butchers are kept in check (or, if you have a more benign view of human possibilities, in which they are persuaded to give up their murderous fears), so that intellectuals can continue to argue about universals versus particulars and artists can go on painting and writing and making music of whatever kind they feel moved to make? How can one help create a world where dialogue is not only valued over butchery, but actually prevails?

In order to make the world safe for dialogue, will one have to resort to blows? Now there is a familiar paradox. Is it a postmodernist repetition (as in "the war to end all wars")? Is it ironic? Perhaps. But it's not funny at all.[24]

NOTES

INDEX

NOTES

Introduction

1. Nancy K. Miller, *Getting Personal: Feminist Occasions and Other Autobiographical Acts* (New York: Routledge, 1991), pp. ix–x.
2. Jan Kott, *Shakespeare Our Contemporary*, trans. Boleslaw Taborski (New York: Norton, 1974).
3. Nancy Miller has sought to distinguish truly personal criticism (which itself has many varieties, she recognizes) from criticism that merely introduces a "biographeme" in the beginning, after which "the personal vanishes" (Miller, *Getting Personal*, p. 26). She considers "Writing and Motherhood" an example of the latter; but I believe that the concept of mediated autobiography can allow one to consider "personal" even works where the critic's self-figuration is minimal. Mary Ann Caws has suggested (as discussed by Miller) that the personal may reveal itself less in explicit self-disclosure than in an intensity of tone and voice when one treats certain subjects.

1. Writing and Motherhood

This chapter was conceived when my sons were very young (and I myself was much younger), as a paper delivered at a session on motherhood organized by Carolyn Burke at the 1979 MLA Convention in San Francisco. It was revised for publication in 1984, and appeared in S. Garner, C. Kahane, and M. Sprengnether, eds., *The (M)Other Tongue: Essays in Feminist Psychoanalytic Interpretation* (Ithaca: Cornell University Press, 1985). The only pages I now consider dated are those devoted to the question of *l'écriture féminine*, which in the early 1980s was still a subject of lively debate among feminist theorists. I have not altered those pages (by putting them into the past tense, for example), because they have some documentary interest. Nor have I added references to the many works on motherhood, in life and literature, that have appeared since then. Three recent works that have especially contributed to my ongoing thinking about motherhood are Jessica Benjamin, *The Bonds of Love: Psychoanalysis, Feminism, and the Problem of Domination* (New York: Pantheon, 1988); Marianne Hirsch, *The Mother/Daughter Plot:*

Narrative, Psychoanalysis, Feminism (Bloomington: Indiana University Press, 1989); and Sara Ruddick, *Maternal Thinking: Toward a Politics of Peace* (Boston: Beacon, 1989).

1. Helene Deutsch, *The Psychology of Women* (New York: Bantam, 1973; orig. pub. 1945), vol. 2, p. 479. Other quotations from Helene Deutsch are all from this book; page references will be given in parentheses in the text.

2. Julia Kristeva, "Un nouveau type d'intellectuel: le dissident," *Tel Quel* 74 (Winter 1977): 6. Unless otherwise indicated, all translations from the French are mine.

3. Quoted in Joel Kovel, "The Castration Complex Reconsidered," in Jean Strouse, ed., *Women and Analysis* (New York: Viking, 1974), p. 136.

4. Juliet Mitchell, "On Freud and the Distinction between the Sexes," in Strouse, ed., *Women and Analysis*, p. 32.

5. Nancy Chodorow, *The Reproduction of Mothering: Psychoanalysis and the Sociology of Gender* (Berkeley: University of California Press, 1978), p. 39.

6. Ibid., pp. 77, 82, 84–85.

7. See in particular Klein's 1937 essay, "Love, Guilt, and Reparation," reprinted in Melanie Klein, *"Love, Guilt, and Reparation" and Other Works, 1921–1945* (New York: Doubleday, 1977), pp. 306–343.

8. My readers will certainly have noticed that almost all of the analysts I have been quoting are women. Their statements show either a remarkable alienation from their own experience (surely they did not become analysts and writers by adapting without problems to the "passive-masochistic gratifications" of femininity) or else a remarkable degree of self-hatred (their own development was "abnormal," since they chose the route of the masculinity complex in their own lives). What seems astonishing is that Helene Deutsch declared herself to be a long-standing feminist, whose greatest hope for her women patients was that they would "have a passionate interest in something other than the possible man and children in [their lives]." That is a curious statement, coming as it does from the most orthodoxly Freudian theorist of "normal" femininity. As Marcia Cavell rightly points out, the statement suggests at the very least a deep split between Deutsch the therapist and Deutsch the theorist. (See Cavell, "Since 1924: Toward a New Psychology of Women," in Strouse, ed., *Women and Analysis*, p. 167.)

9. Karen Horney, "Maternal Conflicts," in Horney, *Feminine Psychology* (New York: Norton, 1973), pp. 175–181.

10. Adrienne Rich, *Of Woman Born: Motherhood as Experience and Institution* (New York: Bantam, 1977), p. 17.

11. Sigmund Freud, "Creative Writers and Day-Dreaming" (1908), in *The Standard Edition of the Complete Psychological Works*, trans. James Strachey (London: Hogarth, 1953–1974), vol. 9, p. 152.

12. See D. W. Winnicott, *Playing and Reality* (New York: Basic, 1971), p. 107 and passim.

13. Klein, *"Love, Guilt, and Reparation,"* p. 334.

14. Roland Barthes, *Le Plaisir du texte* (Paris: Seuil, 1973), p. 60.

15. Susan Suleiman, "Reading Robbe-Grillet: Sadism and Text in *Projet pour une révolution à New York,"* *Romanic Review* 68 (January 1977): 43–62.

16. Tillie Olsen, *Silences* (New York: Doubleday, 1979), pp. 16, 31.

17. Elaine Showalter, "Women Writers and the Double Standard," in Vivian Gornick and Barbara Moran, eds., *Woman in Sexist Society* (New York: Basic, 1971), p. 333.

18. Elaine Showalter, *A Literature of Their Own: British Women Novelists from Brontë to Lessing* (Princeton: Princeton University Press, 1977), p. 65.

19. Phyllis Rose, as paraphrased in Showalter, *A Literature of Their Own,* p. 270.

20. Nina Auerbach, "Artists and Mothers: A False Alliance," *Women and Literature* 6 (Spring 1978): 9, 14.

21. Kristeva, "Un nouveau type d'intellectuel," pp. 6–7.

22. Liv Ullman, *Changing* (New York: Bantam, 1978), pp. 36, 37.

23. Jane Lazarre, *The Mother Knot* (New York: Dell, 1977), pp. 55–56.

24. Rich, *Of Woman Born,* p. 12.

25. Kathleen E. Woodiwiss, interviewed by Judy Klemensrud, *New York Times Book Review,* November 4, 1979, p. 52.

26. Olsen, *Silences,* p. 19.

27. Susan Hill, "On Ceasing to Be a Novelist" (interview with Robert Robinson), *The Listener,* February 2, 1978, p. 154.

28. Woodiwiss, interviewed by Klemensrud.

29. Karen Horney, "Neurotic Disturbances in Work," in Horney, *Neurosis and Human Growth: The Struggle toward Self-Realization* (New York: Norton, 1970), pp. 319–20, emphasis added.

30. I am struck, however, by how closely Horney's description corresponds to Simone de Beauvoir's explanation for the lack of audaciousness in women writers: "To please is her first care; and often she fears she will be displeasing as a woman from the mere fact that she writes . . . The writer of originality, unless dead, is always shocking, scandalous; novelty disturbs and repels. Woman is still astonished and flattered at being admitted to the world of thought, of art—a masculine world. She is on her best behavior; *she is afraid to disarrange, to investigate, to explode;* she feels she should seek pardon for literary pretensions through her modesty and good taste. She takes on the reliable value of conformity." Simone de Beauvoir, *The Second Sex,* trans. and ed. H. M. Parshley (New York: Bantam, 1961), p. 666, emphasis added. I discuss Beauvoir's views on women writers in Chapter 4.

31. Quoted by Jean Ricardou in Simone de Beauvoir et al., *Que peut la littérature?* (Paris: Union Générale, 1965), p. 59.

32. Olsen, *Silences,* p. 19.

33. Phyllis Chesler, *With Child: A Diary of Motherhood* (New York: Crowell, 1979), p. 246.

34. Rich, *Of Woman Born,* p. 9.

35. Lazarre, *Mother Knot*, p. 216.

36. Kristeva, "Un nouveau type d'intellectuel," p. 6.

37. Julia Kristeva, "Héréthique de l'amour," *Tel Quel* 74 (Winter 1977): 31. Reprinted as "Stabat Mater" in Kristeva, *Histoires d'amour* (Paris: Denoël, 1983). An English translation by Arthur Goldhammer appeared in Susan Rubin Suleiman, ed., *The Female Body in Western Culture: Contemporary Perspectives* (Cambridge, Mass.: Harvard University Press, 1986).

38. Rich, *Of Woman Born*, p. 1.

39. Kristeva, "Un nouveau type d'intellectuel," p. 6.

40. See Cixous' essay "Sorties," in Catherine Clément and Hélène Cixous, *La Jeune Née* (Paris: Union Générale, 1975), esp. pp. 169–180.

41. Chantal Chawaf, *Maternité* (Paris: Stock, 1979), p. 20.

42. The debate over *l'écriture féminine,* whose implications have properly been seen as political rather than merely stylistic, has been long and sometimes acrimonious among French feminists. The issues are clearly defined in the dialogue that concludes Cixous and Clément's *La Jeune Née,* as well as in Clément's essay "Enslaved Enclave" and Cixous' "Laugh of the Medusa," in Elaine Marks and Isabelle de Courtivron, eds., *New French Feminisms* (New York: Schocken, 1981). Like Clément, but from a different perspective, Kristeva has criticized the concept of *l'écriture féminine;* see in particular "A partir de *Polylogue,*" *Revue des sciences humaines* 168 (December 1977): 495–501.

43. Olsen, *Silences*, p. 32.

44. "Good Housekeeping" first appeared in *American Review* 18 (1973), and was reprinted in Pat Rotter, ed., *Bitches and Sad Ladies: An Anthology of Fiction by and about Women* (New York: Dell, 1976), pp. 68–70. *The Autobiography of My Mother* was published in 1976 (New York: Doubleday). Rosellen Brown is the mother of two young daughters.

45. Katherine Anne Porter, "Notes on Writing," in Brewster Ghiselin, ed., *The Creative Process* (New York: New American Library, n.d.; orig. pub. 1952), p. 199.

46. There is an interesting contrast between this scene and one of the culminating scenes in Margaret Drabble's novel *The Garrick Year* (1964), where the heroine sees her young daughter fall into a river and immediately jumps in to save her. In Drabble's fiction, as I suggest below, the mother-child bond is never problematic.

47. Showalter, *Literature of Their Own*, p. 305.

2. Maternal Splitting

This chapter first appeared in a slightly different version in *Signs* (Fall 1988), © by the University of Chicago; all rights reserved. I am grateful to the "other mothers" in the Cambridge mothers' group—Mieke Bal, Teresa Bernardez, Carol Gilligan, Marianne Hirsch, Evelyn Keller, Amy Lang, Ruth Perry, and Gail Reimer—for our ongoing discussions, in 1985 and 1986, of the issues treated here.

1. Nancy Friday, *Jealousy* (New York: Morrow, 1985); Phyllis Chesler, *Mothers on Trial: The Battle for Children and Custody* (New York: McGraw-Hill, 1986).

2. Bruno Bettelheim, *The Uses of Enchantment: The Meaning and Importance of Fairy Tales* (New York: Vintage, 1987), pp. 67, 69.

3. Melanie Klein, "Weaning," in *"Love, Guilt, and Reparation" and Other Works, 1921–1945* (New York: Doubleday, 1977), p. 290.

4. Ibid., p. 293.

5. Margaret Mahler, Fred Pine, and Anni Bergman, *The Psychological Birth of the Human Infant* (New York: Basic, 1975), p. 99. Subsequent page references will be given in parentheses in the text.

6. Bettelheim, *The Uses of Enchantment*, p. 68.

7. Freud's 1912 essay can be found in Sigmund Freud, *Sexuality and the Psychology of Love* (New York: Collier, 1963), pp. 58–69. James Swan, "*Mater* and Nannie: Freud's Two Mothers and the Discovery of the Oedipus Complex," *American Imago* 31 (1974): 50 and passim.

8. The question of the mother's sexuality is once again foregrounded in Sue Miller's best-selling novel, *The Good Mother* (New York: Harper and Row, 1986)—in which, perhaps most significantly, the mother's sexuality becomes a determining factor in a legal conflict over what is beneficial or destructive to the child. The cultural-ideological implications of this novel and of its extraordinary popular success ("Can a truly good mother have a passionate sex life?") are yet to be fully explored.

9. The phrase "unique love-object" occurs in Mahler, Pine, and Bergman, *The Psychological Birth of the Human Infant*, p. 110.

10. Erik H. Erikson, *Childhood and Society,* 2nd ed. (New York: Norton, 1963); Nancy Chodorow, *The Reproduction of Mothering: Psychoanalysis and the Sociology of Gender* (Berkeley: University of California Press, 1978); Dorothy Dinnerstein, *The Mermaid and the Minotaur: Sexual Arrangements and the Human Malaise* (New York: Harper and Row, 1976); Jessica Benjamin, *The Bonds of Love: Psychoanalysis, Feminism, and the Problem of Domination* (New York: Pantheon, 1989).

11. E. Ann Kaplan, "Mothering, Feminism and Representation: The Maternal in Melodrama and the Woman's Film, 1910–1940," in Christine Gledhill, ed., *Home Is Where the Heart Is* (London: British Film Institute, 1987), pp. 113–137.

12. Nancy Chodorow and Susan Contratto, "The Fantasy of the Perfect Mother," in Barrie Thorne and Marilyn Yalom, eds., *Rethinking the Family* (New York: Longman, 1982), p. 71. Subsequent page references to this essay will be given in parentheses in the text.

13. Among the works that Chodorow and Contratto critique are Adrienne Rich, *Of Woman Born: Motherhood as Experience and Institution* (New York: Norton, 1976); Jane Lazarre, *The Mother Knot* (New York: McGraw-Hill, 1976); and *Feminist Studies* 4, no. 2 (Summer 1978), a special issue entitled "Toward a Feminist Theory of Motherhood."

14. Carol Gilligan, *In a Different Voice: Psychological Theory and Women's Development* (Cambridge, Mass.: Harvard University Press, 1982), p. 159.

15. Mary Gordon, "On Mothership and Authorhood," *New York Times Book Review,* February 10, 1985, p. 1.

16. "A Cabin of One's Own," *New York Times Book Review,* March 31, 1985, p. 30.

17. Margaret Drabble, "The Limits of Mother Love," *New York Times Book Review,* March 31, 1985, p. 30.

18. Mary Gordon, *Men and Angels* (New York: Random House, 1985), p. 45. Subsequent page references will be given in parentheses in the text.

19. I call my reading of *Men and Angels* both detailed and partial because, although it explores at length the phenomenon of maternal splitting and uses it to make sense of the novel as a whole, that is all it does. In other words, it make *one* sense of a work that invites many other readings and constructions of sense. Such a partial reading is inevitable, given my theoretical frame; in any case, no reading of a novel can claim completeness, although some readings may be more complete than others.

20. Alice Balint, "Love for the Mother and Mother Love," in Michael Balint, *Primary Love and Psychoanalytic Technique* (New York: Liveright, 1965), p. 101.

21. Erik H. Erikson, "Human Strength and the Cycle of Generations," in Erikson, *Insight and Responsibility* (New York: Norton, 1964), p. 116.

22. Lenore J. Weitzman, *The Divorce Revolution: The Unexpected Social and Economic Consequences for Women and Children in America* (New York: Free Press, 1985), chs. 9, 10.

23. This is even clearer in Chesler's more recent book, based on her involvement on behalf of Mary Beth Whitehead in the "Baby M" case; see Phyllis Chesler, *Sacred Bond: The Legacy of Baby M* (New York: Times Books, 1988). Here, too, although Chesler's claims may be sweeping, the cases she documents are sobering. See also Daniel Golden, "What Makes Mommy Run?" *Boston Globe Magazine,* April 24, 1988.

3. Motherhood and Identity Politics

1. Thomás Rivera, *Y no se lo trago la tierra* (Houston: Arte Publico, 1987).

2. Thelma Ravella-Pinto, "Buchi Emecheta at Spelman College," *Sage* 2, no. 1 (Spring 1985): 50–56, esp. 50.

3. Mary Gordon, *Men and Angels* (New York: Random House, 1985).

4. Buchi Emecheta, *The Joys of Motherhood* (New York: George Braziller, 1979).

4. Simone de Beauvoir and the Writing Self

This chapter first appeared in a slightly different version in *L'Esprit créateur* (Winter 1989), special issue titled *Writing Lives: Sartre, Beauvoir, and (Auto)biography,* ed. Susan R. Suleiman.

1. Hélène Cixous, "La venue à l'écriture," in Hélène Cixous, Madeleine Gagnon, and Annie Leclerc, *La venue à l'écriture* (Paris: Union Générale, 1977),

p. 20. Unless otherwise indicated, all translations from French works are my own.

2. Simone de Beauvoir, *La Force de l'âge* (Paris: Gallimard, 1960).

3. *Le Deuxième Sexe* (Paris: Gallimard, collection "Idées," 1949), vol. 2, pp. 427, 478, 479. Subsequent page references to this edition will be given in parentheses in the text.

4. Christine Brooke-Rose, "Illiterations," in Ellen G. Friedman and Miriam Fuchs, eds., *Breaking the Sequence: Women's Experimental Fiction* (Princeton: Princeton University Press, 1989), p. 59.

5. Simone de Beauvoir, *Mémoires d'une jeune fille rangée* (Paris: Gallimard, 1958), p. 193.

6. Nancy K. Miller, "Women's Autobiography in France: For a Dialectics of Identification," in Sally McConnell-Ginet, Ruth Borker, and Nelly Furman, eds., *Women and Language in Literature and Society* (New York: Praeger, 1980), pp. 259–271.

7. Emery Snyder, unpublished paper on *Les Mandarins*, written for my course on twentieth-century French fiction, Fall 1986.

8. Simone de Beauvoir, *La Force des choses* (Paris: Gallimard, 1963), p. 188. Subsequent page references will be given in parentheses in the text.

9. Sandra Gilbert and Susan Gubar's analysis of this "classic" male trope is well known—see their book *The Madwoman in the Attic* (New Haven: Yale University Press, 1979), ch. 1. See also Nancy K. Miller, "Rereading as a Woman: The Body in Practice," in Susan Rubin Suleiman, ed., *The Female Body in Western Culture: Contemporary Perspectives* (Cambridge, Mass.: Harvard University Press, 1986).

10. This argument is made, for example, by Michèle Le Doeff, "Simone de Beauvoir and Existentialism," *Feminist Studies* 6, no. 2 (Summer 1980): 277–289.

11. Jacques Lacan, "La Question hystérique (II): 'Qu'est-ce qu'une femme?'" in *Le Séminaire, III: Les Psychoses* (Paris: Seuil, 1981), p. 198.

12. Luce Irigaray, *Speculum de l'autre femme* (Paris: Minuit, 1974).

13. Alice Jardine, "Interview with Simone de Beauvoir," *Signs* 5, no. 2 (1979): 231.

14. In this regard, it becomes especially interesting (and paradoxical) that the "discreet" profession with which Beauvoir endowed Anne in *The Mandarins* is that of psychoanalyst, for psychoanalysis appears valuable to many people today to the degree that it allows one to work through the question of sexual difference. Beauvoir's choice not to make Anne's profession meaningful, either to Anne herself or to the reader, may be thought of as a missed oppportunity. On the other hand, as I have suggested à propos of Lacan, there are blind spots concerning female sexuality and the female sex in classical (and not-so-classical) psychoanalysis as well.

5. The Passion According to Hélène Cixous

This chapter first appeared as an introductory essay to Hélène Cixous, *"Coming to Writing" and Other Essays,* ed. Deborah Jenson (Cambridge, Mass.: Harvard University Press, 1991). Unless otherwise identified, all of the quotations and page numbers refer to that book. The epigraph is from "From the Scene of the Unconscious to the Scene of History," trans. Deborah W. Carpenter [Jenson], in Ralph Cohen, ed., *The Future of Literary Theory* (New York: Routledge, 1989), p. 11. The initials H.C. (originally, the subtitle of my introductory essay was "The Passion According to H.C.") are an allusion to Clarice Lispector's novel *The Passion According to G.H.*, about which Cixous has written and lectured extensively.

1. The "Bibliography," prepared by Marguerite Sandré and Christa Stevens, is in Françoise van Rossum-Guyon and Myriam Diaz-Diocaretz, eds., *Hélène Cixous: Chemins d'une écriture* (Paris: Presses Universitaires de Vincennes, 1990).

2. Françoise van Rossum-Guyon, "A propos de *Manne*: Entretien avec Hélène Cixous," in *Hélène Cixous: Chemins d'une écriture*, pp. 222, 223. My translation.

3. Hélène Cixous, "From the Scene of the Unconscious to the Scene of History," trans. Deborah W. Carpenter, in Ralph Cohen, ed., *The Future of Literary Theory* (New York: Routledge, 1989), p. 10.

4. Quoted in Robert Hughes, "The Art of Frank Auerbach," *New York Review of Books*, October 11, 1990, p. 28. It may be worth noting that Frank Auerbach is himself a "displaced person," having left his native Berlin at age eight; his parents, who stayed behind, were both killed at Auschwitz (Hughes, p. 28).

5. Clarice Lispector has been one of the authors treated in Hélène Cixous' seminar at the University of Paris for more than ten years. The other authors vary, and have included in recent years Isak Dinesen, Marina Tsvetaeva, and Osip Mandelstam, as well as Rilke, Kafka, and Kleist, who are constantly referred to in H.C.'s work. For a selection from the seminar in English, see Hélène Cixous, *Reading with Clarice Lispector* (Minneapolis: University of Minnesota Press, 1990).

6. This early version is in *Souffles* (Paris: Editions des Femmes, 1975), pp. 180–181. I have discussed Cixous' "angry ironic" mode in chapters 2 and 7 of my book *Subversive Intent: Gender, Politics, and the Avant-Garde* (Cambridge, Mass.: Harvard University Press, 1990).

7. Besides those who are "there without writing," one might mention a number of important intellectual presences whose work and thought have made a huge difference for Cixous without being explicitly mentioned in her writing. Two who come immediately to mind are Antoinette Fouque, the founder of Editions des Femmes, the publishing house that with a short interruption in the early 1980s has published all of Cixous' books since 1975; and Jacques Derrida, another native of Oran (although they did not know each other in Algeria, he has spoken with affection about their common background), who has been her friend and a major intellectual ally for many years.

8. Hélène Cixous, *Vivre l'orange / To Live the Orange* (Paris: Editions des Femmes, 1979), p. 111.

9. "Entretien avec Renée el Kaïm," February 1985, unpublished manuscript, pp. 4–5. All quotes from this text are my translations and are quoted by permission of Hélène Cixous.

10. Ibid., pp. 2–3. Cixous' father, born in Algeria, technically had the status of an overseas French citizen. His family had lived in Morocco before settling in Algeria, and like many other Sephardic Jewish families in the Middle East they still spoke Spanish at home; Cixous recalls, however, that he felt politically and culturally close to France during the 1930s, especially during the Popular Front government (1936–1937) headed by the Socialists. Cixous' mother left Germany in 1933 after Hitler came to power, and was joined in Algeria in 1938 by her mother, who had lived in Alsace before World War I and was able to leave Germany thanks to her Franco-German passport. Cixous' maternal grandfather, of Hungarian-Czech extraction, was killed on the Russian front in 1915. During World War II, many family members were deported and perished in concentration camps. (Information on family background from Hélène Cixous, personal communication, October 22, 1990.)

11. Ibid., p. 9.

12. "From the Scene of the Unconscious to the Scene of History," p. 5.

13. Van Rossum-Guyon, "A Propos de *Manne*," p. 215.

14. Julia Kristeva, *Etrangers à nous-mêmes* (Paris: Fayard, 1988), p. 58; my translation.

15. "From the Scene of the Unconscious to the Scene of History," p. 2.

16. Ibid., p. 10.

6. Artists in Love (and Out)

A slightly shorter version of this chapter appeared in Whitney Chadwick and Isabelle de Courtivron, eds., *Significant Others: Creativity and Intimate Partnership* (London: Thames and Hudson, 1993). The first epigraph is from a personal conversation, Oak Park, Illinois, December 27, 1990; other personal quotations are from that interview, or from my earlier meetings with Leonora Carrington in November 1988 and April 1989. The second epigraph is from an interview with Paul de Angelis, June 1990 (see note 3 for full citation). Unfortunately, it was not possible to give color reproductions of the works by Carrington and Ernst discussed here. Good color reproductions are to be found in the exhibition catalogues mentioned in note 4.

1. The facts mentioned in this hypothetical movie script were culled from various published sources, most of which are mentioned in the notes that follow. In addition, I wish to thank Leonora Carrington, Whitney Chadwick, Andrea Schlieker, and Marina Warner for their indispensable help in gathering materials for this essay. The argument and interpretations are, of course, my own.

2. Max Ernst, *"Beyond Painting" and Other Writings by the Artist and His Friends* (New York: Wittenborn, Schultz, 1948), pp. 28–29.

3. Paul de Angelis, "Interview with Leonora Carrington," in *Leonora Carrington: The Mexican Years, 1943–1985*, exhibition catalogue (The Mexican Museum, San Francisco, and University of New Mexico Press, 1991), p. 34.

4. See *Leonora Carrington: Paintings, Drawings and Sculptures, 1940–1990*, exhibi-

tion catalogue (London: Serpentine Gallery, 1991), plate 14 (p. 65). Ernst's *Two Children Threatened by a Nightingale* has been widely reproduced, most recently in Werner Spies, ed., *Max Ernst: A Retrospective,* exhibition catalogue (London: Tate Gallery, and Munich: Prestel Verlag, 1991).

5. De Angelis, "Interview with Leonora Carrington," p. 42.

6. I have discussed this painting in detail in my book *Subversive Intent: Gender, Politics, and the Avant-Garde* (Cambridge, Mass.: Harvard University Press, 1990), ch. 7.

7. Max Ernst, "Les Mystères de la forêt," in *Ecritures* (Paris: Gallimard, 1970), p. 223; my translation.

8. See Sarah Wilson, "Max Ernst and England," in Spies, ed., *Max Ernst: A Retrospective,* pp. 365–366. Wilson's essay was extremely helpful in my efforts to track the works produced by Ernst and Carrington during their relationship. Another indispensable source is Whitney Chadwick's classic work, *Women Artists and the Surrealist Movement* (London: Thames and Hudson, 1985).

9. Uwe Schneede, *The Essential Max Ernst,* trans. R. W. Last (London: Thames and Hudson, 1972), p. 95.

10. *The Mythology of All Races,* vol. 2: *Eddic,* ed. Canon John Arnott MacCulloch (Boston: Marshall Jones, 1930), p. 207.

11. Andrew Graham-Dixon, "The Rocking-Horse Winner" (review of the Carrington retrospective exhibition at the Serpentine Gallery), *The Independent,* December 17, 1991.

12. Interview with Marina Warner, July 4, 1987; parts of this interview are reported in Marina Warner's introduction to Carrington's *The House of Fear: Notes from Down Below.* My thanks to her for sharing the complete version with me.

13. Marina Warner, "Introduction" to *The House of Fear: Notes from Down Below,* p. 10. Page references to "Little Francis," given in parentheses, are to this edition.

14. "Pigeon, Fly," in Carrington, *"The Seventh Horse" and Other Tales* (New York: Dutton, 1988), p. 28. Other page references to this story and to "The Seventh Horse" will be given in parentheses in the text.

15. Peggy Guggenheim, *Out of This Century: Confessions of an Art Addict* (New York: Universe Books, 1979), p. 239. For a recent scholarly discussion of the Ernst-Carrington relationship, see Renée Riese Hubert, "Leonora Carrington and Max Ernst: Artistic Partnership and Feminist Liberation," *New Literary History,* 22, no. 3 (Summer 1991): 715–745.

16. Jimmy Ernst, *A Not-So-Still-Life* (New York: St. Martin's/Marek, 1984), pp. 213–214.

17. Coincidentally, all three women artists had a personal link to Ernst. Leonor Fini accepted the invitation, but did not deliver a painting in time. The other painters in the competition were Ivan Le Lorrain Albright, Eugene Berman, Luis Guglielmi, Horace Pippin, Abraham Rattner, and Stanley Spencer. All of the above information, as well as the quotations to come, are from the cata-

logue that accompanied the traveling exhibition. See *The Temptation of Saint Anthony: Bel Ami International Art Competition and Exhibition of New Paintings by Eleven American and European Artists, 1946–1947* (Washington, D.C.: American Federation of Arts, 1946). Page references to this volume will be given in parentheses in the text.

18. The Bel Ami exhibition, which opened at the Knoedler Gallery in New York in September 1946, was widely reviewed in the press. The review in the *New York Times* of September 22 (signed E.A.J.) mentioned the judges' difficulty in reaching a decision, and noted that "several of the canvases, indeed, seem peculiarly persuasive, among them the exquisite, so finely imaginative account by Leonora Carrington." Other reviews include those in *Art News*, September 1946, and *Art Digest*, September 15, 1946. *Art News* had announced the existence of the competition in its February issue, and reported Ernst's winning the prize in April. (The date given for Carrington's *Temptation of St. Anthony* in the catalogue of the Serpentine Gallery exhibition is thus off by one year; the correct date is 1946, not 1947.) Ernst's painting was duly featured in Albert Lewin's film *The Private Affairs of Bel Ami* (1947), where it appeared in two shots, the first one in a sudden burst of Technicolor—the rest of the film was black and white. Unfortunately, the film is quite mediocre despite starring roles by George Sanders and the young Angela Lansbury.

19. For a detailed discussion of this novel, written in the early 1950s and first published in 1976, see Suleiman, *Subversive Intent*, ch. 7.

7. The Fate of the Surrealist Imagination in the Society of the Spectacle

1. Ado Kyrou, *Le Surréalisme au cinéma* (Paris: Arcanes, 1953); *Amour-érotisme et cinéma* (Paris: Le Terrain Vague, 1957).

2. Angela Carter, "Tokyo Pastoral," in *Nothing Sacred: Selected Writings* (London: Virago, 1982), p. 33.

3. Ibid., p. 28.

4. The unidentified quotes attributed to Angela Carter in the preceding pages are from that telephone conversation, London, May 16, 1991. My memory of the conversation remains especially vivid and poignant, for Angela Carter was already undergoing daily treatments for lung cancer; yet her extraordinary sense of humor (including her ability to laugh at the doctors' disagreements about how to treat her illness), as well as her kindness and interest in others, remained as alive as ever. She died less than a year later, on February 16, 1992, at the age of fifty-one. I dedicate this chapter to her memory.

5. Brian McHale, *Postmodernist Fiction* (New York: Methuen, 1987), p. 10.

6. Angela Carter, *The Infernal Desire Machines of Dr. Hoffman* (London: Penguin, 1982), p. 97. The novel was first published in 1972. Subsequent page references to the Penguin edition will be given in parentheses in the text.

7. André Breton, "Introduction au discours sur le peu de réalité," in *Point du jour*

(Paris: Gallimard, 1970), p. 26. The essay was first published in September 1924. The translation used here is my own.

8. Susan Rubin Suleiman, *Subversive Intent: Gender, Politics, and the Avant-Garde* (Cambridge, Mass.: Harvard University Press, 1990), p. xv.

9. Linda Hutcheon, *A Poetics of Postmodernism* (New York: Routledge, 1988), p. 5.

10. Auberon Waugh, "The Surreal Thing," *Spectator,* May 20, 1972, p. 772.

11. David Punter, "Angela Carter: Supersessions of the Masculine," *Critique* 25, no. 4 (Summer 1984): 211. Subsequent page references will be given in parentheses in the text.

12. Ricarda Smith, "The Journey of the Subject in Angela Carter's Fiction," *Textual Practice* 3, no. 1 (1990): n5.

13. Herbert Marcuse, *Eros and Civilization,* with a new preface by the author (New York: Vintage, 1962), p. 135.

14. Guy Debord, *La Société du spectacle* (Paris: Champ Libre, 1971), p. 9; my translation.

15. Donna Haraway's "A Manifesto for Cyborgs: Science, Technology, and Socialist Feminism in the 1980's," first published in 1984 (*Socialist Review* 50), has often been reprinted and has acquired an international audience. Lyotard's hopefulness about computers and postmodern society, expressed in *La Condition postmoderne* (Paris: Minuit, 1979; English trans. 1981), has been somewhat tempered since then; see Jean-François Lyotard, *Le Postmoderne expliqué aux enfants* (Paris: Galilée, 1986).

16. Gilles Deleuze and Félix Guattari, *L'Anti-Oedipe* (Paris: Minuit, 1972); the phrases in quotation marks are on p. 34.

17. Angela Carter, *The Passion of New Eve* (London: Victor Gollancz, 1977); idem, *Nights at the Circus* (London: Chatto and Windus, 1984).

18. This essay has benefited greatly from the discussions I have had with various audiences who heard it as a public lecture—in Austin, Texas, in 1992 and in Amsterdam and Valencia in 1993. My special thanks to Giulia Colaizzi and Thomas Elsaesser, whose questions and challenges concerning postmodernism and technology pushed me to define Carter's position more clearly.

8. Alternatives to Beauty in Contemporary Art

This chapter was conceived as my contribution to the conference "Whatever Happened to Beauty?" organized by Richard Shiff, director of the Center for the Study of Modernism at the University of Texas at Austin, held at the Center on February 7–8, 1992. The public included artists, art historians, academics in other fields, and students, as well as a considerable number of nonspecialists. The epigraph by Van Gogh is taken from the source cited in note 1 below. The epigraph by Magdalena Campos-Pons is from an interview with Lillian Mansour conducted in Boston in 1988 and communicated to me in manuscript. The epigraph by Gertrude Stein is from "Composition as Explanation," p. 513 (see note 2 below).

1. Herschel B. Chipp, ed., *Theories of Modern Art* (Berkeley: University of California Press, 1968), p. 36. Subsequent references to this useful volume will be given in parentheses in the text.

2. "Composition as Explanation," in *Selected Writings of Gertrude Stein*, ed. Carl Van Vechten (New York: Vintage, 1990), p. 515. I wish to thank Robin Lydenberg for calling this passage to my attention.

3. The exhibition was curated by Elisabeth Sussman and Matthew Teitelbaum of the Institute of Contemporary Art, and Olivier Debroise from Mexico. My heartfelt thanks to Matthew Teitelbaum for providing me with slides and background materials and sharing his knowledge about the artists in the show; and to Elisabeth Sussman, who had moved to the Whitney Museum in New York by the time the show opened but who provided help from afar. See the excellent exhibition catalogue edited by the three curators: *El Corazón Sangrante / The Bleeding Heart* (Seattle: University of Washington Press, and Boston: Institute of Contemporary Art, 1991).

4. For a brief discussion and some examples of *milagros* in Latin American folk art, see Marion Oettinger, Jr., *The Folk Art of Latin America: Visiones del Pueblo* (New York: Dutton Studio Books and the Museum of American Folk Art, 1992), pp. 42–43.

5. Quoted in the article by Brian Alexander, "S.D. Border Art Leaves Folks in Ohio Unmoved," *Los Angeles Times*, July 28, 1990.

6. David Avalos, "Welcome to Café Mestizo," in *Café Mestizo*, exhibition catalogue (New York: Intar Gallery, 1989). The New York installation differed in some details from the 1991 installation in Boston. Avalos told me he does not worry about variations from one installation to another, although he obviously remembers them, no matter how minor. For the Boston installation, he worked long distance with ICA curator Matthew Siegel.

7. Avalos explained to me that in the actual installation at the Intar Gallery, Cooper's novel did not appear—it was placed next to the *Straight-Razor Taco* only for the cover photograph (telephone conversation with the artist, September 9, 1993). Be that as it may, the juxtaposition is meaningful and interesting; the cover photo simply actualizes one of the possible interpretations of the *Straight-Razor Taco*.

9. Living Between

This chapter is the considerably expanded version of an essay first published in *The Review of Contemporary Fiction* 9, no. 3 (Fall 1989): 124–127. The second epigraph is taken from "A Conversation with Christine Brooke-Rose" (see note 7 below).

1. *Alleinstehende Frau*, whose colloquial translation is "single woman" or "independent woman" (not leaning on anyone), can be rendered literally as "stand-

ing alone." The German phrase, never translated, recurs several times in *Between* and has a particular significance, as we shall see.

2. Roland Barthes, *The Pleasure of the Text,* trans. Richard Miller (New York: Hill and Wang, 1975), pp. 3–4. Miller translates the French phrase *"Babel heureuse"* ("happy Babel") as "sanctioned Babel." I prefer the more expressive literal meaning.

3. Christine Brooke-Rose, *Between* (1968), in *The Christine Brooke-Rose Omnibus: Four Novels* (Manchester, England: Carcanet, 1986), p. 447. Hereafter page references to this edition will be given in parentheses in the text.

4. Richard Martin, "'Just Words on a Page': The Novels of Christine Brooke-Rose," *Review of Contemporary Fiction* 9, no. 3 (Fall 1989): 114. This issue of the journal is devoted to the work of Brooke-Rose, Kathy Acker, and Dorothy Richardson.

5. Jean Baudrillard, "The Precession of Simulacra," in Brian Wallis, ed., *Art after Modernism: Rethinking Representation* (New York: New Museum of Contemporary Art, 1984), p. 254.

6. In flattened English: "He likes ready-made stories the dirtier the funnier with a burst of crude laughter right off and the more off the righter." This does away with the bilingual punning on *tout de suite,* but succeeds in creating a pun on "off." Of course my reader-friendly attempt to "translate Brooke-Rose into English" is absurd (like trying to translate *Finnegans Wake*). If she had wanted to write *Between* in English, she would have. Tant pis for the monolingual reader, nicht wahr?

7. Ellen G. Friedman and Miriam Fuchs, "A Conversation with Christine Brooke-Rose," *Review of Contemporary Fiction* 9, no. 3 (Fall 1989): 85. The second epigraph to this chapter is taken from this interview (p. 84).

8. Friedman and Fuchs, "A Conversation," p. 84.

9. Zygmunt Bauman, *Legislators and Interpreters: On Modernity, Postmodernity and Intellectuals* (Cambridge: Polity, 1987); Rosi Braidotti, "L'Usure des langues," *Cahiers du GRIF* 39 (1988): 73–81.

10. Life-Story, History, Fiction

This chapter first appeared in *Contention: Debates in Society, Culture, and Science* 2 (January 1992). I wish to thank the following people for their helpful comments on an earlier version of this essay: Dorrit Cohn, Natalie Davis, Dorothy Kaufmann, Nikki Keddie, and Gerald Prince.

1. Deirdre Bair, *Simone de Beauvoir: A Biography* (New York: Summit, 1990).

2. Simone de Beauvoir, *Mémoires d'une jeune fille rangée* (Paris: Gallimard, 1958), p. 168. Unless otherwise indicated, all translations from the French are my own.

3. Simone de Beauvoir, *La Force de l'âge* (Paris: Gallimard, 1960), p. 613.

4. Simone de Beauvoir, *Journal de guerre* (Paris: Gallimard, 1990); idem, *Lettres à Sartre,* 2 vols. (Paris: Gallimard, 1990). The letters have been published in an

abridged English translation: *Letters to Sartre*, ed. and trans. Quintin Hoare (New York: Arcade, 1992).

5. See *La Force des choses* (Paris: Gallimard, 1963), p. 50. The English title of this book is *The Force of Circumstance*.

6. Jean-Paul Sartre, *Lettres au Castor et à quelques autres* (Paris: Gallimard, 1983), vol. 2, p. 21.

7. Beauvoir, *Lettres à Sartre*, vol. 2, p. 26.

8. Sartre, *Lettres*, vol. 2, p. 22.

9. Beauvoir, *Journal de guerre*, p. 29. Subsequent page references will be given in parentheses in the text.

10. Bianca Lamblin, *Mémoires d'une jeune fille dérangée* (Paris: Balland, 1993). Bianca Lamblin (Lamblin is her married name), who was one of Beauvoir's *lycée* students around 1938, indicts Sartre and Beauvoir not only for their cynical treatment of her as a sex object, but also for the brutal way they dropped her at a time when their friendship would have been especially important to her, since she was Jewish. Beauvoir got a ride out of Paris with Bianca and her father when the Germans entered in June 1940, but did not see her again until after the war.

11. Alice Schwarzer, *After "The Second Sex": Conversations with Simone de Beauvoir*, trans. Marianne Howarth (New York: Pantheon, 1984), p. 85.

12. Ibid., pp. 112–113.

13. Marianne Alphant, "Abus de Beauvoir," *Libération* 22 (February 1990): 21.

14. Sylvie Le Bon de Beauvoir, the editor of these volumes, gives no explanation for the gap in the *Journal* between February 22 and June 9. The letters to Sartre continue through March 23, then stop as well. Sartre was in Paris on leave in April, and correspondence in May was impossible because of the German invasion. Simone started writing to him again on July 11, when Sartre was in a prisoner of war camp in southern France.

15. Beauvoir, *Lettres*, vol. 2, pp. 192, 193.

16. Beauvoir, *La Force des choses*, p. 16.

17. It is not clear why Sylvie Le Bon de Beauvoir decided to end the *Journal* in 1941. She writes in her brief introduction that Beauvoir kept a diary all her life, intermittently, and that the *Journal de guerre* is but a small part of a much vaster whole. She does not indicate, however, whether more diaries exist for the war years—and if so, whether they will be published. One can only hope that the negative reactions to the *Journal de guerre* and the *Lettres à Sartre* will not prevent publication of the rest of Beauvoir's private writings in the near future.

18. See Beauvoir, *La Force de l'âge*, pp. 555–561.

19. Simone de Beauvoir, *Le Sang des autres* (Paris: Gallimard, 1945), p. 163. Subsequent page references will be given in parentheses in the text.

20. Beauvoir, *Journal de guerre*, p. 368.

21. Beavoir, *Lettres à Sartre*, vol. 2, p. 246.

22. Beauvoir, *La Force de l'âge*, p. 528.

23. Ibid., pp. 554–555.

24. Beauvoir, *La Force de l'âge*, p. 555.

25. See, in this regard, the recent volume edited by Marianne Hirsch and Evelyn Fox Keller, *Conflicts in Feminism* (New York: Routledge, 1990).

26. Joan W. Scott, "Rewriting History," in M. Higonnet, J. Jenson, S. Michel, and M. Weitz, eds., *Behind the Lines: Gender and the Two World Wars* (New Haven: Yale University Press, 1987), p. 25.

27. Schwarzer, *After "The Second Sex,"* p. 37.

28. Hélène Vivienne Wenzel, "Interview with Simone de Beauvoir," *Yale French Studies* 72 (1986): 25.

29. A comparative reading of diaries and memoirs by French women intellectuals of Beauvoir's generation would be extremely enlightening. Dorothy Kaufmann's current work on Edith Thomas, a novelist and active member of the Resistance who also kept a diary during the war (as yet unpublished) is one case in point. See Kaufmann, "'Le Témoin compromis': Diaries of Resistance and Collaboration by Edith Thomas," *L'Esprit Créateur* 33, no. 1 (Spring 1993): 17–29.

11. War Memories

A slightly shorter version of this chapter appeared in *New Literary History*, Summer 1993. I wish to thank Jack Beatty, Lawrence Kritzman, and Doris Sommer for their close reading of an earlier version of this essay and their excellent suggestions for revision.

1. Harry James Cargas, *In Conversation with Elie Wiesel* (New York: Paulist Press, 1976), p. 89.

2. Ibid., p. 86.

3. Elie Wiesel, *Night Dawn Day* (New York: Aronson / B'nai B'rith, 1985), p. 271; subsequent page references will be given in parentheses following the quotation. *Day* was first published in English as *The Accident* (New York: Hill and Wang, 1972). The translation is by Anne Borchardt.

4. Cargas, *In Conversation with Elie Wiesel*, p. 87.

5. Harry James Cargas, for example, sees this as a novel of emotional and spiritual recovery, fueled by love and friendship—a possible reading, but one that has to ignore a great deal. See ibid., p. 120.

6. Alvin H. Rosenfeld, "The Problematics of Holocaust Literature," in Alvin H. Rosenfeld and Irving Greenberg, eds., *Confronting the Holocaust: The Impact of Elie Wiesel* (Bloomington: Indiana University Press, 1978), p. 22.

7. Citations for Lesèvre's and Delbo's works are given in notes 11, 12, and 14. Other first-person accounts of concentration camp experiences in French include David Rousset, *L'Univers concentrationnaire* (Paris: Pavois, 1946); Robert Antelme, *L'Espèce humaine* (Paris: Gallimard, 1957); and Germaine Tillion, *Ravensbrück* (Paris: Seuil, 1973; rev. ed., 1988).

8. For a full-scale study on the fate of Jewish children during World War II, see

Deborah Dwork, *Children with a Star: Jewish Youth in Nazi Europe* (New Haven: Yale University Press, 1991). Besides official documents and historical works, Dwork based her study on oral testimonies rather than on written accounts by survivors.

9. Shoshana Felman quotes the videotaped testimony of a child survivor: "I was unable to read any books . . . I didn't read a word about the Holocaust." After years of refusal, this witness, Menachem S., nevertheless agreed to tell his story for the Fortunoff Video Archive at Yale University. See Shoshana Felman and Dori Laub, *Testimony: Crises of Witnessing in Literature, Psychoanalysis, and History* (New York: Routledge, 1992), p. 46.

10. According to Lejeune in *Le Pacte autobiographique* (Paris: Seuil, 1975), the sign of true autobiography—as opposed to, say, autobiographical fiction—is the single, identical name of author, narrator, and character; this identity signals that what the author recounts is to be understood as having "really happened" to him or her—whence the notion of an "autobiographical pact" between author and reader. Lejeune's criterion of identity has been criticized by some theorists, and is challenged by postmodern writing which blurs the line between fiction and autobiography—for example, by giving the main character of an autobiographical novel the same name as the author's. The classic example in French (written, the author has said, as a response to Lejeune) is Serge Doubrovsky's novel *Fils* (Paris: Galilée, 1977).

11. Lise Lesèvre, *Face à Barbie: Souvenirs-cauchemars de Montluc à Ravensbrück* (Paris: Pavillon, 1987), p. 75; my translation. Subsequent page references will be given in parentheses in the text.

12. Charlotte Delbo, *La Mémoire et les jours* (Paris: Berg International, 1985), p. 14. Lawrence Langer discusses Delbo's concepts and makes extensive use of them in his study of oral testimonies from the Fortunoff Video Archives at Yale, *Holocaust Testimonies: The Ruins of Memory* (New Haven: Yale University Press, 1991).

13. Lucie Aubrac, *Ils partiront dans l'ivresse: Lyon, mai '43—Londres, février '44* (Paris: Seuil, 1984). In English: *Outwitting the Gestapo*, trans. Konrad Bieber with the assistance of Betsy Wing (Lincoln: University of Nebraska Press, 1992).

14. Charlotte Delbo, *Aucun de nous ne reviendra* (Paris: Gonthier, 1965). Delbo's other books include (besides *La Mémoire et les jours,* already cited) *Une Connaissance inutile* (Paris: Minuit, 1970), *Mesure de nos jours* (Paris: Minuit, 1971), and *Le Convoi du 24 janvier* [*1943*] (Paris: Minuit, 1965). *Le Convoi* gives short biographies (including their camp numbers) of each of the 230 French women who were in the convoy that took Delbo to Auschwitz. Of the 230, forty-nine survived. Delbo's powerful writings about the experience of Auschwitz are not sufficiently well known outside France (or inside).

15. Claudine Vegh, *I Didn't Say Goodbye,* trans. Ros Schwartz (New York: Dutton, 1984), p. 150. Subsequent page references will be given in parentheses in the text.

16. Saul Friedländer, *When Memory Comes*, trans. Helen R. Lane (New York: Farrar

Straus Giroux, 1979), pp. 73–74. Subsequent page reference will be given in parentheses in the text.

17. Georges Perec, *W ou le souvenir d'enfance* (Paris: Denoël, 1975), p. 135; my translation, here and in subsequent quotations from this work.

18. Deborah Dwork, *Children with a Star: Jewish Youth in Nazi Europe* (New Haven: Yale University Press, 1991), p. xxxiii.

19. Bruno Bettelheim, "Postface" to Vegh, *I Didn't Say Goodbye*, p. 164. I have modified the translation.

20. Cathy Caruth, "Introduction" to *Psychoanalysis, Culture and Trauma*, special issue of *American Imago* 48, no. 1 (Spring 1991): 8. The unusually intense recent interest, by analysts, historians, and literary critics, in the question of trauma and memory, specifically as it relates to representations of the Holocaust, may itself be a phenomenon of "delayed reaction" analogous to that of trauma. Besides works already cited, see for example Saul Friedländer, ed., *Probing the Limits of Representation: Nazism and the "Final Solution"* (Cambridge, Mass.: Harvard University Press, 1992).

21. Friedländer, *When Memory Comes*, p. 159; I have modified Helen R. Lane's translation slightly in this instance.

12. My War in Four Episodes

This chapter was first published in *Agni* 33 (Spring 1991). A Hungarian acquaintance who read that version recently pointed out an inaccuracy in the last section: no bridges in Budapest had "survived the bombing" (as I had written) during the last year of the war. The Russian army put up a makeshift temporary bridge, which is the one I must have crossed with my parents when we walked back home. At first I decided to take the liberty offered by literary autobiography and not alter my original sentence, whose rhythm I liked. But factual scruples eventually won out over poetic license: I rewrote the sentence. I mention this because the struggle and its outcome have a certain interest of their own, both theoretical and autobiographical. A companion piece to this memoir is "Reading in Tongues," *Boston Review* (May–August 1992).

Epilogue

1. Michael Ignatieff, "The Balkan Tragedy," *New York Review of Books*, May 13, 1993, p. 5.

2. Hélène Cixous, "We Who Are Free, Are We Free?" *Critical Inquiry* 19, no. 2 (Winter 1993): 202–203. I have substituted "self-identification" for "auto-identification" in the translation, for reasons of euphony.

3. Ignatieff, "The Balkan Tragedy," p. 4.

4. Okay, okay, I will name a few. I take sole responsibility for assigning them to their respective groups, and apologize in advance for those I have overlooked.

Among the members of each group, significant differences may exist. Pro-post-modernists: Hal Foster, Linda Hutcheon, Andreas Huyssen, Rosalind Krauss, Jean-François Lyotard, Craig Owens, Richard Rorty (sometimes), Gayatri Spivak. Pro-modernists: Terry Eagleton, Fredric Jameson, Jürgen Habermas, Christopher Norris. Cultural pessimists: Jean Baudrillard, Gilles Lipovetsky, and all the "occasional" visitors from among the first two groups.

5. For a good summing up of the issues, see Linda J. Nicholson, ed., *Feminism and Postmodernism* (New York: Routledge, 1990). Among the most recent position statements are Naomi Schor's defense of "essentialism" in "This Essentialism Which Is Not One: Coming to Grips with Irigaray," *Differences* 1, no. 2 (1989): 38–58; and Drucilla Cornell's defense of the "postmodern subject" in *Beyond Accommodation: Ethical Feminism, Deconstruction, and the Law* (New York: Routledge, 1991).

6. Susan Rubin Suleiman, *Subversive Intent: Gender, Politics, and the Avant-Garde* (Cambridge, Mass.: Harvard University Press, 1990), p. 205. The argument about putting the self into play is made fully in ch. 7; the quote from Winnicott, also quoted there, is from *Playing and Reality* (New York: Basic, 1971), p. 64.

7. Christopher Norris, *Uncritical Theory: Postmodernism, Intellectuals, and the Gulf War* (Amherst: University of Massachusetts Press, 1992); Norris' account of postmodernism in this work is surprisingly reductive for such a well-informed critic. Equally surprising is his attempt to "divorce" Derrida from other poststructuralist philosophers such as Lyotard or Rorty, by arguing that Derrida is essentially an Enlightenment philosopher! Norris seems to want to "save" Derrida by showing that his philosophy is (unlike postmodernism, in Norris' view) compatible with ethical and political positions. As Norris himself admits, his reading of Derrida entails a lot of omissions—and, I would add, no small degree of interpretive arm-twisting.

8. Norris, *Uncritical Theory,* p. 28.

9. Richard Rorty, *Contingency, Irony, and Solidarity* (Cambridge: Cambridge University Press, 1989), p. 189. Subsequent page references to this book will be given in parentheses in the text.

10. Barbara Herrnstein Smith, *Contingencies of Value* (Cambridge, Mass.: Harvard University Press, 1988), p. 161.

11. Zygmunt Bauman, *Intimations of Postmodernity* (New York: Routledge, 1992), p. xxii.

12. A number of commentators, including some of the first reviewers of Rorty's much-discussed book, have criticized his attempt to separate the public from the private, though not exactly in the terms in which I will argue here. One of the most extended of these critiques is Nancy Fraser, "Solidarity or Singularity? Richard Rorty between Romanticism and Technocracy," in *Unruly Practices: Power, Discourse, and Gender in Contemporary Social Theory* (Minneapolis: University of Minnesota Press, 1989), pp. 93–112. See also David Lachterman, review essay, *Clio* 18, no. 4 (1989): 390–399; and Michael S. Roth, review essay, *History and Theory* 29, no. 3 (1990): 339–357.

13. Donna Haraway, "A Manifesto for Cyborgs: Science, Technology, and Socialist Feminism in the 1980's," *Socialist Review* 50 (1984): 100.

14. Nancy Fraser makes a somewhat similar point when she notes that in Rorty's system, radical social theory "becomes aestheticized, narcissized, bourgeoisified"; for Rorty, in other words, ironist theory must be apolitical ("Solidarity or Singularity?" 103).

15. "Editors' Introduction: Multiplying Identities," *Critical Inquiry* 18, no. 4 (Summer 1992), p. 625. See also Hohmi K. Bhabha, "Introduction: Narrating the Nation," in Bhabha, ed., *Nation and Narration* (London: Routledge, 1990); Bhabha proposes hybridity and the "crossing" of national boundaries as positive values. The hope for a "new transnational culture" (p. 4) may strike one today as even more utopian than it appeared in 1990.

16. Guy Scarpetta, *Eloge du cosmopolitisme* (Paris: Grasset & Fasquelle, 1981), p. 25; my translation.

17. See Mirko Kovac, "Les Jeux olympiques de la mort," *La Règle du jeu* 9 (January 1993): 237. This issue of the journal is devoted largely to writings about Sarajevo, most of them by eyewitnesses, some by people still living there.

18. Salman Rushdie, "Le Roman est la preuve de la démocratie," *La Règle du jeu* 9 (January 1993): 178; my translation.

19. Zygmunt Bauman, *Legislators and Interpreters: On Modernity, Postmodernity and Intellectuals* (Cambridge: Polity, 1987), p. 5. Subsequent page references to this book will be given in parentheses in the text. For an interesting recent reflection on the possibilities (and impossibilities) of postmodernism in Hungary, by a younger but no less ironic Central European sociologist, see Tibor Dessewffy's essay (originally published in Hungarian in *2000*, February 1993), "Meeting the 'Posties': Postmodern Goulash in Hungary," forthcoming.

20. Lonnie D. Kliever, "Authority in a Pluralist World," in R. Rubenstein, ed., *Modernisation: The Humanist Response to Its Promise and Problems*; quoted in Bauman, *Legislators and Interpreters*, p. 129.

21. Vladimir Pistalo, "Mr. Hyde dans les Balkans," *La Règle du jeu* 9 (January 1993): 198.

22. The theory of "greater Serbia," which has provided the ideological justification for the current war, is the work of intellectuals, many of them writers and university professors. Dobrice Cosic, the recently ousted Yugoslav president, was among them—he is now considered too "moderate" by the extreme Serbian nationalists. See the articles by John Darnton in the *New York Times* (June 1, June 2, and June 3, 1993), as well as Juan Goytisolo's essay (one of four published under the general title "Sarajevo mon amour") in *La Règle du jeu* 9, (January 1993). Goytisolo considers "a core of intellectuals from the Academy of Sciences in Belgrade" as the real driving force behind the current war; they are the ones who "made themselves into the spokesmen for *the purest essences of the nation*" and "elaborated the expansionist doctrine of greater Serbia" (p. 248).

23. Wayne Booth, "Individualism and the Mystery of the Social Self; or, Does

Amnesty Have a Leg to Stand On?" in Barbara Johnson, ed., *Freedom and Interpretation: The Oxford Amnesty Lectures, 1992* (New York: Basic, 1993), p. 95. Subsequent references to this essay will be given in parentheses in the text.

24. I wish to thank Michael Suleiman, whose comments about the necessity of "taking a stand" forced me to rework the last section of the essay; Veronika Görög, whose comments after my public lecture in Budapest helped me sharpen my argument about the rhetoric of doubt; and Richard Rorty, who pointed out to me the all too familiar status of the paradox I mention in the last paragraph. (Rorty does not consider it a paradox, but I do.)

INDEX

Page numbers in italics refer to illustrations.

Abraham, Karl, 14
Adorno, Theodor, 175
Albright, Ivan Le Lorrain, 254n17
Algren, Nelson, 71
Alice's Adventures in Wonderland (Carroll),
    132
Alphant, Marianne, 185, 186
Alta, 34
Andrássy, Julius, Count, 233
Appiah, Anthony, 236
Aubrac, Lucie, 206
Auden, W. H., 171
Auerbach, Frank, 82, 85
Auerbach, Nina, 20
Aurenche, Marie-Berthe, 102
Austen, Jane, 20
Avalos, David, 150–159; *Hubcap Milagro—
    Junipero Serra's Next Miracle: Turning
    Blood into Thunderbird Wine, 150, 155, 151–
    153; Café Mestizo, 153–159, 155; Hubcap
    Milagro—Combination Platter 2: The
    Manhattan Special, 156; Hubcap
    Milagro—Combination Platter 3: The
    Straight-Razor Taco, 158, 257n7*

Bacon, Francis, 143
Bair, Deirdre, 179, 181, 182, 194
Balint, Alice, 16, 51
Barr, Alfred H., Jr., 117–118
Barrès, Maurice, 71, 77

Barthes, Roland, 18, 126, 147, 170, 172
Bataille, Georges, 239
Baudelaire, Charles, 81, 173
Baudrillard, Jean, 172, 228, 230, 241, 262n4
Bauman, Raquel Portillo, 55–59
Bauman, Zygmunt, 176, 233, 240
Beauvoir, Hélène de, 193
Beauvoir, Simone de, 4, 8, 9, 67–77, 179–
    198; as autobiographer, 67, 69, 71, 179–
    191; on women and writing, 70–71, 74–77,
    247n30; *The Second Sex,* 69–71, 75, 77,
    180, 196–197; *The Mandarins,* 71–76, 180,
    251n14; *The Force of Circumstance,* 73–75,
    191; *Memoirs of a Dutiful Daughter,* 179,
    180; *The Prime of Life,* 179, 180–181, 182,
    184–185, 191, 194–195; *Journal de Guerre,*
    182, 185–191, 192, 195, 197; *The Blood of
    Others,* 182, 183, 191–194
Beauvoir, Sylvie le Bon de, 259nn14,17
Bel Ami (Lewin film) International Compe-
    tition, 255nn17,18
Bellmer, Hans, 157
Benjamin, Jessica, 41, 245n
Berger, John, 160
Bergerac, Cyrano de: *Trip to the Moon,* 6
Berman, Eugene, 254n17
Bettelheim, Bruno, 39–40, 211
The Bleeding Heart/El corazón sangrante (ex-
    hibition), 147–168, 257n3
Booth, Wayne, 241–242

Bosnia, 225, 230, 232, 238–239, 241, 264n22
Bost, Jacques-Laurent, 186, 187, 194
Braidotti, Rosi, 176
Brassaï, 163
Breton, André, 93, 94, 96, 101, 103, 127, 128, 133
Brontës, Charlotte and Emily, 20
Brooke-Rose, Christine, 6, 70, 169–176; - Between, 170–176; Amalgamemnon, 173; Thru, 173
Brown, Rosellen, 32–37; "Good Housekeeping," 32–34; The Autobiography of My Mother, 32, 35–37
Budapest, 171, 214–218, 220, 223–224, 225, 226, 233, 262n
Burke, Carolyn, 29

The Cabinet of Dr. Caligari, 129
Campos-Pons, Maria Magdalena, 4, 140, 159–160; I Am a Fountain, 159, 159–160
Camus, Albert, 71
Cargas, Harry James, 201
Carrington, Leonora, 89–121, 132; "The Bird Superior, Max Ernst," 92, 96, 113; The Inn of the Dawn Horse (self-portrait), 94–95, 95, 96; "The Debutante," 95; Portrait of Max Ernst, 96, 97; Femme et Oiseau, 96, 98, 108, 109, 111; The Horses of Lord Candlestick, 101, 108; "The House of Fear," 101, 107, 108; "The Seventh Horse," 106, 113, 115–117; Rencontre (with Ernst), 109; The House Opposite, 113; Temptation of Saint Anthony, 118, 120, 121; "Little Francis," 109–111; "Pigeon, Fly," 111–112
Carroll, Lewis, 112; Alice in Wonderland, 132
Carter, Angela, 6, 93, 125–139, 255n4; The Infernal Desire Machines of Dr. Hoffmann, 125, 126, 127–136, 137–139
Cavalcanti, Guido, 171, 173
Cavell, Marcia, 246n8
Caws, Mary Ann, 245n3
Cézanne, Paul, 143
Chamberlain, Neville, 173
Chateaubriand, René François de: René, 72
Chawaf, Chantal, 30
Chesler, Phyllis, 24, 26, 39, 52–53, 250n23
Chicago, Judy, 76

Chodorow, Nancy, 15, 16, 41, 42–44, 50, 51, 60
Cixous, Hélène, 78–88, 169, 226, 234, 252nn5,7, 253n10; as theorist of women's writing, 29–30, 68, 80, 82–85, 248n42; on history, 78, 85–88, 179, 226; "Coming to Writing," 68, 79–80, 84, 86, 87
Claudel, Paul, 71, 77
Clément, Catherine, 248
Coetzee, J. M.: Waiting for the Barbarians, 242
Colette, 209
Contratto, Susan, 42–44, 50, 60
Cooper, James Fenimore: The Last of the Mohicans, 157, 158, 257n7
Cornell, Drucilla, 263n5
Correa, Juan: The Allegory of the Sacrament, 148, 149, 151
Cosic, Dobrice, 264n22
Critical Inquiry ("Identities" issue), 236

Dali, Salvador, 118, 128
Darnton, John, 264n22
De Angelis, Paul, 99
Debord, Guy, 126, 134–135
Debroise, Olivier, 257n3
Delbo, Charlotte, 204; Aucun de nous ne reviendra, 206
Deleuze, Gilles, 136, 169
Delvaux, Paul, 118, 128
De Man, Paul, 198
Derrida, Jacques, 80, 234, 235, 236, 252n7, 263n7
Desnos, Robert, 135–136
Deutsch, Helene, 14, 16, 17, 18–19, 246n8
Dinesen, Isak, 252n5
Dinnerstein, Dorothy, 41, 51
Dostoevsky, Fyodor, 69
Doubrovsky, Serge: Fils, 261n10
Drabble, Margaret, 37, 45
Drieu la Rochelle, Pierre, 190
Duchamp, Marcel, 117–118, 128, 137
Duras, Marguerite: La Douleur, 239
Dwork, Deborah, 208

Eagleton, Terry, 262n4
Eliot, George, 20
Eliot, T. S., 171

Emecheta, Buchi, 57–58, 61–63; *The Joys of Motherhood,* 61–63
Erikson, Erik, 41, 52, 60
Ernst, Max, 89–119, 128, 157; *Europe after the Rain,* 91, 115, *116; Leonora in the Morning Light,* 92, 103, *104; La Femme 100 têtes,* 96; *Deux enfants menacés par un rossignol,* 98–99, 103; "Les Mystères de la forêt," 102, 109; *The Bride of the Wind* (oil), 104–106, *105; The Bride of the Wind* (pencil), 104–106, *106; Rencontre* (with Carrington), *109; The Robing of the Bride,* 114, 115; *Temptation of Saint Anthony,* 118, *119*
Ernst, Jimmy, 102

Felman, Shoshana, 261n9
Fini, Leonor, 118, 254n17
Finnegans Wake (Joyce), 258n6
Foster, Hal, 262n4
Foucault, Michel, 169, 235, 236
Fouque, Antoinette, 82, 252n7
Frank, Anne, 196
Fraser, Nancy, 263n12, 264n14
Freud, Sigmund, 20, 76; on women, 14, 15, 29, 40–41; on creativity, 17, 31
Friday, Nancy, 39
Friedländer, Saul: *When Memory Comes,* 199, 207, 208, 209, 210, 211, 212
Friedrich, Caspar David, 103

Gaskell, Elizabeth, 19
Gates, Henry Louis, Jr., 236
Gauguin, Paul, 143
Genet, Jean, 239
Gide, André, 71, 77
Gilligan, Carol, 43
Goethe, Johann Wolfgang von, 171, 173
Gombrowicz, Witold, 239
The Good Mother (Miller), 52, 249n8
Gordon, Mary, 7, 38, 44–51; *Men and Angels,* 45–51, 53, 56, 60, 61, 250n19
Goytisolo, Juan, 264n22
Grenier, Jean, 182
Grimm, Jacob: *Teutonic Mythology,* 105
Guattari, Félix, 136
Guggenheim, Peggy, 91, 92, 102, 112

Guiglielmi, Luis, 254n17
Gulliver's Travels (Swift), 130, 132

Haacke, Hans, 144
Habermas, Jürgen, 234, 236, 262n4
The Hand That Rocks the Cradle (film), 38
Haraway, Donna, 135, 234
Hegel, Georg Wilhelm Friedrich, 188–189, 190, 235
Heidegger, Martin, 198, 235, 239
Hill, Susan, 21–22
Hillesum, Ettie, 196
Hitler, Adolf, 173
Hoffmann, E. T. A., 130; *Tales of Hoffmann,* 125, 129–130
Hokusai, Katsushika, 78
Horney, Karen, 14–15, 16, 23–24, 247n30
Hutcheon, Linda, 129, 262n4
Huyssen, Andreas, 262n4

Irigaray, Luce, 29–30, 76

Jameson, Fredric, 262n4
Janeway, Elizabeth, 14–15
Janis, Harriet, 117
Janis, Sidney, 117, 118
Jardine, Alice, 77
Johnson, Barbara, 238
Joyce, James, 85; *Finnegans Wake,* 258n6

Kafka, Franz, 69, 81, 82, 85, 239, 252n5
Kahlo, Frida, 147, 167; *The Miscarriage, 165,* 167; *Self-Portrait with Cropped Hair, 166,* 167
Kant, Immanuel, 146
Kaplan, E. Ann, 41
Kaplan, Janet, 93
Karadzic, Radovan, 239, 240
Kaufmann, Dorothy, 260n29
Klein, Melanie, 16, 17, 40
Kleist, Heinrich von, 252n5
Kliever, Lonnie, 240
Kokoschka, Oskar, 104
Kott, Jan, 4
Krauss, Rosalind, 262n4
Kristeva, Julia, 18, 20–21, 25, 30, 45, 229, 234, 235; on motherhood and creativity, 26–29

Kruger, Barbara, 144
Kyrou, Ado, 125–126

Lacan, Jacques, 27, 70, 76, 169
Lamba, Jacqueline, 103
Lamblin, Bianca Bienenfeld (Louise
 Védrine), 184, 185; *Mémoires d'une jeune
 fille dérangée,* 259n10
The Last of the Mohicans (Cooper), 157, 158
Lawrence, T. E., 69
Lazarre, Jane, 21, 25–26
Lejeune, Philippe: *Le Pacte autobiog-*
 raphique, 205, 261n10
Lesèvre, Lise, 204–206
Levi, Primo, 204
Lewin, Albert, 117, 255n18
Lipovetsky, Gilles, 262n4
Lispector, Clarice, 82–85, 252n5
Louis, Morris, 160
Lyotard, François, 135, 256n15, 262n4, 263n7

The Magic Flute (Mozart), 128
Magritte, René, 128
Mahler, Alma, 104
Mahler, Margaret, 40, 50
La Malinche, 157
Mandelstam, Osip, 252n5
Manon Lescaut (Prévost), 72
Man Ray, 157, 163; *Gift,* 151–152, *152*
Mapplethorpe, Robert, 228
Marcuse, Herbert, 132, 133–135
Martin, Richard, 172
Matisse, Henri, 143
Maupassant, Guy de: *Bel Ami,* 117, 118
McHale, Brian, 127
Melville, Hermann, 69
Mendieta, Ana, 147, 159, 167; *Body Tracks,*
 159, 160, *162*
Miller, Nancy K., 2, 71, 245n3
Miller, Sue: *The Good Mother,* 52, 249n8
Mitchell, Juliet, 14–15
Mitgang, Herbert, 45
Mnouchkine, Ariane, 87
Monet, Claude, 78, 83
Morrison, Toni, 61; *Beloved,* 61, 62
Mussolini, Benito, 173

Nadja (Breton), 101
Nietzsche, Friedrich, 235, 239

Norris, Christopher, 230, 231, 241, 262n4,
 263n7

O'Keeffe, Georgia, 76
Olsen, Tillie, 18, 21, 24, 26, 31
Ophuls, Marcel: *The Sorrow and the Pity,* 188
Oppenheim, Meret: *Ma Gouvernante, My*
 Nurse, Mein Kindermädchen, 154–157, 156
Owens, Craig, 262n4

Perec, Georges: *W ou le souvenir d'enfance,*
 199, 207, 208–209, 210, 211–212
Pétain, Henri Philippe, 173
Picasso, Pablo, 143
Pippin, Horace, 254n17
Pistalo, Vladimir, 241
Poe, Edgar Allan, 18
Porter, Katherine Anne, 34
Prévost, Antoine François, Abbé: *Manon*
 Lescaut, 72
Proust, Marcel, 18, 130, 206
Punter, David, 132–133

Rattner, Abraham, 254n17
Rauschenberg, Robert: *Coca-Cola Plan,* 152–
 153, *153,* 158
Ravella-Pinto, Thelma, 57
Read, Herbert: *Surrealism,* 98
Réage, Pauline: *Story of O,* 130
Reich, Wilhelm, 132
Rembrandt Harmensz van Rijn, 5, 78, 83
René (Chateaubriand), 72
Rich, Adrienne, 17, 21, 23, 25–26
Rilke, Rainer Maria, 85, 252n5
Rimbaud, Arthur, 128, 238
Rivera, Tomás, 57
Robbe-Grillet, Alain, 18
Rorty, Richard, 3, 263nn7,12; *Contingency,*
 Irony, and Solidarity, 231, 232, 233–236,
 237–238, 239, 262n4, 263n12, 264n14
Rosemont, Franklin, 94
Rossini, Gioacchino Antonio: *Tancredi,* 80–
 81
Rousseau, Jean-Jacques, 69, 70
Rubin, Lillian (mother), 215–216, 218–221,
 222, 223
Rubin, Michael (father), 218, 219, 220, 221,
 222, 223
Ruddick, Sara, 43

Rushdie, Salman, 225, 226, 240; *Satanic Verses*, 93

Sade, Marquis de, 130, 239
Sage: A Scholarly Journal on Black Women, 57
Saint Theresa, 70
Sartre, Jean-Paul, 24, 67, 71, 76, 77, 180–189 passim, 190, 194, 195
Scarpetta, Guy, 234, 236
Schneede, Uwe, 104
Schor, Naomi, 263n5
Schwarzer, Alice, 185, 196
Scorsese, Martin: *The Last Temptation of Christ*, 117
Scott, Joan, 196
Serra, Father Junipero, 151
Shakespeare, William, 5, 171, 173
Sherman, Cindy, 144
Shklar, Judith, 239
Showalter, Elaine, 19
Signs, 55, 56, 57, 59, 61
Silence of the Lambs (film), 95
Smith, Barbara Herrnstein, 231, 232
Smith, Kiki, 144
Smith, Ricarda, 133
Snyder, Emery, 72
Sorokine, Nathalie, 181, 184, 188
The Sorrow and the Pity (film), 188
Spencer, Stanley, 254n17
Spivak, Gayatri, 234, 262n4
Stalin, Joseph, 233
Stein, Gertrude, 36, 140, 145–146, 147, 167, 168
Stendhal, 18, 69, 70
Story of O (Réage), 130
Surrealist Manifesto (Breton), 127, 128, 133
Sussman, Elizabeth, 257n3

Swan, Jim, 41
Swift, Jonathan: *Gulliver's Travels*, 130, 132

Tales of Hoffmann (Hoffmann), 129–130
Tanning, Dorothea, 116, 118
Teitelbaum, Matthew, 257n3
Tel Quel, 26
Thomas, Edith, 260n29
Thompson, Clara, 14–15
Tsvetaeva, Maria, 85, 242n5

Ullman, Liv, 21, 24

Valéry, Paul, 71, 77
Van Gogh, Vincent, 140, 142–143
Vargas, Eugenia, 160–164; *Untitled 1*, *163*; *Untitled 5*, *164*
Varo, Remedios, 93
Védrine, Louise. *See* Lamblin, Bianca Bienenfeld
Vegh, Claudine: *I Didn't Say Goodbye*, 207–208, 209–210, 211, 212
Vermeer, Jan, 5

Walker, Alice, 63
Warner, Marina, 99, 110
Waugh, Auberon, 132
Weitzman, Lenore, 52–53
Wenzel, Hélène, 197
Wiesel, Elie, 200, 201; *Night*, 200–201, 203–204, 206; *Day*, 200-204, 205; *Dawn*, 203–204
Williams, Patricia, 57
Winnicott, D. W., 16, 17, 229
Wojnarowicz, David, 144, 229
Woodiwiss, Kathleen, 21, 22
Woolf, Virginia, 18, 20